THE LESSON OF THE MASTER

AND OTHER STORIES

THE LESSON OF THE MASTER

THE MARRIAGES   THE PUPIL

BROOKSMITH

THE SOLUTION   SIR EDMUND ORME

BY

HENRY JAMES

New York

MACMILLAN AND CO.

AND LONDON

1892

CONTENTS

THE LESSON OF THE MASTER.[1]

I.

HE had been informed that the ladies were at church, but that was corrected by what he saw from the top of the steps (they descended from a great height in two arms, with a circular sweep of the most charming effect) at the threshold of the door which, from the long, bright gallery, overlooked the immense lawn. Three gentlemen, on the grass, at a distance, sat under the great trees; but the fourth figure was not a gentleman, the one in the crimson dress which made so vivid a spot, told so as a "bit of colour" amid the fresh, rich green. The servant had come so far with Paul Overt to show him the way and had asked him if he wished first to go to his room. The young man declined this privilege, having no disorder to repair after so short and easy a journey and liking to take a general perceptive possession of the new scene immediately, as he always did. He stood there a little with his eyes on the group and on the admirable picture — the wide grounds of an old country-house near London (that only made it better,) on a splendid Sunday in June. "But that lady, who is she?" he said to the servant before the man went away.

"I think it's Mrs. St. George, sir."

[1] *Copyright, 1891, by Macmillan & Co.*

"Mrs. St. George, the wife of the distinguished ——"
Then Paul Overt checked himself, doubting whether the
footman would know.

"Yes, sir — probably, sir," said the servant, who appeared to wish to intimate that a person staying at
Summersoft would naturally be, if only by alliance, distinguished. His manner, however, made poor Overt feel
for the moment as if he himself were but little so.

"And the gentlemen?" he inquired.

"Well, sir, one of them is General Fancourt."

"Ah yes, I know; thank you." General Fancourt was
distinguished, there was no doubt of that, for something
he had done, or perhaps even had not done (the young
man could not remember which) some years before in
India. The servant went away, leaving the glass doors
open into the gallery, and Paul Overt remained at the
head of the wide double staircase, saying to himself that
the place was sweet and promised a pleasant visit, while
he leaned on the balustrade of fine old ironwork which,
like all the other details, was of the same period as the
house. It all went together and spoke in one voice — a
rich English voice of the early part of the eighteenth
century. It might have been church-time on a summer's
day in the reign of Queen Anne; the stillness was too
perfect to be modern, the nearness counted so as distance
and there was something so fresh and sound in the
originality of the large smooth house, the expanse of
whose beautiful brickwork, which had been kept clear
of messy creepers (as a woman with a rare complexion
disdains a veil,) was pink rather than red. When Paul
Overt perceived that the people under the trees were
noticing him he turned back through the open doors into
the great gallery which was the pride of the place. It
traversed the mansion from end to end and seemed —

with its bright colours, its high panelled windows, its
faded, flowered chintzes, its quickly-recognised portraits
and pictures, the blue and white china of its cabinets
and the attenuated festoons and rosettes of its ceiling —
a cheerful upholstered avenue into the other century.

The young man was slightly nervous; that belonged
in general to his disposition as a student of fine prose,
with his dose of the artist's restlessness; and there was
a particular excitement in the idea that Henry St. George
might be a member of the party. For the younger writer
he had remained a high literary figure, in spite of the
lower range of production to which he had fallen after
his three first great successes, the comparative absence
of quality in his later work. There had been moments
when Paul Overt almost shed tears upon this; but now
that he was near him (he had never met him,) he was
conscious only of the fine original source and of his own
immense debt. After he had taken a turn or two up
and down the gallery he came out again and descended
the steps. He was but slenderly supplied with a certain
social boldness (it was really a weakness in him,) so
that, conscious of a want of acquaintance with the four
persons in the distance, he indulged in a movement as to
which he had a certain safety in feeling that it did not
necessarily appear to commit him to an attempt to join
them. There was a fine English awkwardness in it —
he felt this too as he sauntered vaguely and obliquely
across the lawn, as if to take an independent line. Fortunately there was an equally fine English directness in
the way one of the gentlemen presently rose and made
as if to approach him, with an air of conciliation and
reassurance. To this demonstration Paul Overt instantly
responded, though he knew the gentleman was not his
host. He was tall, straight and elderly, and had a pink,

smiling face and a white moustache. Our young man met him half way while he laughed and said: "A—— Lady Watermouth told us you were coming; she asked me just to look after you." Paul Overt thanked him (he liked him without delay,) and turned round with him, walking toward the others. "They've all gone to church — all except us," the stranger continued as they went; "we're just sitting here — it's so jolly." Overt rejoined that it was jolly indeed — it was such a lovely place; he mentioned that he had not seen it before — it was a charming impression.

"Ah, you've not been here before?" said his companion. "It's a nice little place — not much to *do*, you know." Overt wondered what he wanted to "do" — he felt as if he himself were doing a good deal. By the time they came to where the others sat he had guessed his initiator was a military man, and (such was the turn of Overt's imagination,) this made him still more sympathetic. He would naturally have a passion for activity — for deeds at variance with the pacific, pastoral scene. He was evidently so good-natured, however, that he accepted the inglorious hour for what it was worth. Paul Overt shared it with him and with his companions for the next twenty minutes ; the latter looked at him and he looked at them without knowing much who they were, while the talk went on without enlightening him much as to what it was about. It was indeed about nothing in particular, and wandered, with casual, pointless pauses and short terrestrial flights, amid the names of persons and places — names which, for him, had no great power of evocation. It was all sociable and slow, as was right and natural on a warm Sunday morning.

Overt's first attention was given to the question, privately considered, of whether one of the two younger men would be Henry St. George. He knew many of his distinguished contemporaries by their photographs, but he had never, as it happened, seen a portrait of the great misguided novelist. One of the gentlemen was out of the question — he was too young; and the other scarcely looked clever enough, with such mild, undiscriminating eyes. If those eyes were St. George's the problem presented by the ill-matched parts of his genius was still more difficult of solution. Besides, the deportment of the personage possessing them was not, as regards the lady in the red dress, such as could be natural, towards his wife, even to a writer accused by several critics of sacrificing too much to manner. Lastly, Paul Overt had an indefinite feeling that if the gentleman with the sightless eyes bore the name that had set his heart beating faster (he also had contradictory, conventional whiskers — the young admirer of the celebrity had never in a mental vision seen *his* face in so vulgar a frame), he would have given him a sign of recognition or of friendliness — would have heard of him a little, would know something about *Ginistrella*, would have gathered at least that that recent work of fiction had made an impression on the discerning. Paul Overt had a dread of being grossly proud, but it seemed to him that his self-consciousness took no undue license in thinking that the authorship of *Ginistrella* constituted a degree of identity. His soldierly friend became clear enough; he was "Fancourt," but he was also the General; and he mentioned to our young man in the course of a few moments that he had but lately returned from twenty years' service abroad.

"And do you mean to remain in England?" Overt asked.

"Oh yes, I have bought a little house in London."

"And I hope you like it," said Overt, looking at Mrs. St. George.

"Well, a little house in Manchester Square — there's a limit to the enthusiasm that that inspires."

"Oh, I meant being at home again — being in London."

"My daughter likes it — that's the main thing. She's very fond of art and music and literature and all that kind of thing. She missed it in India and she finds it in London, or she hopes she will find it. Mr. St. George has promised to help her — he has been awfully kind to her. She has gone to church — she's fond of that too — but they'll all be back in a quarter of an hour. You must let me introduce you to her — she will be so glad to know you. I dare say she has read every word you have written."

"I shall be delighted — I haven't written very many," said Overt, who felt without resentment that the General at least was very vague about that. But he wondered a little why, since he expressed this friendly disposition, it did not occur to him to pronounce the word which would put him in relation with Mrs. St. George. If it was a question of introductions Miss Fancourt (apparently she was unmarried,) was far away and the wife of his illustrious *confrère* was almost between them. This lady struck Paul Overt as a very pretty woman, with a surprising air of youth and a high smartness of aspect which seemed to him (he could scarcely have said why,) a sort of mystification. St. George certainly had every right to a charming wife, but he himself would never have taken the important little woman in the aggressively Parisian dress for the domestic partner of a man of letters. That partner in general, he knew, was far from presenting herself in a single type: his observation had instructed him that she was not inveterately, not necessarily dreary. But he had never before seen her look so much as if her prosperity had deeper foundations than an ink-spotted study-table littered with proof-sheets. Mrs. St. George might have been the wife of a gentleman who "kept" books rather than wrote them, who carried on great affairs in the City and made better bargains than those that poets make with publishers. With this she hinted at a success more personal, as if she had been the most characteristic product of an age in which society, the world of conversation, is a great drawing-room with the City for its antechamber. Overt judged her at first to be about thirty years of age; then, after a while, he perceived that she was much nearer fifty. But she juggled away the twenty years somehow — you only saw them in a rare glimpse, like the rabbit in the conjurer's sleeve. She was extraordinarily white, and everything about her was pretty — her eyes, her ears, her hair, her voice, her hands, her feet (to which her relaxed attitude in her wicker chair gave a great publicity,) and the numerous ribbons and trinkets with which she was bedecked. She looked as if she had put on her best clothes to go to church and then had decided that they were too good for that and had stayed at home. She told a story of some length about the shabby way Lady Jane had treated the Duchess, as well as an anecdote in relation to a purchase she had made in Paris (on her way back from Cannes,) for Lady Egbert, who had never refunded the money. Paul Overt suspected her of a tendency to figure great people as larger than life, until he noticed the manner in which she handled Lady Egbert, which was so subversive that it reassured him. He felt that he should have understood her better if he might have met her eye; but she scarcely looked at him. "Ah, here they come — all the good ones!" she said at

last; and Paul Overt saw in the distance the return of
the churchgoers — several persons, in couples and threes,
advancing in a flicker of sun and shade at the end of a
large green vista formed by the level grass and the
overarching boughs.

"If you mean to imply that we are bad, I protest,"
said one of the gentlemen — "after making oneself
agreeable all the morning!"

"Ah, if they've found you agreeable!" Mrs. St. George
exclaimed, smiling. "But if we are good the others are
better."

"They must be angels then," observed the General.

"Your husband was an angel, the way he went off at
your bidding," the gentleman who had first spoken said
to Mrs. St. George.

"At my bidding?"

"Didn't you make him go to church?"

"I never made him do anything in my life but once,
when I made him burn up a bad book. That's all!" At
her "That's all!" Paul broke into an irrepressible laugh;
it lasted only a second, but it drew her eyes to him. His
own met them, but not long enough to help him to understand her; unless it were a step towards this that he felt
sure on the instant that the burnt book (the way she
alluded to it!) was one of her husband's finest things.

"A bad book?" her interlocutor repeated.

"I didn't like it. He went to church because your
daughter went," she continued, to General Fancourt. "I
think it my duty to call your attention to his demeanour
to your daughter."

"Well, if you don't mind it, I don't," the General
laughed.

"*Il s'attache à ses pas.* But I don't wonder — she's so
charming."

"I hope she won't make him burn any books!" Paul Overt ventured to exclaim.

"If she would make him write a few it would be more to the purpose," said Mrs. St. George. "He has been of an indolence this year!"

Our young man stared — he was so struck with the lady's phraseology. Her "Write a few" seemed to him almost as good as her "That's all." Didn't she, as the wife of a rare artist, know what it was to produce *one* perfect work of art? How in the world did she think they were turned off? His private conviction was that admirably as Henry St. George wrote, he had written for the last ten years, and especially for the last five, only too much, and there was an instant during which he felt the temptation to make this public. But before he had spoken a diversion was effected by the return of the absent guests. They strolled up dispersedly — there were eight or ten of them — and the circle under the trees rearranged itself as they took their place in it. They made it much larger; so that Paul Overt could feel (he was always feeling that sort of thing, as he said to himself,) that if the company had already been interesting to watch it would now become a great deal more so. He shook hands with his hostess, who welcomed him without many words, in the manner of a woman able to trust him to understand — conscious that, in every way, so pleasant an occasion would speak for itself. She offered him no particular facility for sitting by her, and when they had all subsided again he found himself still next General Fancourt, with an unknown lady on his other flank.

"That's my daughter — that one opposite," the General said to him without loss of time. Overt saw a tall girl, with magnificent red hair, in a dress of a pretty grey-green tint and of a limp silken texture, in which every

modern effect had been avoided. It had therefore somehow the stamp of the latest thing, so that Overt quickly
perceived she was eminently a contemporary young lady.

"She's very handsome — very handsome," he repeated,
looking at her. There was something noble in her head,
and she appeared fresh and strong.

Her father surveyed her with complacency; then he
said: "She looks too hot — that's her walk. But she'll
be all right presently. Then I'll make her come over
and speak to you."

"I should be sorry to give you that trouble; if you
were to take me over there — " the young man murmured.

"My dear sir, do you suppose I put myself out that
way? I don't mean for you, but for Marian," the General added.

"*I* would put myself out for her, soon enough," Overt
replied; after which he went on: "Will you be so good
as to tell me which of those gentlemen is Henry St.
George?"

"The fellow talking to my girl. By Jove, he *is* making up to her — they're going off for another walk."

"Ah, is that he, really?" The young man felt a certain surprise, for the personage before him contradicted
a preconception which had been vague only till it was
confronted with the reality. As soon as this happened
the mental image, retiring with a sigh, became substantial
enough to suffer a slight wrong. Overt, who had spent
a considerable part of his short life in foreign lands, made
now, but not for the first time, the reflection that whereas
in those countries he had almost always recognised the
artist and the man of letters by his personal "type," the
mould of his face, the character of his head, the expression of his figure and even the indications of his dress, in
England this identification was as little as possible a

matter of course, thanks to the greater conformity, the habit of sinking the profession instead of advertising it, the general diffusion of the air of the gentleman — the gentleman committed to no particular set of ideas. More than once, on returning to his own country, he had said to himself in regard to the people whom he met in society: "One sees them about and one even talks with them; but to find out what they *do* one would really have to be a detective." In respect to several individuals whose work he was unable to like (perhaps he was wrong) he found himself adding, "No wonder they conceal it — it's so bad!" He observed that oftener than in France and in Germany his artist looked like a gentleman (that is, like an English one,) while he perceived that outside of a few exceptions his gentleman didn't look like an artist. St. George was not one of the exceptions; that circumstance he definitely apprehended before the great man had turned his back to walk off with Miss Fancourt. He certainly looked better behind than any foreign man of letters, and beautifully correct in his tall black hat and his superior frock coat. Somehow, all the same, these very garments (he wouldn't have minded them so much on a weekday,) were disconcerting to Paul Overt, who forgot for the moment that the head of the profession was not a bit better dressed than himself. He had caught a glimpse of a regular face, with a fresh colour, a brown moustache and a pair of eyes surely never visited by a fine frenzy, and he promised himself to study it on the first occasion. His temporary opinion was that St. George looked like a lucky stockbroker — a gentleman driving eastward every morning from a sanitary suburb in a smart dog-cart. That carried out the impression already derived from his wife. Paul Overt's glance, after a moment, travelled back to this lady, and he saw that her own had followed her husband as he moved off with Miss Fancourt. Overt permitted himself to wonder a little whether she were jealous when another woman took him away. Then he seemed to perceive that Mrs. St. George was not glaring at the indifferent maiden — her eyes rested only on her husband, and with unmistakable serenity. That was the way she wanted him to be — she liked his conventional uniform. Overt had a great desire to hear more about the book she had induced him to destroy.

II.

As they all came out from luncheon General Fancourt took hold of Paul Overt and exclaimed, "I say, I want you to know my girl!" as if the idea had just occurred to him and he had not spoken of it before. With the other hand he possessed himself of the young lady and said: "You know all about him. I've seen you with his books. She reads everything — everything!" he added to the young man. The girl smiled at him and then laughed at her father. The General turned away and his daughter said:

"Isn't papa delightful?"

"He is indeed, Miss Fancourt."

"As if I read you because I read 'everything'!"

"Oh, I don't mean for saying that," said Paul Overt. "I liked him from the moment he spoke to me. Then he promised me this privilege."

"It isn't for you he means it, it's for me. If you flatter yourself that he thinks of anything in life but me you'll find you are mistaken. He introduces every one to me. He thinks me insatiable."

"You speak like him," said Paul Overt, laughing.

"Ah, but sometimes I want to," the girl replied, colouring. "I don't read everything — I read very little. But I *have* read you."

"Suppose we go into the gallery," said Paul Overt. She pleased him greatly, not so much because of this last remark (though that of course was not disagreeable to him,) as because, seated opposite to him at luncheon, she had given him for half an hour the impression of her beautiful face. Something else had come with it — a sense of generosity, of an enthusiasm which, unlike many enthusiasms, was not all manner. That was not spoiled for him by the circumstance that the repast had placed her again in familiar contact with Henry St. George. Sitting next to her he was also opposite to our young man, who had been able to observe that he multiplied the attentions which his wife had brought to the General's notice. Paul Overt had been able to observe further that this lady was not in the least discomposed by these demonstrations and that she gave every sign of an unclouded spirit. She had Lord Masham on one side of her and on the other the accomplished Mr. Mulliner, editor of the new high-class, lively evening paper which was expected to meet a want felt in circles increasingly conscious that Conservatism must be made amusing, and unconvinced when assured by those of another political colour that it was already amusing enough. At the end of an hour spent in her company Paul Overt thought her still prettier than she had appeared to him at first, and if her profane allusions to her husband's work had not still rung in his ears he should have liked her — so far as it could be a question of that in connection with a woman to whom he had not yet spoken and to whom probably he should never speak if it were left to her. Pretty women evidently were necessary to Henry St. George, and for the moment it was Miss Fancourt who

was most indispensable. If Overt had promised himself
to take a better look at him the opportunity now was of
the best, and it brought consequences which the young
man felt to be important. He saw more in his face, and
he liked it the better for its not telling its whole story
in the first three minutes. That story came out as one
read, in little instalments (it was excusable that Overt's
mental comparisons should be somewhat professional,)
and the text was a style considerably involved — a language not easy to translate at sight. There were shades
of meaning in it and a vague perspective of history which
receded as you advanced. Of two facts Paul Overt had
taken especial notice. The first of these was that he
liked the countenance of the illustrious novelist much
better when it was in repose than when it smiled ; the
smile displeased him (as much as anything from that
source could,) whereas the quiet face had a charm which
increased in proportion as it became completely quiet.
The change to the expression of gaiety excited on
Overt's part a private protest which resembled that of
a person sitting in the twilight and enjoying it, when
the lamp is brought in too soon. His second reflection
was that, though generally he disliked the sight of a
man of that age using arts to make himself agreeable to
a pretty girl, he was not struck in this case by the ugliness of the thing, which seemed to prove that St. George
had a light hand or the air of being younger than he
was, or else that Miss Fancourt showed that *she* was not
conscious of an anomaly.

Overt walked with her into the gallery, and they
strolled to the end of it, looking at the pictures, the
cabinets, the charming vista, which harmonised with the
prospect of the summer afternoon, resembling it in its
long brightness, with great divans and old chairs like

hours of rest. Such a place as that had the added merit of giving persons who came into it plenty to talk about. Miss Fancourt sat down with Paul Overt on a flowered sofa, the cushions of which, very numerous, were tight, ancient cubes, of many sizes, and presently she said: "I'm so glad to have a chance to thank you."

"To thank me?"

"I liked your book so much. I think it's splendid."

She sat there smiling at him, and he never asked himself which book she meant; for after all he had written three or four. That seemed a vulgar detail, and he was not even gratified by the idea of the pleasure she told him — her bright, handsome face told him — he had given her. The feeling she appealed to, or at any rate the feeling she excited, was something larger — something that had little to do with any quickened pulsation of his own vanity. It was responsive admiration of the life she embodied, the young purity and richness of which appeared to imply that real success was to resemble *that*, to live, to bloom, to present the perfection of a fine type, not to have hammered out headachy fancies with a bent back at an ink-stained table. While her grey eyes rested on him (there was a wideish space between them, and the division of her rich-coloured hair, which was so thick that it ventured to be smooth, made a free arch above them,) he was almost ashamed of that exercise of the pen which it was her present inclination to eulogise. He was conscious that he should have liked better to please her in some other way. The lines of her face were those of a woman grown, but there was something childish in her complexion and the sweetness of her mouth. Above all she was natural — that was indubitable now — more natural than he had supposed at first, perhaps on account of her æsthetic drapery, which was conventionally uncon-

ventional, suggesting a tortuous spontaneity. He had
feared that sort of thing in other cases, and his fears
had been justified; though he was an artist to the
essence, the modern reactionary nymph, with the bram-
bles of the woodland caught in her folds and a look as if
the satyrs had toyed with her hair, was apt to make him
uncomfortable. Miss Fancourt was really more candid
than her costume, and the best proof of it was her supposing that such garments suited her liberal character.
She was robed like a pessimist, but Overt was sure she
liked the taste of life. He thanked her for her appreciation — aware at the same time that he didn't appear
to thank her enough and that she might think him un-
gracious. He was afraid she would ask him to explain
something that he had written, and he always shrank
from that (perhaps too timidly,) for to his own ear the
explanation of a work of art sounded fatuous. But he
liked her so much as to feel a confidence that in the long
run he should be able to show her that he was not rudely
evasive. Moreover it was very certain that she was not
quick to take offence; she was not irritable, she could be
trusted to wait. So when he said to her, "Ah! don't
talk of anything I have done, *here;* there is another
man in the house who is the actuality!" when he uttered
this short, sincere protest, it was with the sense that she
would see in the words neither mock humility nor the
ungraciousness of a successful man bored with praise.

"You mean Mr. St. George — isn't he delightful?"

Paul Overt looked at her a moment; there was a
species of morning-light in her eyes.

"Alas, I don't know him. I only admire him at a
distance."

"Oh, you must know him — he wants so to talk to
you," rejoined Miss Fancourt, who evidently had the

habit of saying the things that, by her quick calculation, would give people pleasure. Overt divined that she would always calculate on everything's being simple between others.

"I shouldn't have supposed he knew anything about me," Paul said, smiling.

"He does then — everything. And if he didn't, I should be able to tell him."

"To tell him everything?"

"You talk just like the people in your book!" the girl exclaimed.

"Then they must all talk alike."

"Well, it must be so difficult. Mr. St. George tells me it is, terribly. I've tried too and I find it so. I've tried to write a novel."

"Mr. St. George oughtn't to discourage you," said Paul Overt.

"You do much more — when you wear that expression."

"Well, after all, why try to be an artist?" the young man went on. "It's so poor — so poor!"

"I don't know what you mean," said Marian Fancourt, looking grave.

"I mean as compared with being a person of action — as living your works."

"But what is art but a life — if it be real?" asked the girl. "I think it's the only one — everything else is so clumsy!" Paul Overt laughed, and she continued: "It's so interesting, meeting so many celebrated people."

"So I should think; but surely it isn't new to you."

"Why, I have never seen any one — any one: living always in Asia."

"But doesn't Asia swarm with personages? Haven't you administered provinces in India and had captive rajahs and tributary princes chained to your car?"

"I was with my father, after I left school to go out there. It was delightful being with him — we are alone together in the world, he and I — but there was none of the society I like best. One never heard of a picture — never of a book, except bad ones."

"Never of a picture? Why, wasn't all life a picture?" Miss Fancourt looked over the delightful place where they sat. "Nothing to compare with this. I adore England!" she exclaimed.

"Ah, of course I don't deny that we must do something with it yet."

"It hasn't been touched, really," said the girl.

"Did Henry St. George say that?"

There was a small and, as he felt it, venial intention of irony in his question; which, however, the girl took very simply, not noticing the insinuation. "Yes, he says it has not been touched — not touched comparatively," she answered, eagerly. "He's so interesting about it. To listen to him makes one want so to do something."

"It would make me want to," said Paul Overt, feeling strongly, on the instant, the suggestion of what she said and of the emotion with which she said it, and what an incentive, on St. George's lips, such a speech might be.

"Oh, you — as if you hadn't! I should like so to hear you talk together," the girl added, ardently.

"That's very genial of you; but he would have it all his own way. I'm prostrate before him."

Marian Fancourt looked earnest for a moment. "Do you think then he's so perfect?"

"Far from it. Some of his later books seem to me awfully queer."

"Yes, yes — he knows that."

Paul Overt stared. "That they seem to me awfully queer?"

" Well yes, or at any rate that they are not what they should be. He told me he didn't esteem them. He has told me such wonderful things — he's so interesting."

There was a certain shock for Paul Overt in the knowledge that the fine genius they were talking of had been reduced to so explicit a confession and had made it, in his misery, to the first comer; for though Miss Fancourt was charming, what was she after all but an immature girl encountered at a country-house ? Yet precisely this was a part of the sentiment that he himself had just expressed; he would make way completely for the poor peccable great man, not because he didn't read him clear, but altogether because he did. His consideration was half composed of tenderness for superficialities which he was sure St. George judged privately with supreme sternness and which denoted some tragic intellectual secret. He would have his reasons for his psychology à fleur de peau, and these reasons could only be cruel ones, such as would make him dearer to those who already were fond of him. "You excite my envy. I judge him, I discriminate — but I love him," Overt said in a moment. "And seeing him for the first time this way is a great event for me."

"How momentous — how magnificent!" cried the girl. "How delicious to bring you together!"

" Your doing it — that makes it perfect," Overt responded.

"He's as eager as you," Miss Fancourt went on. "But it's so odd you shouldn't have met."

"It's not so odd as it seems. I've been out of England so much — repeated absences during all these last years."

"And yet you write of it as well as if you were always here."

"It's just the being away perhaps. At any rate the

best bits, I suspect, are those that were done in dreary places abroad."

"And why were they dreary?"

"Because they were health-resorts — where my poor mother was dying."

"Your poor mother?" the girl murmured, kindly.

"We went from place to place to help her to get better. But she never did. To the deadly Riviera (I hate it!) to the high Alps, to Algiers, and far away — a hideous journey — to Colorado."

"And she isn't better?" Miss Fancourt went on.

"She died a year ago."

"Really? — like mine! Only that is far away. Some day you must tell me about your mother," she added.

Overt looked at her a moment. "What right things you say! If you say them to St. George I don't wonder he's in bondage."

"I don't know what you mean. He doesn't make speeches and professions at all — he isn't ridiculous."

"I'm afraid you consider that I am."

"No, I don't," the girl replied, rather shortly. "He understands everything."

Overt was on the point of saying jocosely: "And I don't — is that it?" But these words, before he had spoken, changed themselves into others slightly less trivial: "Do you suppose he understands his wife?"

Miss Fancourt made no direct answer to his question; but after a moment's hesitation she exclaimed: "Isn't she charming?"

"Not in the least!"

"Here he comes. Now you must know him," the girl went on. A small group of visitors had gathered at the other end of the gallery and they had been joined for a moment by Henry St. George, who strolled in from a neighbouring room. He stood near them a moment, not, apparently, falling into the conversation, but taking up an old miniature from a table and vaguely examining it. At the end of a minute he seemed to perceive Miss Fancourt and her companion in the distance; whereupon, laying down his miniature, he approached them with the same procrastinating air, with his hands in his pockets, looking to right and left at the pictures. The gallery was so long that this transit took some little time, especially as there was a moment when he stopped to admire the fine Gainsborough. "He says she has been the making of him," Miss Fancourt continued, in a voice slightly lowered.

"Ah, he's often obscure!" laughed Paul Overt.

"Obscure?" she repeated, interrogatively. Her eyes rested upon her other friend, and it was not lost upon Paul that they appeared to send out great shafts of softness. "He is going to speak to us!" she exclaimed, almost breathlessly. There was a sort of rapture in her voice; Paul Overt was startled. "Bless my soul, is she so fond of him as that — is she in love with him?" he mentally inquired. "Didn't I tell you he was eager?" she added, to her companion.

"It's eagerness dissimulated," the young man rejoined, as the subject of their observation lingered before his Gainsborough. "He edges toward us shyly. Does he mean that she saved him by burning that book?"

"That book? what book did she burn?" The girl turned her face quickly upon him.

"Hasn't he told you, then?"

"Not a word."

"Then he doesn't tell you everything!" Paul Overt had guessed that Miss Fancourt pretty much supposed

he did. The great man had now resumed his course
and come nearer; nevertheless Overt risked the profane
observation: "St. George and the dragon, the anecdote
suggests!"

Miss Fancourt, however, did not hear it; she was
smiling at her approaching friend. "He *is* eager — he
is!" she repeated.

"Eager for you — yes."

The girl called out frankly, joyously: "I know you
want to know Mr. Overt. You'll be great friends, and
it will always be delightful to me to think that I was
here when you first met and that I had something to do
with it."

There was a freshness of intention in this speech which
carried it off; nevertheless our young man was sorry for
Henry St. George, as he was sorry at any time for any
one who was publicly invited to be responsive and delightful. He would have been so contented to believe
that a man he deeply admired attached an importance to
him that he was determined not to play with such a presumption if it possibly were vain. In a single glance of
the eye of the pardonable master he discovered (having
the sort of divination that belonged to his talent,) that
this personage was full of general good-will, but had not
read a word he had written. There was even a relief, a
simplification, in that: liking him so much already for
what he had done, how could he like him more for having
been struck with a certain promise? He got up, trying
to show his compassion, but at the same instant he found
himself encompassed by St. George's happy personal art
— a manner of which it was the essence to conjure away
false positions. It all took place in a moment. He was
conscious that he knew him now, conscious of his hand-
shake and of the very quality of his hand; of his face,

seen nearer and consequently seen better, of a general
fraternising assurance, and in particular of the circumstance that St. George didn't dislike him (as yet at
least,) for being imposed by a charming but too gushing
girl, valuable enough without such danglers.   At any
rate no irritation was reflected in the voice with which
he questioned Miss Fancourt in respect to some project
of a walk — a general walk of the company round the
park.   He had said something to Overt about a talk —
"We must have a tremendous lot of talk; there are so
many things, aren't there ? " — but Paul perceived that
this idea would not in the present case take very immediate effect.   All the same he was extremely happy, even
after the matter of the walk had been settled (the three
presently passed back to the other part of the gallery,
where it was discussed with several members of the
party,) even when, after they had all gone out together,
he found himself for half an hour in contact with Mrs.
St. George.   Her husband had taken the advance with
Miss Fancourt, and this pair were quite out of sight.   It
was the prettiest of rambles for a summer afternoon —
a grassy circuit, of immense extent, skirting the limit of
the park within.   The park was completely surrounded
by its old mottled but perfect red wall, which, all the
way on their left, made a picturesque accompaniment.
Mrs. St. George mentioned to him the surprising number
of acres that were thus enclosed, together with numerous other facts relating to the property and the family,
and its other properties: she could not too strongly urge
upon him the importance of seeing their other houses.
She ran over the names of these and rang the changes on
them with the facility of practice, making them appear
an almost endless list.   She had received Paul Overt
very amiably when he broke ground with her by telling

her that he had just had the joy of making her husband's acquaintance, and struck him as so alert and so accommodating a little woman that he was rather ashamed of his *mot* about her to Miss Fancourt; though he reflected that a hundred other people, on a hundred occasions, would have been sure to make it.   He got on with Mrs. St. George, in short, better than he expected; but this did not prevent her from suddenly becoming aware that she was faint with fatigue and must take her way back to the house by the shortest cut.   She hadn't the strength of a kitten, she said— she was awfully seedy; a state of things that Overt had been too preoccupied to perceive — preoccupied with a private effort to ascertain in what sense she could be held to have been the making of her husband.   He had arrived at a glimmering of the answer when she announced that she must leave him, though this perception was of course provisional.   While he was in the very act of placing himself at her disposal for the return the situation underwent a change; Lord Masham suddenly turned up, coming back to them, overtaking them, emerging from the shrubbery — Overt could scarcely have said how he appeared, and Mrs. St. George had protested that she wanted to be left alone and not to break up the party.   A moment later she was walking off with Lord Masham.   Paul Overt fell back and joined Lady Watermouth, to whom he presently mentioned that Mrs. St. George had been obliged to renounce the attempt to go further.

"She oughtn't to have come out at all," her ladyship remarked, rather grumpily.

"Is she so very much of an invalid?"

"Very bad indeed."   And his hostess added, with still greater austerity: "She oughtn't to come to stay with one!"   He wondered what was implied by this, and presently gathered that it was not a reflection on the lady's conduct or her moral nature: it only represented that her strength was not equal to her aspirations.

III.

THE smoking-room at Summersoft was on the scale of the rest of the place; that is it was high and light and commodious, and decorated with such refined old carvings and mouldings that it seemed rather a bower for ladies who should sit at work at fading crewels than a parliament of gentlemen smoking strong cigars. The gentlemen mustered there in considerable force on the Sunday evening, collecting mainly at one end, in front of one of the cool fair fireplaces of white marble, the entablature of which was adorned with a delicate little Italian "subject." There was another in the wall that faced it, and, thanks to the mild summer night, there was no fire in either; but a nucleus for aggregation was furnished on one side by a table in the chimney-corner laden with bottles, decanters and tall tumblers. Paul Overt was an insincere smoker; he puffed cigarettes occasionally for reasons with which tobacco had nothing to do. This was particularly the case on the occasion of which I speak; his motive was the vision of a little direct talk with Henry St. George. The "tremendous" communion of which the great man had held out hopes to him earlier in the day had not yet come off, and this saddened him considerably, for the party was to go its several ways immediately after breakfast on the morrow. He had, however, the disappointment of finding that apparently the author of *Shadowmere* was not disposed to prolong his vigil. He was not among the gentlemen assembled in the smoking-room when Overt entered it, nor was he one of those who turned up, in bright habiliments, during the next ten minutes. The young man waited a little, wondering whether he had only gone to put on something extraordinary; this would account for his delay as well as contribute further to Overt's observation of his tendency to do the approved superficial thing. But he didn't arrive — he must have been putting on something more extraordinary than was probable. Paul gave him up, feeling a little injured, a little wounded at his not having managed to say twenty words to him. He was not angry, but he puffed his cigarette sighingly, with the sense of having lost a precious chance. He wandered away with his regret, moved slowly round the room, looking at the old prints on the walls. In this attitude he presently felt a hand laid on his shoulder and a friendly voice in his ear. "This is good. I hoped I should find you. I came down on purpose." St. George was there, without a change of dress and with a kind face — his graver one — to which Overt eagerly responded. He explained that it was only for the Master — the idea of a little talk — that he had sat up and that, not finding him, he had been on the point of going to bed.

"Well, you know, I don't smoke — my wife doesn't let me," said St. George, looking for a place to sit down. "It's very good for me — very good for me. Let us take that sofa."

"Do you mean smoking is good for you?"

"No, no, her not letting me. It's a great thing to have a wife who proves to one all the things one can do without. One might never find them out for oneself. She doesn't allow me to touch a cigarette."

They took possession of the sofa, which was at a distance from the group of smokers, and St. George went on: "Have you got one yourself?"

"Do you mean a cigarette?"

"Dear no! a wife."

"No; and yet I would give up my cigarette for one."

"You would give up a good deal more than that," said St. George. "However, you would get a great deal in return. There is a great deal to be said for wives," he added, folding his arms and crossing his outstretched legs. He declined tobacco altogether and sat there without returning fire. Paul Overt stopped smoking, touched by his courtesy; and after all they were out of the fumes, their sofa was in a far-away corner. It would have been a mistake, St. George went on, a great mistake for them to have separated without a little chat; "for I know all about you," he said, "I know you're very remarkable. You've written a very distinguished book."

"And how do you know it?" Overt asked.

"Why, my dear fellow, it's in the air, it's in the papers, it's everywhere," St. George replied, with the immediate familiarity of a *confrère* — a tone that seemed to his companion the very rustle of the laurel. "You're on all men's lips and, what's better, you're on all women's. And I've just been reading your book."

"Just? You hadn't read it this afternoon," said Overt.

"How do you know that?"

"You know how I know it," the young man answered, laughing.

"I suppose Miss Fancourt told you."

"No, indeed; she led me rather to suppose that you had."

"Yes; that's much more what she would do. Doesn't she shed a rosy glow over life? But you didn't believe her?" asked St. George.

"No, not when you came to us there."

"Did I pretend? did I pretend badly?" But without waiting for an answer to this St. George went on: "You ought always to believe such a girl as that — always, always. Some women are meant to be taken with allowances and reserves; but you must take *her* just as she is."

"I like her very much," said Paul Overt.

Something in his tone appeared to excite on his companion's part a momentary sense of the absurd; perhaps it was the air of deliberation attending this judgment. St. George broke into a laugh and returned: "It's the best thing you can do with her. She's a rare young lady! In point of fact, however, I confess I hadn't read you this afternoon."

"Then you see how right I was in this particular case not to believe Miss Fancourt."

"How right? how can I agree to that, when I lost credit by it?"

"Do you wish to pass for exactly what she represents you? Certainly you needn't be afraid," Paul said.

"Ah, my dear young man, don't talk about passing — for the likes of me! I'm passing away — nothing else than that. She has a better use for her young imagination (isn't it fine?) than in 'representing' in any way such a weary, wasted, used-up animal!" St. George spoke with a sudden sadness which produced a protest on Paul's part; but before the protest could be uttered he went on, reverting to the latter's successful novel: "I had no idea you were so good — one hears of so many things. But you're surprisingly good."

"I'm going to be surprisingly better," said Overt.

"I see that and it's what fetches me. I don't see so much else — as one looks about — that's going to be surprisingly better. They're going to be consistently worse — most of the things. It's so much easier to be worse

—heaven knows I've found it so. I'm not in a great glow, you know, about what's being attempted, what's being done. But you *must* be better — you must keep it up. I haven't, of course. It's very difficult — that's the devil of the whole thing; but I see you can. It will be a great disgrace if you don't."

"It's very interesting to hear you speak of yourself; but I don't know what you mean by your allusions to your having fallen off," Paul Overt remarked, with pardonable hypocrisy. He liked his companion so much now that it had ceased for the moment to be vivid to him that there had been any decline.

"Don't say that — don't say that," St. George replied gravely, with his head resting on the top of the back of the sofa and his eyes on the ceiling. "You know perfectly what I mean. I haven't read twenty pages of your book without seeing that you can't help it."

"You make me very miserable," Paul murmured.

"I'm glad of that, for it may serve as a kind of warning. Shocking enough it must be, especially to a young, fresh mind, full of faith, — the spectacle of a man meant for better things sunk at my age in such dishonour." St. George, in the same contemplative attitude, spoke softly but deliberately, and without perceptible emotion. His tone indeed suggested an impersonal lucidity which was cruel — cruel to himself — and which made Paul lay an argumentative hand on his arm. But he went on, while his eyes seemed to follow the ingenuities of the beautiful Adams ceiling: "Look at me well and take my lesson to heart, for it *is* a lesson. Let that good come of it at least that you shudder with your pitiful impression and that this may help to keep you straight in the future. Don't become in your old age what I am in mine — the depressing, the deplorable illustration of the worship of false gods!"

"What do you mean by your old age?" Paul Overt asked.

"It has made me old.   But I like your youth."

Overt answered nothing — they sat for a minute in silence.   They heard the others talking about the governmental majority.   Then, "What do you mean by false gods?" Paul inquired.

"The idols of the market — money and luxury and 'the world,' placing one's children and dressing one's wife — everything that drives one to the short and easy way.   Ah, the vile things they make one do!"

"But surely one is right to want to place one's children."

"One has no business to have any children," St. George declared, placidly.   "I mean of course if one wants to do something good."

"But aren't they an inspiration — an incentive?"

"An incentive to damnation, artistically speaking."

"You touch on very deep things — things I should like to discuss with you," Paul Overt said.   "I should like you to tell me volumes about yourself.   This is a festival for *me!*"

"Of course it is, cruel youth.   But to show you that I'm still not incapable, degraded as I am, of an act of faith, I'll tie my vanity to the stake for you and burn it to ashes.   You must come and see me — you must come and see us.   Mrs. St. George is charming; I don't know whether you have had any opportunity to talk with her. She will be delighted to see you; she likes great celebrities, whether incipient or predominant.   You must come and dine — my wife will write to you.   Where are you to be found?"

"This is my little address" — and Overt drew out his pocketbook and extracted a visiting-card.   On second thoughts, however, he kept it back, remarking that he would not trouble his friend to take charge of it but would come and see him straightway in London and leave it at his door if he should fail to obtain admittance.

"Ah! you probably will fail; my wife's always out, or when she isn't out she's knocked up from having been out. You must come and dine — though that won't do much good either, for my wife insists on big dinners. You must come down and see us in the country, that's the best way; we have plenty of room, and it isn't bad."

"You have a house in the country?" Paul asked, enviously.

"Ah, not like this! But we have a sort of place we go to — an hour from Euston. That's one of the reasons."

"One of the reasons?"

"Why my books are so bad."

"You must tell me all the others!" Paul exclaimed, laughing.

St. George made no direct rejoinder to this; he only inquired rather abruptly: "Why have I never seen you before?"

The tone of the question was singularly flattering to his new comrade; it seemed to imply that he perceived now that for years he had missed something. "Partly, I suppose, because there has been no particular reason why you should see me. I haven't lived in the world — in your world. I have spent many years out of England, in different places abroad."

"Well, please don't do it any more. You must do England — there's such a lot of it."

"Do you mean I must write about it?" Paul asked, in a voice which had the note of the listening candour of a child.

"Of course you must. And tremendously well, do you mind? That takes off a little of my esteem for this thing of yours — that it goes on abroad. Hang abroad! Stay at home and do things here — do subjects we can measure."

"I'll do whatever you tell me," said Paul Overt, deeply attentive. "But excuse me if I say I don't understand how you have been reading my book," he subjoined. "I've had you before me all the afternoon, first in that long walk, then at tea on the lawn, till we went to dress for dinner, and all the evening at dinner and in this place."

St. George turned his face round with a smile. "I only read for a quarter of an hour."

"A quarter of an hour is liberal, but I don't understand where you put it in. In the drawing-room, after dinner, you were not reading, you were talking to Miss Fancourt."

"It comes to the same thing, because we talked about *Ginistrella*. She described it to me — she lent it to me."

"Lent it to you?"

"She travels with it."

"It's incredible," Paul Overt murmured, blushing.

"It's glorious for you; but it also turned out very well for me. When the ladies went off to bed she kindly offered to send the book down to me. Her maid brought it to me in the hall and I went to my room with it. I hadn't thought of coming here, I do that so little. But I don't sleep early, I always have to read for an hour or two. I sat down to your novel on the spot, without undressing, without taking off anything but my coat. I think that's a sign that my curiosity had been strongly roused about it. I read a quarter of an hour, as I tell you, and even in a quarter of an hour I was greatly struck."

" Ah, the beginning isn't very good — it's the whole thing!" said Overt, who had listened to this recital with extreme interest. "And you laid down the book and came after me ?" he asked.

"That's the way it moved me. I said to myself, 'I see it's off his own bat, and he's there, by the way, and the day's over and I haven't said twenty words to him.' It occurred to me that you would probably be in the smoking-room and that it wouldn't be too late to repair my omission. I wanted to do something civil to you, so I put oɔ my coat and came down. I shall read your book again when I go up."

Paul Overt turned round in his place — he was exceedingly touched by the picture of such a demonstration in his favour. "You're really the kindest of men. *Cela s'est passé comme ça?* and I have been sitting here with you all this time and never apprehended it and never thanked you!"

"Thank Miss Fancourt — it was she who wound me up. She has made me feel as if I had read your novel."

"She's an angel from heaven!" Paul Overt exclaimed.

"She is indeed. I have never seen anyone like her. Her interest in literature is touching — something quite peculiar to herself; she takes it all so seriously. She feels the arts and she wants to feel them more. To those who practise them it's almost humiliating — her curiosity, her sympathy, her good faith. How can anything be as fine as she supposes it ?"

"She's a rare organisation," Paul Overt sighed.

"The richest I have ever seen — an artistic intelligence really of the first order. And lodged in such a form!" St. George exclaimed.

"One would like to paint such a girl as that," Overt continued.

C

"Ah, there it is — there's nothing like life! When you're finished, squeezed dry and used up and you think the sack's empty, you're still spoken to, you still get touches and thrills, the idea springs up — out of the lap of the actual — and shows you there's always something to be done. But I shan't do it — she's not for me!"

"How do you mean, not for you?"

"Oh, it's all over — she's for you, if you like."

"Ah, much less!" said Paul Overt. "She's not for a dingy little man of letters; she's for the world, the bright rich world of bribes and rewards. And the world will take hold of her — it will carry her away."

"It will try; but it's just a case in which there may be a fight. It would be worth fighting, for a man who had it in him, with youth and talent on his side."

These words rang not a little in Paul Overt's consciousness — they held him silent a moment. "It's a wonder she has remained as she is — giving herself away so, with so much to give away."

"Do you mean so ingenuous — so natural? Oh, she doesn't care a straw — she gives away because she overflows. She has her own feelings, her own standards; she doesn't keep remembering that she must be proud. And then she hasn't been here long enough to be spoiled; she has picked up a fashion or two, but only the amusing ones. She's a provincial — a provincial of genius; her very blunders are charming, her mistakes are interesting. She has come back from Asia with all sorts of excited curiosities and unappeased appetites. She's first-rate herself and she expends herself on the second-rate. She's life herself and she takes a rare interest in imitations. She mixes all things up, but there are none in regard to which she hasn't perceptions. She sees things in a perspective — as if from the top of the Himalayas — and she enlarges everything she touches. Above all she exaggerates — to herself, I mean. She exaggerates you and me!"

There was nothing in this description to allay the excitement produced in the mind of our younger friend by such a sketch of a fine subject. It seemed to him to show the art of St. George's admired hand, and he lost himself in it, gazing at the vision (it hovered there before him,) of a woman's figure which should be part of the perfection of a novel. At the end of a moment he became aware that it had turned into smoke, and out of the smoke — the last puff of a big cigar — proceeded the voice of General Fancourt, who had left the others and come and planted himself before the gentlemen on the sofa. "I suppose that when you fellows get talking you sit up half the night."

"Half the night?—*jamais de la vie!* I follow a hygiene," St. George replied, rising to his feet.

"I see, you're hothouse plants," laughed the General. "That's the way you produce your flowers."

"I produce mine between ten and one every morning; I bloom with a regularity!" St. George went on.

"And with a splendour!" added the polite General, while Paul Overt noted how little the author of *Shadowmere* minded, as he phrased it to himself, when he was addressed as a celebrated story-teller. The young man had an idea that *he* should never get used to that — it would always make him uncomfortable (from the suspicion that people would think they had to,) and he would want to prevent it. Evidently his more illustrious congener had toughened and hardened — had made himself a surface. The group of men had finished their cigars and taken up their bedroom candlesticks; but before they all passed out Lord Watermouth invited St.

George and Paul Overt to drink something. It happened that they both declined, upon which General Fancourt said: "Is that the hygiene? You don't sprinkle the flowers?"

"Oh, I should drown them!" St. George replied; but leaving the room beside Overt he added whimsically, for the latter's benefit, in a lower tone: "My wife doesn't let me."

"Well, I'm glad I'm not one of you fellows!" the General exclaimed.

The nearness of Summersoft to London had this consequence, chilling to a person who had had a vision of sociability in a railway-carriage, that most of the company, after breakfast, drove back to town, entering their own vehicles, which had come out to fetch them, while their servants returned by train with their luggage. Three or four young men, among whom was Paul Overt, also availed themselves of the common convenience; but they stood in the portico of the house and saw the others roll away. Miss Fancourt got into a victoria with her father, after she had shaken hands with Paul Overt and said, smiling in the frankest way in the world — "I *must* see you more. Mrs. St. George is so nice: she has promised to ask us both to dinner together." This lady and her husband took their places in a perfectly-appointed brougham (she required a closed carriage,) and as our young man waved his hat to them in response to their nods and flourishes he reflected that, taken together, they were an honourable image of success, of the material rewards and the social credit of literature. Such things were not the full measure, but all the same he felt a little proud for literature.

IV.

BEFORE a week had elapsed Paul Overt met Miss Fancourt in Bond Street, at a private view of the works of a young artist in "black and white" who had been so good as to invite him to the stuffy scene. The drawings were admirable, but the crowd in the one little room was so dense that he felt as if he were up to his neck in a big sack of wool. A fringe of people at the outer edge endeavoured by curving forward their backs and presenting, below them, a still more convex surface of resistance to the pressure of the mass, to preserve an interval between their noses and the glazed mounts of the pictures; while the central body, in the comparative gloom projected by a wide horizontal screen, hung under the skylight and allowing only a margin for the day, remained upright, dense and vague, lost in the contemplation of its own ingredients. This contemplation sat especially in the sad eyes of certain female heads, surmounted with hats of strange convolution and plumage, which rose on long necks above the others. One of the heads, Paul Overt perceived, was much the most beautiful of the collection, and his next discovery was that it belonged to Miss Fancourt. Its beauty was enhanced by the glad smile that she sent him across surrounding obstructions, a smile which drew him to her as fast as he could make his way. He had divined at Summersoft that the last thing her nature contained was an affectation of indifference; yet even with this circumspection he had a freshness of pleasure in seeing that she did not pretend to await his arrival with composure. She smiled as radiantly as if she wished to make him hurry, and as soon as he came within earshot she said to him, in her voice of joy: " He's here — he's here — he's coming back in a moment!"

"Ah, your father?" Paul responded, as she offered him her hand.

"Oh dear no, this isn't in my poor father's line. I mean Mr. St. George. He has just left me to speak to some one — he's coming back. It's he who brought me — wasn't it charming?"

"Ah, that gives him a pull over me — I couldn't have 'brought' you, could I?"

"If you had been so kind as to propose it — why not you as well as he?" the girl asked, with a face which expressed no cheap coquetry, but simply affirmed a happy fact.

"Why, he's a *père de famille*. They have privileges," Paul Overt explained. And then, quickly: "Will you go to see places with *me?*" he broke out.

"Anything you like!" she smiled. "I know what you mean, that girls have to have a lot of people ——" She interrupted herself to say: "I don't know; I'm free. I have always been like that," she went on; "I can go anywhere with any one. I'm so glad to meet you," she added, with a sweet distinctness that made the people near her turn round.

"Let me at least repay that speech by taking you out of this squash," said Paul Overt. "Surely people are not happy here!"

"No, they are *mornes*, aren't they? But I am very happy indeed, and I promised Mr. St. George to remain in this spot till he comes back. He's going to take me away. They send him invitations for things of this sort — more than he wants. It was so kind of him to think of me."

"They also send me invitations of this kind — more than I want. And if thinking of *you* will do it ——!" Paul went on.

"Oh, I delight in them — everything that's life — everything that's London!"

"They don't have private views in Asia, I suppose. But what a pity that for this year, in this fertile city, they are pretty well over."

"Well, next year will do, for I hope you believe we are going to be friends always. Here he comes!" Miss Fancourt continued, before Paul had time to respond.

He made out St. George in the gaps of the crowd, and this perhaps led to his hurrying a little to say : "I hope that doesn't mean that I'm to wait till next year to see you."

"No, no; are we not to meet at dinner on the 25th?" she answered, with an eagerness greater even than his own.

"That's almost next year. Is there no means of seeing you before?"

She stared, with all her brightness. "Do you mean that you would *come?*"

"Like a shot, if you'll be so good as to ask me!"

"On Sunday, then — this next Sunday?"

"What have I done that you should doubt it?" the young man demanded, smiling.

Miss Fancourt turned instantly to St. George, who had now joined them, and announced triumphantly : "He's coming on Sunday — this next Sunday!"

"Ah, my day — my day too!" said the famous novelist, laughing at Paul Overt.

"Yes, but not yours only. You shall meet in Manchester Square; you shall talk — you shall be wonderful!"

"We don't meet often enough," St. George remarked, shaking hands with his disciple. "Too many things — ah, too many things! But we must make it up in the country in September. You won't forget that you've promised me that?"

"Why, he's coming on the 25th; you'll see him then," said Marian Fancourt.

"On the 25th?" St. George asked, vaguely.

"We dine with you; I hope you haven't forgotten. He's dining out," she added gaily to Paul Overt.

"Oh, bless me, yes; that's charming! And you're coming? My wife didn't tell me," St. George said to Paul. "Too many things — too many things!" he repeated.

"Too many people — too many people!" Paul exclaimed, giving ground before the penetration of an elbow.

"You oughtn't to say that; they all read you."

"Me? I should like to see them! Only two or three at most," the young man rejoined.

"Did you ever hear anything like that? he knows how good he is!" St. George exclaimed, laughing, to Miss Fancourt. "They read *me*, but that doesn't make me like them any better. Come away from them, come away!" And he led the way out of the exhibition.

"He's going to take me to the Park," the girl said, with elation, to Paul Overt, as they passed along the corridor which led to the street.

"Ah, does he go there?" Paul asked, wondering at the idea as a somewhat unexpected illustration of St. George's *moeurs*.

"It's a beautiful day; there will be a great crowd. We're going to look at the people, to look at types," the girl went on. "We shall sit under the trees; we shall walk by the Row."

"I go once a year, on business," said St. George, who had overheard Paul's question.

"Or with a country cousin, didn't you tell me? I'm the country cousin!" she went on, over her shoulder, to

Paul, as her companion drew her toward a hansom to which he had signalled. The young man watched them get in; he returned, as he stood there, the friendly wave of the hand with which, ensconced in the vehicle beside Miss Fancourt, St. George took leave of him. He even lingered to see the vehicle start away and lose itself in the confusion of Bond Street. He followed it with his eyes; it was embarrassingly suggestive. "She's not for me!" the great novelist had said emphatically at Summersoft; but his manner of conducting himself toward her appeared not exactly in harmony with such a conviction. How could he have behaved differently if she *had* been for him? An indefinite envy rose in Paul Overt's heart as he took his way on foot alone, and the singular part of it was that it was directed to each of the occupants of the hansom. How much he should like to rattle about London with such a girl! How much he should like to go and look at "types" with St. George!

The next Sunday, at four o'clock, he called in Manchester Square, where his secret wish was gratified by his finding Miss Fancourt alone. She was in a large, bright, friendly, occupied room, which was painted red all over, draped with the quaint, cheap, florid stuffs that are represented as coming from southern and eastern countries, where they are fabled to serve as the counterpanes of the peasantry, and bedecked with pottery of vivid hues, ranged on casual shelves, and with many water-colour drawings from the hand (as the visitor learned,) of the young lady, commemorating, with courage and skill, the sunsets, the mountains, the temples and palaces of India. Overt sat there an hour — more than an hour, two hours — and all the while no one came in. Miss Fancourt was so good as to remark, with her liberal humanity, that it was delightful they were not interrupted; it was so rare in London, especially at that season, that people got a good talk. But fortunately now, of a fine Sunday, half the world went out of town, and that made it better for those who didn't go, when they were in sympathy. It was the defect of London (one of two or three, the very short list of those she recognised in the teeming world-city that she adored,) that there were too few good chances for talk; one never had time to carry anything far.

"Too many things — too many things!" Paul Overt said, quoting St. George's exclamation of a few days before.

"Ah yes, for him there are too many; his life is too complicated."

"Have you seen it *near?* That's what I should like to do; it might explain some mysteries," Paul Overt went on. The girl asked him what mysteries he meant, and he said: "Oh, peculiarities of his work, inequalities, superficialities. For one who looks at it from the artistic point of view it contains a bottomless ambiguity."

"Oh, do describe that more — it's so interesting. There are no such suggestive questions. I'm so fond of them. He thinks he's a failure — fancy!" Miss Fancourt added.

"That depends upon what his ideal may have been. Ah, with his gifts it ought to have been high. But till one knows what he really proposed to himself—— Do *you* know, by chance?" the young man asked, breaking off.

"Oh, he doesn't talk to me about himself. I can't make him. It's too provoking."

Paul Overt was on the point of asking what then he did talk about; but discretion checked this inquiry, and he said instead: "Do you think he's unhappy at home?"

"At home?"

"I mean in his relations with his wife. He has a mystifying little way of alluding to her."

"Not to me," said Marian Fancourt, with her clear eyes. "That wouldn't be right, would it?" she asked, seriously.

"Not particularly; so I am glad he doesn't mention her to you. To praise her might bore you, and he has no business to do anything else. Yet he knows you better than me."

"Ah, but he respects *you!*" the girl exclaimed, enviously.

Her visitor stared a moment; then he broke into a laugh. "Doesn't he respect you?"

"Of course, but not in the same way. He respects what you've done — he told me so, the other day."

"When you went to look at types?"

"Ah, we found so many — he has such an observation of them! He talked a great deal about your book. He says it's really important."

"Important! Ah! the grand creature," Paul murmured, hilarious.

"He was wonderfully amusing, he was inexpressibly droll, while we walked about. He sees everything; he has so many comparisons, and they are always exactly right. *C'est d'un trouvé!* as they say."

"Yes, with his gifts, such things as he ought to have done!" Paul Overt remarked.

"And don't you think he *has* done them?"

He hesitated a moment. "A part of them — and of course even that part is immense. But he might have been one of the greatest! However, let us not make this an hour of qualifications. Even as they stand, his writings are a mine of gold."

To this proposition Marian Fancourt ardently responded, and for half an hour the pair talked over the master's principal productions. She knew them well —

she knew them even better than her visitor, who was struck with her critical intelligence and with something large and bold in the movement in her mind. She said things that startled him and that evidently had come to her directly; they were not picked-up phrases, she placed them too well. St. George had been right about her being first-rate, about her not being afraid to gush, not remembering that she must be proud. Suddenly something reminded her, and she said: "I recollect that he did speak of Mrs. St. George to me once. He said, à propos of something or other, that she didn't care for perfection."

"That's a great crime, for an artist's wife," said Paul Overt.

"Yes, poor thing!" and the young lady sighed, with a suggestion of many reflections, some of them mitigating. But she added in a moment, "Ah, perfection, perfection — how one ought to go in for it! I wish I could."

"Every one can, in his way," said Paul Overt.

"In *his* way, yes; but not in hers. Women are so hampered — so condemned! But it's a kind of dishonour if you don't, when you want to *do* something, isn't it?" Miss Fancourt pursued, dropping one train in her quickness to take up another, an accident that was common with her. So these two young persons sat discussing high themes in their eclectic drawing-room, in their London season — discussing, with extreme seriousness, the high theme of perfection. And it must be said, in extenuation of this eccentricity, that they were interested in the business; their tone was genuine, their emotion real; they were not posturing for each other or for some one else.

The subject was so wide that they found it necessary to contract it; the perfection to which for the moment

they agreed to confine their speculations was that of
which the valid work of art is susceptible. Miss Fancourt's imagination, it appeared, had wandered far in that
direction, and her visitor had the rare delight of feeling
that their conversation was a full interchange.   This
episode will have lived for years in his memory and even
in his wonder; it had the quality that fortune distils in
a single drop at a time — the quality that lubricates ensuing weeks and months. He has still a vision of the
room, whenever he likes — the bright, red, sociable, talk-
ative room, with the curtains that, by a stroke of successful audacity, had the note of vivid blue. He remembers
where certain things stood, the book that was open on
the table and the particular odour of the flowers that
were placed on the left, somewhere behind him. These
facts were the fringe, as it were, of a particular consciousness which had its birth in those two hours and of which
perhaps the most general description would be to mention that it led him to say over and over again to himself: "I had no idea there was any one like this — I had
no idea there was any one like this!" Her freedom
amazed him and charmed him — it seemed so to simplify
the practical question. She was on the footing of an independent personage — a motherless girl who had passed
out of her teens and had a position, responsibilities, and
was not held down to the limitations of a little miss.
She came and went without the clumsiness of a chaperon;
she received people alone and, though she was totally
without hardness, the question of protection or patron-
age had no relevancy in regard to her. She gave such
an impression of purity combined with naturalness that,
in spite of her eminently modern situation, she suggested
no sort of sisterhood with the "fast" girl. Modern she
was, indeed, and made Paul Overt, who loved old colour,

the golden glaze of time, think with some alarm of the muddled palette of the future. He couldn't get used to her interest in the arts he cared for; it seemed too good to be real — it was so unlikely an adventure to tumble into such a well of sympathy. One might stray into the desert easily — that was on the cards and that was the law of life; but it was too rare an accident to stumble on a crystal well. Yet if her aspirations seemed at one moment too extravagant to be real, they struck him at the next as too intelligent to be false. They were both noble and crude, and whims for whims, he liked them better than any he had met. It was probable enough she would leave them behind — exchange them for politics, or "smartness," or mere prolific maternity, as was the custom of scribbling, daubing, educated, flattered girls, in an age of luxury and a society of leisure. He noted that the water-colours on the walls of the room she sat in had mainly the quality of being *naïves,* and reflected that *naïveté* in art is like a cipher in a number: its importance depends upon the figure it is united with. But meanwhile he had fallen in love with her.

Before he went away he said to Miss Fancourt: "I thought St. George was coming to see you to-day — but he doesn't turn up."

For a moment he supposed she was going to reply, "*Comment donc?* Did you come here only to meet him?" But the next he became aware of how little such a speech would have fallen in with any flirtatious element he had as yet perceived in her. She only replied: "Ah yes, but I don't think he'll come. He recommended me not to expect him." Then she added, laughing: "He said it wasn't fair to you. But I think I could manage two."

"So could I," Paul Overt rejoined, stretching the

point a little to be humorous. In reality his appreciation of the occasion was so completely an appreciation
of the woman before him that another figure in the
scene, even so esteemed a one as St. George, might for
the hour have appealed to him vainly. As he went away
he wondered what the great man had meant by its not
being fair to him; and, still more than that, whether he
had actually stayed away out of the delicacy of such an
idea. As he took his course, swinging his stick, through
the Sunday solitude of Manchester Square, with a good
deal of emotion fermenting in his soul, it appeared to
him that he was living in a world really magnanimous.
Miss Fancourt had told him that there was an uncertainty about her being, and her father's being, in town
on the following Sunday, but that she had the hope of a
visit from him if they should not go away. She promised to let him know if they stayed at home, then he could
act accordingly. After he had passed into one of the
streets that lead out of the square, he stopped, without
definite intentions, looking sceptically for a cab. In a
moment he saw a hansom roll through the square from
the other side and come a part of the way toward him.
He was on the point of hailing the driver when he perceived that he carried a fare; then he waited, seeing him
prepare to deposit his passenger by pulling up at one of
the houses. The house was apparently the one he himself had just quitted; at least he drew that inference as
he saw that the person who stepped out of the hansom
was Henry St. George. Paul Overt turned away quickly,
as if he had been caught in the act of spying. He
gave up his cab — he preferred to walk; he would go
nowhere else. He was glad St. George had not given
up his visit altogether — that would have been too absurd.
Yes, the world was magnanimous, and Overt felt so too

as, on looking at his watch, he found it was only six o'clock, so that he could mentally congratulate his successor on having an hour still to sit in Miss Fancourt's drawing-room. He himself might use that hour for another visit, but by the time he reached the Marble Arch the idea of another visit had become incongruous to him. He passed beneath that architectural effort and walked into the Park till he got upon the grass. Here he continued to walk; he took his way across the elastic turf and came out by the Serpentine. He watched with a friendly eye the diversions of the London people, and bent a glance almost encouraging upon the young ladies paddling their sweethearts on the lake, and the guardsmen tickling tenderly with their bearskins the artificial flowers in the Sunday hats of their partners. He prolonged his meditative walk; he went into Kensington Gardens — he sat upon the penny chairs — he looked at the little sail-boats launched upon the round pond — he was glad he had no engagement to dine. He repaired for this purpose, very late, to his club, where he found himself unable to order a repast and told the waiter to bring whatever he would. He did not even observe what he was served with, and he spent the evening in the library of the establishment, pretending to read an article in an American magazine. He failed to discover what it was about; it appeared in a dim way to be about Marian Fancourt.

Quite late in the week she wrote to him that she was not to go into the country — it had only just been settled. Her father, she added, would never settle anything — he put it all on her. She felt her responsibility — she had to — and since she was forced that was the way she had decided. She mentioned no reasons, which gave Paul Overt all the clearer field for bold conjecture about them. In Manchester Square, on this second Sunday, he esteemed his fortune less good, for she had three or four other visitors. But there were three or four compensations; the greatest, perhaps, of which was that, learning from her that her father had, after all, at the last hour, gone out of town alone, the bold conjecture I just now spoke of found itself becoming a shade more bold. And then her presence was her presence, and the personal red room was there and was full of it, whatever phantoms passed and vanished, emitting incomprehensible sounds. Lastly, he had the resource of staying till every one had come and gone and of supposing that this pleased her, though she gave no particular sign. When they were alone together he said to her: "But St. George did come — last Sunday. I saw him as I looked back."

"Yes; but it was the last time."

"The last time?"

"He said he would never come again."

Paul Overt stared. "Does he mean that he wishes to cease to see you?"

"I don't know what he means," the girl replied, smiling. "He won't, at any rate, see me here."

"And, pray, why not?"

"I don't know," said Marian Fancourt; and her visitor thought he had not yet seen her more beautiful than in uttering these unsatisfactory words.

V.

"Oh, I say, I want you to remain," Henry St. George said to him at eleven o'clock, the night he dined with the head of the profession. The company had been numerous and they were taking their leave; our young man, after bidding good-night to his hostess, had put out his hand

D

in farewell to the master of the house. Besides eliciting from St. George the protest I have quoted this movement provoked a further observation about such a chance to have a talk, their going into his room, his having still everything to say. Paul Overt was delighted to be asked to stay; nevertheless he mentioned jocularly the literal fact that he had promised to go to another place, at a distance.

"Well then, you'll break your promise, that's all. You humbug!" St. George exclaimed, in a tone that added to Overt's contentment.

"Certainly, I'll break it; but it was a real promise."

"Do you mean to Miss Fancourt? You're following her?" St. George asked.

Paul Overt answered by a question. "Oh, is *she* going?"

"Base impostor!" his ironic host went on; "I've treated you handsomely on the article of that young lady: I won't make another concession. Wait three minutes — I'll be with you." He gave himself to his departing guests, went with the long-trained ladies to the door. It was a hot night, the windows were open, the sound of the quick carriages and of the linkmen's call came into the house. The company had been brilliant; a sense of festal things was in the heavy air: not only the influence of that particular entertainment, but the suggestion of the wide hurry of pleasure which, in London, on summer nights, fills so many of the happier quarters of the complicated town. Gradually Mrs. St. George's drawing-room emptied itself; Paul Overt was left alone with his hostess, to whom he explained the motive of his waiting. "Ah yes, some intellectual, some *professional*, talk," she smiled; "at this season doesn't one miss it? Poor dear Henry, I'm so glad!" The young man looked out of the window a moment, at the called hansoms that lurched up, at the smooth broughams that rolled away. When he turned round Mrs. St. George had disappeared; her husband's voice came up to him from below — he was laughing and talking, in the portico, with some lady who awaited her carriage. Paul had solitary possession, for some minutes, of the warm, deserted rooms, where the covered, tinted lamplight was soft, the seats had been pushed about and the odour of flowers lingered. They were large, they were pretty, they contained objects of value; everything in the picture told of a "good house." At the end of five minutes a servant came in with a request from Mr. St. George that he would join him downstairs; upon which, descending, he followed his conductor through a long passage to an apartment thrown out, in the rear of the habitation, for the special requirements, as he guessed, of a busy man of letters.

St. George was in his shirt-sleeves in the middle of a large, high room — a room without windows, but with a wide skylight at the top, like a place of exhibition. It was furnished as a library, and the serried bookshelves rose to the ceiling, a surface of incomparable tone, produced by dimly-gilt "backs," which was interrupted here and there by the suspension of old prints and drawings. At the end furthest from the door of admission was a tall desk, of great extent, at which the person using it could only write standing, like a clerk in a counting-house; and stretching from the door to this structure was a large plain band of crimson cloth, as straight as a garden-path and almost as long, where, in his mind's eye, Paul Overt immediately saw his host pace to and fro during his hours of composition. The servant gave him a coat, an old jacket with an air of experience, from a cupboard in the wall, retiring afterwards with the garment he had taken off. Paul Overt welcomed the coat; it was a coat for talk and promised confidences — it must have received so many — and had pathetic literary elbows. "Ah, we're practical — we're practical!" St. George said, as he saw his visitor looking the place over. "Isn't it a good big cage, to go round and round? My wife invented it and she locks me up here every morning."

"You don't miss a window — a place to look out?"

"I did at first, awfully; but her calculation was just. It saves time, it has saved me many months in these ten years. Here I stand, under the eye of day — in London of course, very often, it's rather a bleared old eye — walled in to my trade. I can't get away, and the room is a fine lesson in concentration. I've learned the lesson, I think; look at that big bundle of proof and admit that I have." He pointed to a fat roll of papers, on one of the tables, which had not been undone.

"Are you bringing out another——?" Paul Overt asked, in a tone of whose deficiencies he was not conscious till his companion burst out laughing, and indeed not even then.

"You humbug — you humbug! Don't I know what you think of them?" St. George inquired, standing before him with his hands in his pockets and with a new kind of smile. It was as if he were going to let his young votary know him well now.

"Upon my word, in that case you know more than I do!" Paul ventured to respond, revealing a part of the torment of being able neither clearly to esteem him nor distinctly to renounce him.

"My dear fellow," said his companion, "don't imagine I talk about my books, specifically; it isn't a decent subject — *il ne manquerait plus que ça* — I'm not so bad as you may apprehend! About myself, a little, if you like; though it wasn't for that I brought you down here. I want to ask you something — very much indeed — I value this chance. Therefore sit down. We are practical, but there *is* a sofa, you see, for she does humour me a little, after all. Like all really great administrators she knows when to." Paul Overt sank into the corner of a deep leathern couch, but his interlocutor remained standing and said: "If you don't mind, in this room this is my habit. From the door to the desk and from the desk to the door. That shakes up my imagination, gently; and don't you see what a good thing it is that there's no window for her to fly out of? The eternal standing as I write (I stop at that bureau and put it down, when anything comes, and so we go on,) was rather wearisome at first, but we adopted it with an eye to the long run; you're in better order (if your legs don't break down!) and you can keep it up for more years. Oh, we're practical — we're practical!" St. George repeated, going to the table and taking up, mechanically, the bundle of proofs. He pulled off the wrapper, he turned the papers over with a sudden change of attention which only made him more interesting to Paul Overt. He lost himself a moment, examining the sheets of his new book, while the younger man's eyes wandered over the room again.

"Lord, what good things I should do if I had such a charming place as this to do them in!" Paul reflected. The outer world, the world of accident and ugliness was so successfully excluded, and within the rich, protecting square, beneath the patronising sky, the figures projected for an artistic purpose could hold their particular revel. It was a prevision of Paul Overt's rather than an observation on actual data, for which the occasions had been too few, that his new friend would have the quality, the charming quality, of surprising him by flashing out in personal intercourse, at moments of suspended, or perhaps even of diminished expectation. A happy relation with him would be a thing proceeding by jumps, not by traceable stages.

"Do you read them — really?" he asked, laying down the proofs on Paul's inquiring of him how soon the work would be published. And when the young man answered, "Oh yes, always," he was moved to mirth again by something he caught in his manner of saying that. "You go to see your grandmother on her birthday — and very proper it is, especially as she won't last for ever. She has lost every faculty and every sense; she neither sees, nor hears, nor speaks; but all customary pieties and kindly habits are respectable. But you're strong if you *do* read 'em! *I* couldn't, my dear fellow. You *are* strong, I know; and that's just a part of what I wanted to say to you. You're very strong indeed. I've been going into your other things — they've interested me exceedingly. Some one ought to have told me about them before — some one I could believe. But whom can one believe? You're wonderfully in the good direction — it's extremely curious work. Now do you mean to keep it up? — that's what I want to ask you."

"Do I mean to do others?" Paul Overt asked, looking up from his sofa at his erect inquisitor and feeling partly like a happy little boy when the schoolmaster is gay and partly like some pilgrim of old who might have consulted the oracle. St. George's own performance had been infirm, but as an adviser he would be infallible.

"Others — others? Ah, the number won't matter; one other would do, if it were really a further step — a throb of the same effort. What I mean is, have you it in your mind to go in for some sort of little perfection?"

"Ah, perfection!" Overt sighed, "I talked of that the other Sunday with Miss Fancourt."

"Oh yes, they'll talk of it, as much as you like! But
they do mighty little to help one to it. There's no obligation, of course; only you strike me as capable," St.
George went on. "You must have thought it all over.
I can't believe you're without a plan. That's the sensation you give me, and it's so rare that it really stirs up
one; it makes you remarkable. If you haven't a plan
and you don't mean to keep it up, of course it's all right,
it's no one's business, no one can force you, and not more
than two or three people will notice that you don't go
straight. The others — *all* the rest, every blessed soul
in England, will think you do — will think you *are* keeping it up: upon my honour they will! I shall be one of
the two or three who know better. Now the question
is whether you can do it for two or three. Is that the
stuff you're made of?"

"I could do it for one, if you were the one."

"Don't say that — I don't deserve it; it scorches me,"
St. George exclaimed, with eyes suddenly grave and glow-
ing. "The 'one' is of course oneself — one's conscience,
one's idea, the singleness of one's aim. I think of that
pure spirit as a man thinks of a woman whom, in some
detested hour of his youth, he has loved and forsaken.
She haunts him with reproachful eyes, she lives for ever
before him. As an artist, you know, I've married for
money." Paul stared and even blushed a little, con-
founded by this avowal; whereupon his host, observing
the expression of his face, dropped a quick laugh and
went on: "You don't follow my figure. I'm not speaking
of my dear wife, who had a small fortune, which, however,
was not my bribe. I fell in love with her, as many other
people have done. I refer to the mercenary muse whom
I led to the altar of literature. Don't do that, my boy.
She'll lead you a life!"

"Haven't you been happy!"

"Happy? It's a kind of hell."

"There are things I should like to ask you," Paul Overt said, hesitating.

"Ask me anything in all the world. I'd turn myself inside out to save you."

"To save me?" Paul repeated.

"To make you stick to it — to make you see it through. As I said to you the other night at Summersoft, let my example be vivid to you."

"Why, your books are not so bad as that," said Paul, laughing and feeling that he breathed the air of art.

"So bad as what?"

"Your talent is so great that it is in everything you do, in what's less good as well as in what's best. You've some forty volumes to show for it — forty volumes of life, of observation, of magnificent ability."

"I'm very clever, of course I know that," St. George replied, quietly. "Lord, what rot they'd all be if I hadn't been! I'm a successful charlatan — I've been able to pass off my system. But do you know what it is? It's *carton-pierre*."

"*Carton-pierre?*"

"Lincrusta-Walton!"

"Ah, don't say such things — you make me bleed!" the younger man protested. "I see you in a beautiful, fortunate home, living in comfort and honour."

"Do you call it honour?" St. George interrupted, with an intonation that often comes back to his companion. "That's what I want *you* to go in for. I mean the real thing. This is brummagaem."

"Brummagaem?" Paul ejaculated, while his eyes wandered, by a movement natural at the moment, over the luxurious room.

"Ah, they make it so well to-day; it's wonderfully deceptive!"

"Is it deceptive that I find you living with every appearance of domestic felicity — blessed with a devoted, accomplished wife, with children whose acquaintance I haven't yet had the pleasure of making, but who *must* be delightful young people, from what I know of their parents?"

"It's all excellent, my dear fellow — heaven forbid I should deny it. I've made a great deal of money; my wife has known how to take care of it, to use it without wasting it, to put a good bit of it by, to make it fructify. I've got a loaf on the shelf; I've got everything, in fact, but the great thing——"

"The great thing?"

"The sense of having done the best — the sense, which is the real life of the artist and the absence of which is his death, of having drawn from his intellectual instrument the finest music that nature had hidden in it, of having played it as it should be played. He either does that or he doesn't — and if he doesn't he isn't worth speaking of. And precisely those who really know don't speak of him. He may still hear a great chatter, but what he hears most is the incorruptible silence of Fame. I have squared her, you may say, for my little hour — but what is my little hour? Don't imagine for a moment I'm such a cad as to have brought you down here to abuse or to complain of my wife to you. She is a woman of very distinguished qualities, to whom my obligations are immense; so that, if you please, we will say nothing about her. My boys — my children are all boys — are straight and strong, thank God! and have no poverty of growth about them, no penury of needs. I receive, periodically, the most satisfactory attestation from Harrow, from Oxford, from Sandhurst (oh, we have done the best for them!) of their being living, thriving, consuming organisms."

"It must be delightful to feel that the son of one's loins is at Sandhurst," Paul remarked enthusiastically.

"It is — it's charming. Oh, I'm a patriot!"

"Then what did you mean — the other night at Summersoft — by saying that children are a curse?"

"My dear fellow, on what basis are we talking?" St. George asked, dropping upon the sofa, at a short distance from his visitor. Sitting a little sideways he leaned back against the opposite arm with his hands raised and interlocked behind his head. "On the supposition that a certain perfection is possible and even desirable — isn't it so? Well, all I say is that one's children interfere with perfection. One's wife interferes. Marriage interferes."

"You think then the artist shouldn't marry?"

"He does so at his peril — he does so at his cost."

"Not even when his wife is in sympathy with his work?"

"She never is — she can't be! Women don't know what work is."

"Surely, they work themselves," Paul Overt objected.

"Yes, very badly. Oh, of course, often, they think they understand, they think they sympathise. Then it is that they are most dangerous. Their idea is that you shall do a great lot and get a great lot of money. Their great nobleness and virtue, their exemplary conscientiousness as British females, is in keeping you up to that. My wife makes all my bargains with my publishers for me, and she has done so for twenty years. She does it consummately well; that's why I'm really pretty well off. Are you not the father of their innocent babes, and will you withhold from them their natural sustenance? You asked me the other night if they were not an immense incentive. Of course they are — there's no doubt of that!"

"For myself, I have an idea I need incentives," Paul Overt dropped.

"Ah well, then, *n'en parlons plus!*" said his companion, smiling.

"You are an incentive, I maintain," the young man went on. "You don't affect me in the way you apparently would like to. Your great success is what I see — the pomp of Ennismore Gardens!"

"Success? — do you call it success to be spoken of as you would speak of me if you were sitting here with another artist — a young man intelligent and sincere like yourself? Do you call it success to make you blush — as you would blush — if some foreign critic (some fellow, of course, I mean, who should know what he was talking about and should have shown you he did, as foreign critics like to show it!) were to say to you: 'He's the one, in this country, whom they consider the most perfect, isn't he?' Is it success to be the occasion of a young Englishman's having to stammer as you would have to stammer at such a moment for old England? No, no; success is to have made people tremble after another fashion. Do try it!"

"Try it?"

"Try to do some really good work."

"Oh, I want to, heaven knows!"

"Well, you can't do it without sacrifices; don't believe that for a moment," said Henry St. George. "I've made none. I've had everything. In other words, I've missed everything."

"You've had the full, rich, masculine, human, general life, with all the responsibilities and duties and burdens and sorrows and joys — all the domestic and social initiations and complications. They must be immensely suggestive, immensely amusing."

" Amusing ? "

" For a strong man — yes."

"They've given me subjects without number, if that's
what you mean; but they've taken away at the same time
the power to use them. I've touched a thousand things,
but which one of them have I turned into gold? The
artist has to do only with that — he knows nothing of
any baser metal. I've led the life of the world, with my
wife and my progeny; the clumsy, expensive, material-
ised, brutalised, Philistine, snobbish life of London.
We've got everything handsome, even a carriage — we
are prosperous, hospitable, eminent people. But, my
dear fellow, don't try to stultify yourself and pretend
you don't know what we *haven't* got. It's bigger than
all the rest. Between artists — come! You know as
well as you sit there that you would put a pistol-ball into
your brain if you had written my books!"

It appeared to Paul Overt that the tremendous talk
promised by the master at Summersoft had indeed come
off, and with a promptitude, a fulness, with which his
young imagination had scarcely reckoned. His companion made an immense impression on him and he
throbbed with the excitement of such deep soundings
and such strange confidences. He throbbed indeed with
the conflict of his feelings — bewilderment and recognition and alarm, enjoyment and protest and assent, all
commingled with tenderness (and a kind of shame in
the participation,) for the sores and bruises exhibited by
so fine a creature, and with a sense of the tragic secret
that he nursed under his trappings. The idea of *his*
being made the occasion of such an act of humility made
him flush and pant, at the same time that his perception,
in certain directions, had been too much awakened to conceal from him anything that St. George **really** meant.

It had been his odd fortune to blow upon the deep waters, to make then surge and break in waves of strange eloquence. He launched himself into a passionate contradiction of his host's last declaration; tried to enumerate to him the parts of his work he loved, the splendid things he had found in it, beyond the compass of any other writer of the day. St. George listened awhile, courteously; then he said, laying his hand on Paul Overt's :

"That's all very well; and if your idea is to do nothing better there is no reason why you shouldn't have as many good things as I — as many human and material appendages, as many sons or daughters, a wife with as many gowns, a house with as many servants, a stable with as many horses, a heart with as many aches." He got up when he had spoken thus, and then stood a moment near the sofa, looking down on his agitated pupil. "Are you possessed of any money ?" it occurred to him to ask.

"None to speak of."

"Oh, well, there's no reason why you shouldn't make a goodish income — if you set about it the right way. Study *me* for that — study me well. You may really have a carriage."

Paul Overt sat there for some moments without speaking. He looked straight before him — he turned over many things. His friend had wandered away from him, taking up a parcel of letters that were on the table where the roll of proofs had lain. "What was the book Mrs. St. George made you burn — the one she didn't like ?" he abruptly inquired.

"The book she made me burn — how did you know that ?"   St. George looked up from his letters.

"I heard her speak of it at Summersoft."

"Ah, yes; she's proud of it. I don't know — it was rather good."

"What was it about?"

"Let me see." And St. George appeared to make an effort to remember. "Oh, yes, it was about myself." Paul Overt gave an irrepressible groan for the disappearance of such a production, and the elder man went on: "Oh, but *you* should write it — *you* should do me. There's a subject, my boy: no end of stuff in it!"

Again Paul was silent, but after a little he spoke. "Are there no women that really understand — that can take part in a sacrifice?"

"How can they take part? They themselves are the sacrifice. They're the idol and the altar and the flame."

"Isn't there even *one* who sees further?" Paul continued.

For a moment St. George made no answer to this; then, having torn up his letters, he stood before his disciple again, ironic. "Of course I know the one you mean. But not even Miss Fancourt."

"I thought you admired her so much."

"It's impossible to admire her more. Are you in love with her?" St. George asked.

"Yes," said Paul Overt.

"Well, then, give it up."

Paul stared. "Give up my love?"

"Bless me, no; your idea."

"My idea?"

"The one you talked with her about. The idea of perfection."

"She would help it — she would help it!" cried the young man.

"For about a year — the first year, yes. After that she would be as a millstone round its neck."

"Why, she has a passion for completeness, for good work — for everything you and I care for most."

"'You and I' is charming, my dear fellow! She has it indeed, but she would have a still greater passion for her children; and very proper too. She would insist upon everything's being made comfortable, advantageous, propitious for them. That isn't the artist's business."

"The artist — the artist! Isn't he a man all the same?"

St. George hesitated. "Sometimes I really think not. You know as well as I what he has to do: the concentration, the finish, the independence that he must strive for, from the moment that he begins to respect his work. Ah, my young friend, his relation to women, especially in matrimony, is at the mercy of this damning fact — that whereas he can in the nature of things have but one standard, they have about fifty. That's what makes them so superior," St. George added, laughing. "Fancy an artist with a plurality of standards," he went on. "To *do* it — to do it and make it divine is the only thing he has to think about. 'Is it done or not?' is his only question. Not 'Is it done as well as a proper solicitude for my dear little family will allow?' He has nothing to do with the relative, nothing to do with a dear little family!"

"Then you don't allow him the common passions and affections of men?"

"Hasn't he a passion, an affection, which includes all the rest? Besides, let him have all the passions he likes — if he only keeps his independence. He must afford to be poor."

Paul Overt slowly got up. "Why did you advise me to make up to her, then?"

St. George laid his hand on his shoulder. "Because she would make an adorable wife! And I hadn't read you then."

"I wish you had left me alone!" murmured the young man.

"I didn't know that that wasn't good enough for you," St. George continued.

"What a false position, what a condemnation of the artist, that he's a mere disfranchised monk and can produce his effect only by giving up personal happiness. What an arraignment of art!" Paul Overt pursued, with a trembling voice.

"Ah, you don't imagine, by chance, that I'm defending art? Arraignment, I should think so! Happy the societies in which it hasn't made its appearance; for from the moment it comes they have a consuming ache, they have an incurable corruption in their bosom. Assuredly, the artist is in a false position. But I thought we were taking him for granted. Pardon me," St. George continued; "*Ginistrella* made me!"

Paul Overt stood looking at the floor — one o'clock struck, in the stillness, from a neighbouring church-tower. "Do you think she would ever look at me?" he asked at last.

"Miss Fancourt — as a suitor? Why shouldn't I think it? That's why I've tried to favour you — I have had a little chance or two of bettering your opportunity."

"Excuse my asking you, but do you mean by keeping away yourself?" Paul said, blushing.

"I'm an old idiot — my place isn't there," St. George replied, gravely.

"I'm nothing, yet; I've no fortune; and there must be so many others."

"You're a gentleman and a man of genius. I think you might do something."

"But if I must give that up — the genius?"

"Lots of people, you know, think I've kept mine."

"You have a genius for torment!" Paul Overt exclaimed; but taking his companion's hand in farewell as a mitigation of this judgment.

"Poor child, I do bother you. Try, try, then! I think your chances are good, and you'll win a great prize."

Paul held the other's hand a minute; he looked into his face. "No, I *am* an artist — I can't help it!"

"Ah, show it then!" St. George broke out — "let me see before I die the thing I most want, the thing I yearn for — a life in which the passion is really intense. If you can be rare, don't fail of it! Think what it is — how it counts — how it lives!" They had moved to the door and St. George had closed both his own hands over that of his companion. Here they paused again and Paul Overt ejaculated — "I want to live!"

"In what sense?"

"In the greatest sense."

"Well then, stick to it — see it through."

"With your sympathy — your help?"

"Count on that — you'll be a great figure to me. Count on my highest appreciation, my devotion. You'll give me satisfaction! — if that has any weight with you." And as Paul appeared still to waver, St. George added: "Do you remember what you said to me at Summersoft?"

"Something infatuated, no doubt!"

"'I'll do anything in the world you tell me.' You said that."

"And you hold me to it?"

"Ah, what am I?" sighed the master, shaking his head.

"Lord, what things I shall have to do!" Paul almost moaned as he turned away.

E

VI.

"It goes on too much abroad — hang abroad!" These, or something like them, had been St. George's remarkable words in relation to the action of *Ginistrella;* and yet, though they had made a sharp impression on Paul Overt, like almost all the master's spoken words, the young man, a week after the conversation I have narrated, left England for a long absence and full of projects of work. It is not a perversion of the truth to say that that conversation was the direct cause of his departure. If the oral utterance of the eminent writer had the privilege of moving him deeply it was especially on his turning it over at leisure, hours and days afterward, that it appeared to yield its full meaning and exhibit its extreme importance. He spent the summer in Switzerland, and having, in September, begun a new task, he determined not to cross the Alps till he should have made a good start. To this end he returned to a quiet corner that he knew well, on the edge of the Lake of Geneva, within sight of the towers of Chillon : a region and a view for which he had an affection springing from old associations, capable of mysterious little revivals and refreshments. Here he lingered late, till the snow was on the nearer hills, almost down to the limit to which he could climb when his stint was done, on the shortening afternoons. The autumn was fine, the lake was blue, and his book took form and direction. These circumstances, for the time, embroidered his life, and he suffered it to cover him with its mantle. At the end of six weeks he appeared to himself to have learned St. George's lesson by heart — to have tested and proved its doctrine. Nevertheless he did a very inconsistent thing : before crossing the Alps he wrote to Marian Fancourt. He was aware of the perversity of this act, and it was only as a luxury, an amusement, the reward of a strenuous autumn, that he justified it. She had not asked any such favour of him when he went to see her three days before he left London — three days after their dinner in Ennismore Gardens. It is true that she had no reason to, for he had not mentioned that he was on the eve of such an excursion. He hadn't mentioned it because he didn't know it; it was that particular visit that made the matter clear. He had paid the visit to see how much he really cared for her, and quick departure, without so much as a farewell, was the sequel to this inquiry, the answer to which had been a distinct superlative. When he wrote to her from Clarens he noted that he owed her an explanation (more than three months after!) for the omission of such a form.

She answered him briefly but very promptly, and gave him a striking piece of news : the death, a week before, of Mrs. St. George. This exemplary woman had succumbed, in the country, to a violent attack of inflammation of the lungs — he would remember that for a long time she had been delicate. Miss Fancourt added that she heard her husband was overwhelmed with the blow; he would miss her unspeakably — she had been everything to him. Paul Overt immediately wrote to St. George. He had wished to remain in communication with him, but had hitherto lacked the right excuse for troubling so busy a man. Their long nocturnal talk came back to him in every detail, but this did not prevent his expressing a cordial sympathy with the head of the profession, for had not that very talk made it clear that the accomplished lady was the influence that ruled his life ? What catastrophe could be more cruel than the extinction of such an influence ? This was exactly the tone that St.

George took in answering his young friend, upwards of a month later. He made no allusion, of course, to their important discussion. He spoke of his wife as frankly and generously as if he had quite forgotten that occasion, and the feeling of deep bereavement was visible in his words. "She took every thing off my hands — off my mind. She carried on our life with the greatest art, the rarest devotion, and I was free, as few men can have been, to drive my pen, to shut myself up with my trade. This was a rare service — the highest she could have rendered me. Would I could have acknowledged it more fitly!"

A certain bewilderment, for Paul Overt, disengaged itself from these remarks: they struck him as a contradiction, a retractation. He had certainly not expected his correspondent to rejoice in the death of his wife, and it was perfectly in order that the rupture of a tie of more than twenty years should have left him sore. But if she was such a benefactress as that, what in the name of consistency had St. George meant by turning *him* upside down that night — by dosing him to that degree, at the most sensitive hour of his life, with the doctrine of renunciation? If Mrs. St. George was an irreparable loss, then her husband's inspired advice had been a bad joke and renunciation was a mistake. Overt was on the point of rushing back to London to show that, for his part, he was perfectly willing to consider it so, and he went so far as to take the manuscript of the first chapters of his new book out of his table-drawer, to insert it into a pocket of his portmanteau. This led to his catching a glimpse of some pages he had not looked at for months, and that accident, in turn, to his being struck with the high promise they contained — a rare result of such retrospections, which it was his habit to avoid as much as possible.

They usually made him feel that the glow of composition might be a purely subjective and a very barren emotion. On this occasion a certain belief in himself disengaged itself whimsically from the serried erasures of his first draft, making him think it best after all to carry out his present experiment to the end. If he could write as well as that under the influence of renunciation, it would be a pity to change the conditions before the termination of the work. He would go back to London of course, but he would go back only when he should have finished his book. This was the vow he privately made, restoring his manuscript to the table-drawer. It may be added that it took him a long time to finish his book, for the subject was as difficult as it was fine and he was literally embarrassed by the fulness of his notes. Something within him told him that he must make it supremely good — otherwise he should lack, as regards his private behaviour, a handsome excuse. He had a horror of this deficiency and found himself as firm as need be on the question of the lamp and the file. He crossed the Alps at last and spent the winter, the spring, the ensuing summer, in Italy, where still, at the end of a twelve-month, his task was unachieved. "Stick to it — see it through:" this general injunction of St. George's was good also for the particular case. He applied it to the utmost, with the result that when in its slow order, the summer had come round again he felt that he had given all that was in him. This time he put his papers into his portmanteau, with the address of his publisher attached, and took his way northward.

He had been absent from London for two years — two years which were a long period and had made such a difference in his own life (through the production of a novel far stronger, he believed, than *Ginistrella*) that he turned out into Piccadilly, the morning after his arrival, with an indefinite expectation of changes, of finding that things had happened. But there were few transformations in Piccadilly (only three or four big red houses where there had been low black ones), and the brightness of the end of June peeped through the rusty railings of the Green Park and glittered in the varnish of the rolling carriages as he had seen it in other, more cursory Junes. It was a greeting that he appreciated; it seemed friendly and pointed, added to the exhilaration of his finished book, of his having his own country and the huge, oppressive, amusing city that suggested everything, that contained everything, under his hand again. "Stay at home and do things here — do subjects we can measure," St. George had said; and now it appeared to him that he should ask nothing better than to stay at home for ever. Late in the afternoon he took his way to Manchester Square, looking out for a number he had not forgotten. Miss Fancourt, however, was not within, so that he turned, rather dejectedly, from the door. This movement brought him face to face with a gentleman who was approaching it and whom he promptly perceived to be Miss Fancourt's father. Paul saluted this personage, and the General returned his greeting with his customary good manner — a manner so good, however, that you could never tell whether it meant that he placed you. Paul Overt felt the impulse to speak to him; then, hesitating, became conscious both that he had nothing particular to say and that though the old soldier remembered him he remembered him wrong. He therefore passed on, without calculating on the irresistible effect that his own evident recognition would have upon the General, who never neglected a chance to gossip. Our young man's face was expressive, and observation seldom let it pass. He had not taken ten steps before he heard himself called after with a friendly, semi-articulate "A —I beg your pardon!" He turned round and the General, smiling at him from the steps, said: "Won't you come in? I won't leave you the advantage of me!" Paul declined to come in, and then was sorry he had done so, for Miss Fancourt, so late in the afternoon, might return at any moment. But her father gave him no second chance; he appeared mainly to wish not to have struck him as inhospitable. A further look at the visitor told him more about him, enough at least to enable him to say — "You've come back, you've come back?" Paul was on the point of replying that he had come back the night before, but he bethought himself to suppress this strong light on the immediacy of his visit, and, giving merely a general assent, remarked that he was extremely sorry not to have found Miss Fancourt. He had come late, in the hope that she would be in. "I'll tell her — I'll tell her," said the old man; and then he added quickly, gallantly, "You'll be giving us something new? It's a long time, isn't it?" Now he remembered him right.

"Rather long. I'm very slow," said Paul. "I met you at Summersoft a long time ago."

"Oh, yes, with Henry St. George. I remember very well. Before his poor wife —— " General Fancourt paused a moment, smiling a little less. "I daresay you know."

"About Mrs. St. George's death? Oh yes, I heard at the time."

"Oh no; I mean — I mean he's to be married."

"Ah! I've not heard that." Just as Paul was about to add, "To whom?" the General crossed his intention with a question.

"When did you come back? I know you've been away — from my daughter. She was very sorry. You ought to give her something new."

"I came back last night," said our young man, to whom something had occurred which made his speech, for the moment, a little thick.

"Ah, most kind of you to come so soon. Couldn't you turn up at dinner?"

"At dinner?" Paul Overt repeated, not liking to ask whom St. George was going to marry, but thinking only of that.

"There are several people, I believe. Certainly St. George. Or afterwards, if you like better. I believe my daughter expects ——." He appeared to notice something in Overt's upward face (on his steps he stood higher) which led him to interrupt himself, and the interruption gave him a momentary sense of awkwardness, from which he sought a quick issue. "Perhaps then you haven't heard she's to be married."

"To be married?" Paul stared.

"To Mr. St. George — it has just been settled. Odd marriage, isn't it?" Paul uttered no opinion on this point: he only continued to stare. "But I daresay it will do — she's so awfully literary!" said the General.

Paul had turned very red. "Oh, it's a surprise — very interesting, very charming! I'm afraid I can't dine — so many thanks!"

"Well, you must come to the wedding!" cried the General. "Oh, I remember that day at Summersoft. He's a very good fellow."

"Charming — charming!" Paul stammered, retreating. He shook hands with the General and got off. His face was red and he had the sense of its growing more and more crimson. All the evening at home — he went straight to his rooms and remained there dinnerless — his cheek burned at intervals as if it had been smitten. He didn't understand what had happened to him, what trick had been played him, what treachery practised. "None, none," he said to himself. "I've nothing to do with it. I'm out of it — it's none of my business." But that bewildered murmur was followed again and again by the incongruous ejaculation — "Was it a plan — was it a plan?" Sometimes he cried to himself, breathless, "Am I a dupe — am I a dupe?" If he was, he was an absurd, and abject one. It seemed to him he had never lost her till now. He had renounced her, yes; but that was another affair — that was a closed but not a locked door. Now he felt as if the door had been slammed in his face. Did he expect her to wait — was she to give him his time like that: two years at a stretch? He didn't know what he had expected — he only knew what he hadn't. It wasn't this — it wasn't this. Mystification, bitterness and wrath rose and boiled in him when he thought of the deference, the devotion, the credulity with which he had listened to St. George. The evening wore on and the light was long; but even when it had darkened he remained without a lamp. He had flung himself on the sofa, and he lay there through the hours with his eyes either closed or gazing into the gloom, in the attitude of a man teaching himself to bear something, to bear having been made a fool of. He had made it too easy — that idea passed over him like a hot wave. Suddenly, as he heard eleven o'clock strike, he jumped up, remembering what General Fancourt had said about his coming after dinner. He would go — he would see her at least; perhaps he should see what it meant. He felt as if some of the elements of a hard sum had been given him and the others were wanting: he couldn't do his sum till he was in possession of them all.

He dressed quickly, so that by half-past eleven he was at
Manchester Square.   There were a good many carriages
at the door — a party was going on; a circumstance which
at the last gave him a slight relief, for now he would
rather see her in a crowd.   People passed him on the
staircase; they were going away, going "on," with the
hunted, herdlike movement of London society at night.
But sundry groups remained in the drawing-room, and it
was some minutes, as she didn't hear him announced, before he discovered her and spoke to her.   In this short
interval he had perceived that St. George was there, talking to a lady before the fireplace; but he looked away
from him, for the moment, and therefore failed to see
whether the author of *Shadowmere* noticed him.   At all
events he didn't come to him.   Miss Fancourt did, as
soon as she saw him; she almost rushed at him, smiling,
rustling, radiant, beautiful.   He had forgotten what her
head, what her face offered to the sight; she was in
white, there were gold figures on her dress, and her hair
was like a casque of gold.   In a single moment he saw
she was happy, happy with a kind of aggressiveness, of
splendour.   But she would not speak to him of that, she
would speak only of himself.

"I'm so delighted; my father told me.   How kind of
you to come!"   She struck him as so fresh and brave,
while his eyes moved over her, that he said to himself,
irresistibly : " Why to *him*, why not to youth, to strength,
to ambition, to a future ?   Why, in her rich young capacity, to failure, to abdication, to superannuation ? "   In
his thought, at that sharp moment, he blasphemed even
against all that had been left of his faith in the peccable master.   " I'm so sorry I missed you," she went on.
" My father told me.   How charming of you to have come
so soon ! "

"Does that surprise you?" Paul Overt asked.

"The first day? No, from you — nothing that's nice." She was interrupted by a lady who bade her good-night, and he seemed to read that it cost her nothing to speak to one in that tone; it was her old bounteous, demonstrative way, with a certain added amplitude that time had brought; and if it began to operate on the spot, at such a juncture in her history, perhaps in the other days too it had meant just as little or as much — a sort of mechanical charity, with the difference now that she was satisfied, ready to give but asking nothing. Oh, she was satisfied — and why shouldn't she be? Why shouldn't she have been surprised at his coming the first day — for all the good she had ever got from him? As the lady continued to hold her attention Paul Overt turned from her with a strange irritation in his complicated artistic soul and a kind of disinterested disappointment. She was so happy that it was almost stupid — it seemed to deny the extraordinary intelligence he had formerly found in her. Didn't she know how bad St. George could be, hadn't she perceived the deplorable thinness —— ? If she didn't she was nothing, and if she did why such an insolence of serenity? This question expired as our young man's eyes settled at last upon the genius who had advised him in a great crisis. St. George was still before the chimney-piece, but now he was alone (fixed, waiting, as if he meant to remain after every one), and he met the clouded gaze of the young friend who was tormented with uncertainty as to whether he had the right (which his resentment would have enjoyed,) to regard himself as his victim. Somehow, the fantastic inquiry I have just noted was answered by St. George's aspect. It was as fine in its way as Marian Fancourt's — it denoted the happy human being; but somehow it represented to Paul Overt that the author of *Shadowmere* had now definitively ceased to count — ceased to count as a writer. As he smiled a welcome across the room he was almost *banal*, he was almost smug. Paul had the impression that for a moment he hesitated to make a movement forward, as if he had a bad conscience; but the next they had met in the middle of the room and had shaken hands, expressively, cordially on St. George's part. Then they had passed together to where the elder man had been standing, while St. George said: "I hope you are never going away again. I have been dining here; the General told me." He was handsome, he was young, he looked as if he had still a great fund of life. He bent the friendliest, most unconfessing eyes upon Paul Overt; asked him about everything, his health, his plans, his late occupations, the new book. "When will it be out — soon, soon, I hope? Splendid, eh? That's right; you're a comfort! I've read you all over again, the last six months." Paul waited to see if he would tell him what the General had told him in the afternoon, and what Miss Fancourt, verbally at least, of course had not. But as it didn't come out he asked at last: "Is it true, the great news I hear, that you're to be married?"

"Ah, you *have* heard it then?"

"Didn't the General tell you?" Paul Overt went on.

"Tell me what?"

"That he mentioned it to me this afternoon?"

"My dear fellow, I don't remember. We've been in the midst of people. I'm sorry, in that case, that I lose the pleasure, myself, of announcing to you a fact that touches me so nearly. It *is* a fact, strange as it may appear. It has only just become one. Isn't it ridiculous?" St. George made this speech without confusion, but on the other hand, so far as Paul could see, without latent impudence. It appeared to his interlocutor that, to talk so comfortably and coolly, he must simply have forgotten what had passed between them. His next words, however, showed that he had not, and they had, as an appeal to Paul's own memory, an effect which would have been ludicrous if it had not been cruel. "Do you recollect the talk we had at my house that night, into which Miss Fancourt's name entered? I've often thought of it since."

"Yes — no wonder you said what you did," said Paul, looking at him.

"In the light of the present occasion? Ah! but there was no light then. How could I have foreseen this hour?"

"Didn't you think it probable?"

"Upon my honour, no," said Henry St. George. "Certainly, I owe you that assurance. Think how my situation has changed."

"I see — I see," Paul murmured.

His companion went on, as if, now that the subject had been broached, he was, as a man of imagination and tact, perfectly ready to give every satisfaction — being able to enter fully into everything another might feel. "But it's not only that — for honestly, at my age, I never dreamed —— a widower, with big boys and with so little else! It has turned out differently from any possible calculation, and I am fortunate beyond all measure. She has been so free, and yet she consents. Better than any one else perhaps — for I remember how you liked her, before you went away, and how she liked you — you can intelligently congratulate me."

"She has been so free!" Those words made a great impression on Paul Overt, and he almost writhed under that irony in them as to which it little mattered whether it was intentional or casual. Of course she had been free and, appreciably perhaps, by his own act; for was not St. George's allusion to her having liked him a part of the irony too? "I thought that by your theory you disapproved of a writer's marrying."

"Surely — surely. But you don't call me a writer?"

"You ought to be ashamed," said Paul.

"Ashamed of marrying again?"

"I won't say that — but ashamed of your reasons."

"You must let me judge of them, my friend."

"Yes; why not? For you judged wonderfully of mine."

The tone of these words appeared suddenly, for Henry St. George, to suggest the unsuspected. He stared as if he read a bitterness in them. "Don't you think I have acted fair?"

"You might have told me at the time, perhaps."

"My dear fellow, when I say I couldn't pierce futurity!"

"I mean afterwards."

St. George hesitated. "After my wife's death?"

"When this idea came to you."

"Ah, never, never! I wanted to save you, rare and precious as you are."

"Are you marrying Miss Fancourt to save me?"

"Not absolutely, but it adds to the pleasure. I shall be the making of you," said St. George, smiling. "I was greatly struck, after our talk, with the resolute way you quitted the country and still more, perhaps, with your force of character in remaining abroad. You're very strong — you're wonderfully strong."

Paul Overt tried to sound his pleasant eyes; the strange thing was that he appeared sincere — not a mocking fiend. He turned away, and as he did so he heard St. George say something about his giving them the proof, being the joy of his old age. He faced him again, taking another look. "Do you mean to say you've stopped writing?"

"My dear fellow, of course I have. It's too late. Didn't I tell you?"

"I can't believe it!"

"Of course you can't — with your own talent! No, no; for the rest of my life I shall only read you."

"Does she know that — Miss Fancourt?"

"She will — she will." Our young man wondered whether St. George meant this as a covert intimation that the assistance he should derive from that young lady's fortune, moderate as it was, would make the difference of putting it in his power to cease to work, ungratefully, an exhausted vein. Somehow, standing there in the ripeness of his successful manhood, he did not suggest that any of his veins were exhausted. "Don't you remember the moral I offered myself to you — that night — as pointing?" St. George continued. "Consider, at any rate, the warning I am at present."

This was too much — he *was* the mocking fiend. Paul separated from him with a mere nod for good-night; the sense that he might come back to him some time in the far future but could not fraternise with him now. It was necessary to his sore spirit to believe for the hour that he had a grievance — all the more cruel for not being a legal one. It was doubtless in the attitude of hugging this wrong that he descended the stairs without taking leave of Miss Fancourt, who had not been in view at the moment he quitted the room. He was glad to get out into the honest, dusky, unsophisticating night, to move fast, to take his way home on foot. He walked a long time, missing his way, not thinking of it. He was thinking of too many other things. His steps recovered their direction, however, and at the end of an hour he found himself before his door, in the small, inexpensive, empty street. He lingered, questioning himself still, before going in, with nothing around and above him but moonless blackness, a bad lamp or two and a few far-away dim stars. To these last faint features he raised his eyes; he had been saying to himself that there would have been mockery indeed if now, on his new foundation, at the end of a year, St. George should put forth something with his early quality — something of the type of *Shadowmere* and finer than his finest. Greatly as he admired his talent Paul literally hoped such an incident would not occur; it seemed to him just then that he scarcely should be able to endure it. St. George's words were still in his ears, "You're very strong — wonderfully strong." Was he really? Certainly, he would have to be; and it would be a sort of revenge. *Is* he? the reader may ask in turn, if his interest has followed the perplexed young man so far. The best answer to that perhaps is that he is doing his best but that it is too soon to say. When the new book came out in the autumn Mr. and Mrs. St. George found it really magnificent. The former still has published nothing, but Paul Overt does not even yet feel safe. I may say for him, however, that if this event were to befall he would really be the very first to appreciate it: which is perhaps a proof that St. George was essentially right and that Nature dedicated him to intellectual, not to personal passion.

THE MARRIAGES.[1]

I.

"WON'T you stay a little longer?" the hostess said, holding the girl's hand and smiling. "It's too early for every one to go; it's too absurd." Mrs. Churchley inclined her head to one side and looked gracious; she held up to her face, in a vague, protecting, sheltering way, an enormous fan of red feathers. Everything about her, to Adela Chart, was enormous. She had big eyes, big teeth, big shoulders, big hands, big rings and bracelets, big jewels of every sort and many of them. The train of her crimson dress was longer than any other; her house was huge; her drawing-room, especially now that the company had left it, looked vast, and it offered to the girl's eyes a collection of the largest sofas and chairs, pictures, mirrors, and clocks that she had ever beheld. Was Mrs. Churchley's fortune also large, to account for so many immensities? Of this Adela could know nothing, but she reflected, while she smiled sweetly back at their entertainer, that she had better try to find out. Mrs. Churchley had at least a high-hung carriage drawn by the tallest horses, and in the Row she was to be seen perched on a mighty hunter. She was high and expansive herself, though not exactly fat; her bones were big,

[1] *Copyright, 1891, by Macmillan & Co.*

her limbs were long, and she had a loud, hurrying voice, like the bell of a steamboat. While she spoke to his daughter she had the air of hiding from Colonel Chart, a little shyly, behind the wide ostrich fan. But Colonel Chart was not a man to be either ignored or eluded.

"Of course every one is going on to something else," he said. "I believe there are a lot of things to-night."

"And where are *you* going?" Mrs. Churchley asked, dropping her fan and turning her bright, hard eyes on the Colonel.

"Oh, I don't do that sort of thing!" he replied, in a tone of resentment just perceptible to his daughter. She saw in it that he thought Mrs. Churchley might have done him a little more justice. But what made the honest soul think that she was a person to look to for a perception of fine shades? Indeed the shade was one that it might have been a little difficult to seize — the difference between "going on" and coming to a dinner of twenty people. The pair were in mourning; the second year had not lightened it for Adela, but the Colonel had not objected to dining with Mrs. Churchley, any more than he had objected, at Easter, to going down to the Millwards', where he had met her, and where the girl had her reasons for believing him to have known he should meet her. Adela was not clear about the occasion of their original meeting, to which a certain mystery attached. In Mrs. Churchley's exclamation now there was the fullest concurrence in Colonel Chart's idea; she didn't say, "Ah, yes, dear friend, I understand!" but this was the note of sympathy she plainly wished to sound. It immediately made Adela say to her, "Surely you must be going on somewhere yourself."

"Yes, you must have a lot of places," the Colonel observed, looking at her shining raiment with a sort of invidious directness. Adela could read the tacit implication : " You're not in sorrow, in desolation."

Mrs. Churchley turned away from her at this, waiting just a moment before answering. The red fan was up again, and this time it sheltered her from Adela. " I'll give everything up — for *you*," were the words that issued from behind it. " *Do* stay a little. I always think this is such a nice hour. One can really talk," Mrs. Churchley went on. The Colonel laughed; he said it wasn't fair. But their hostess continued, to Adela, " Do sit down ; it's the only time to have any talk." The girl saw her father sit down, but she wandered away, turning her back and pretending to look at a picture. She was so far from agreeing with Mrs. Churchley that it was an hour she particularly disliked. She was conscious of the queerness, the shyness, in London, of the gregarious flight of guests, after a dinner, the general *sauve qui peut* and panic fear of being left with the host and hostess. But personally she always felt the contagion, always conformed to the flurry. Besides, she felt herself turning red now, flushed with a conviction that had come over her and that she wished not to show.

Her father sat down on one of the big sofas with Mrs. Churchley ; fortunately he was also a person with a presence that could hold its own. Adela didn't care to sit and watch them while they made love, as she crudely formulated it, and she cared still less to join in their conversation. She wandered further away, went into another of the bright, "handsome," rather nude rooms — they were like women dressed for a ball — where the displaced chairs, at awkward angles to each other, seemed to retain the attitudes of bored talkers. Her heart beat strangely, but she continued to make a pretense of looking at the pictures on the walls and the or-

naments on the tables, while she hoped that, as she
preferred it, it would be also the course that her father
would like best. She hoped "awfully," as she would
have said, that he wouldn't think her rude. She was a
person of courage, and he was a kind, an intensely good-
natured man; nevertheless, she was a good deal afraid of
him. At home it had always been a religion with them to
be nice to the people he liked. How, in the old days, her
mother, her incomparable mother, so clever, so unerring,
so perfect — how in the precious days her mother had
practiced that art! Oh, her mother, her irrecoverable
mother! One of the pictures that she was looking at
swam before her eyes. Mrs. Churchley, in the natural
course, would have begun immediately to climb stair-
cases. Adela could see the high bony shoulders and the
long crimson tail and the universal coruscating nod
wriggle their business-like way through the rest of the
night. Therefore she *must* have had her reasons for de-
taining them. There were mothers who thought every
one wanted to marry their eldest son, and the girl asked
herself if *she* belonged to the class of daughters who
thought every one wanted to marry their father. Her
companions left her alone; and though she didn't want
to be near them, it angered her that Mrs. Churchley
didn't call her. That proved that she was conscious of
the situation. She would have called her, only Colonel
Chart had probably murmured, "Don't." That proved
that he also was conscious. The time was really not
long — ten minutes at the most elapsed — when he cried
out, gayly, pleasantly, as if with a little jocular reproach,
"I say, Adela, we must release this dear lady!" He
spoke, of course, as if it had been Adela's fault that they
lingered. When they took leave she gave Mrs. Churchley, without intention and without defiance, but from

the simple sincerity of her anxiety, a longer look into
the eyes than she had ever given her before. Mrs.
Churchley's onyx pupils reflected the question; they
seemed to say: "Yes, I *am*, if that's what you want to
know!"

What made the case worse, what made the girl more
sure, was the silence preserved by her companion in the
brougham, on their way home. They rolled along in the
June darkness from Prince's Gate to Seymour Street,
each looking out of a window in conscious dumbness;
watching without seeing the hurry of the London night,
the flash of lamps, the quick roll on the wood of hansoms
and other broughams. Adela had expected that her father
would say something about Mrs. Churchley; but when
he said nothing, it was, strangely, still more as if he
had spoken. In Seymour Street he asked the footman if
Mr. Godfrey had come in, to which the servant replied that
he had come in early and gone straight to his room.
Adela had perceived as much, without saying so, by a
lighted window in the third story; but she contributed
no remark to the question. At the foot of the stairs her
father halted a moment, hesitating, as if he had something on his mind; but what it amounted to, apparently,
was only the dry "Good-night" with which he presently ascended. It was the first time since her mother's
death that he had bidden her good-night without kissing her. They were a kissing family, and after her
mother's death the habit had taken a fresh spring. She
had left behind her such a general passion of regret that
in kissing each other they seemed to themselves a little
to be kissing her. Now, as, standing in the hall, with
the stiff watching footman (she could have said to him
angrily, "Go away!") planted near her, she looked with
unspeakable pain at her father's back while he mounted,

the effect was of his having withheld from other and
still more sensitive lips the touch of his own.

He was going to his room, and after a moment she
heard his door close.   Then she said to the servant,
"Shut up the house" (she tried to do everything her
mother had done, to be a little of what she had been,
conscious only of mediocrity), and took her own way upstairs.   After she had reached her room she waited, listening, shaken by the apprehension that she should hear
her father come out again and go up to Godfrey.   He
would go up to tell him, to have it over without delay,
precisely because it would be so difficult.   She asked herself, indeed, why he should tell Godfrey when he had not
taken the occasion — their drive home was an occasion —
to tell herself.   However, she wanted no announcing, no
telling; there was such a horrible clearness in her mind
that what she now waited for was only to be sure her
father wouldn't leave his room.   At the end of ten minutes she saw that this particular danger was over, upon
which she came out and made her way to Godfrey.   Exactly what she wanted to say to him first, if her father
counted on the boy's greater indulgence, and before he
could say anything, was, "Don't forgive him; don't,
don't!"

He was to go up for an examination, poor fellow, and
during these weeks his lamp burned till the small hours.
It was for the diplomatic service, and there was to be
some frightful number of competitors; but Adela had
great hopes of him — she believed so in his talents, and she
saw, with pity, how hard he worked.   This would have
made her spare him, not trouble his night, his scanty
rest, if anything less dreadful had been at stake.   It was
a blessing, however, that one could count upon his cool-
ness, young as he was — his bright, good-looking discre-

tion. Moreover he was the one who would care most. If Leonard was the eldest son — he had, as a matter of course, gone into the army and was in India, on the staff, by good luck, of a governor-general — it was exactly this that would make him comparatively indifferent. His life was elsewhere, and his father and he had been in a measure military comrades, so that he would be deterred by a certain delicacy from protesting; he wouldn't have liked his father to protest in an affair of *his*. Beatrice and Muriel would care, but they were too young to speak, and this was just why her own responsibility was so great.

Godfrey was in working-gear — shirt and trousers and slippers and a beautiful silk jacket. His room felt hot, though a window was open to the summer night; the lamp on the table shed its studious light over a formidable heap of text books and papers, and the bed showed that he had flung himself down to think out a problem. As soon as she got in she said to him: " Father's going to marry Mrs. Churchley ! "

She saw the poor boy's pink face turn pale. " How do you know ? "

" I've seen with my eyes. We've been dining there — we've just come home. He's in love with her — she's in love with him ; they'll arrange it."

" Oh, I say ! " Godfrey exclaimed, incredulous.

" He will, he will, he will ! " cried the girl; and with this she burst into tears.

Godfrey, who had a cigarette in his hand, lighted it at one of the candles on the mantelpiece as if he were embarrassed. As Adela, who had dropped into his arm-chair, continued to sob, he said, after a moment: " He oughtn't to — he oughtn't to."

" Oh, think of mamma — think of mamma ! " the girl went on.

"Yes, he ought to think of mamma;" and Godfrey looked at the tip of his cigarette.

"To such a woman as that, after *her!*"

"Dear old mamma!" said Godfrey, smoking.

Adela rose again, drying her eyes. "It's like an insult to her; it's as if he denied her." Now that she spoke of it, she felt herself tremendously exalted. "It's as if he rubbed out at a stroke all the years of their happiness."

"They were awfully happy," said Godfrey.

"Think what she was — think how no one else will ever again be like her!" the girl cried.

"I suppose he's not very happy now," Godfrey continued vaguely.

"Of course he isn't, any more than you and I are; and it's dreadful of him to want to be."

"Well, don't make yourself miserable till you're sure," the young man said.

But his sister showed him confidently that she *was* sure, from the way the pair had behaved together and from her father's attitude on the drive home. If Godfrey had been there he would have seen everything; it couldn't be explained, but he would have felt. When he asked at what moment the girl had first had her suspicion, she replied that it had all come at once, that evening; or that at least she had had no conscious fear till then. There had been signs for two or three weeks, but she hadn't understood them — ever since the day Mrs. Churchley had dined in Seymour Street. Adela had thought it odd then that her father had wished to invite her, in the quiet way they were living; she was a person they knew so little. He had said something about her having been very civil to him, and that evening, already, she had guessed that he had been to Mrs. Churchley's oftener than she had supposed. To-night it had come to her clearly that he had been to see her every day since the day she dined with them; every afternoon, about the hour she thought he was at his club. Mrs. Churchley was his club, — she was just like a club. At this Godfrey laughed; he wanted to know what his sister knew about clubs. She was slightly disappointed in his laugh, slightly wounded by it, but she knew perfectly what she meant: she meant that Mrs. Churchley was public and florid, promiscuous and mannish.

"Oh, I dare say she's all right," said Godfrey, as if he wanted to get on with his work. He looked at the clock on the mantelshelf; he would have to put in another hour.

"All right to come and take darling mamma's place — to sit where *she* used to sit, to lay her horrible hands on *her* things?" Adela was appalled — all the more that she had not expected it — at her brother's apparent acceptance of such a prospect.

He coloured; there was something in her passionate piety that scorched him. She glared at him with her tragic eyes as if he had profaned an altar. "Oh, I mean nothing will come of it."

"Not if we do our duty," said Adela.

"Our duty?"

"You must speak to him — tell him how we feel; that we shall never forgive him, that we can't endure it."

"He'll think I'm cheeky," returned Godfrey, looking down at his papers, with his back to her and his hands in his pockets.

"Cheeky, to plead for *her* memory?"

"He'll say it's none of my business."

"Then you believe he'll do it?" cried the girl.

"Not a bit. Go to bed!"

"*I*'ll speak to him," said Adela, as pale as a young priestess.

"Don't cry out till you're hurt; wait till he speaks to *you*."

"He won't, he won't!" the girl declared. "He'll do it without telling us."

Her brother had faced round to her again; he started a little at this, and again, at one of the candles, lighted his cigarette, which had gone out. She looked at him a moment; then he said something that surprised her.

"Is Mrs. Churchley very rich?"

"I haven't the least idea. What has that to do with it?"

Godfrey puffed his cigarette. "Does she live as if she were?"

"She has got a lot of showy things."

"Well, we must keep our eyes open," said Godfrey. "And now you *must* let me get on." He kissed his sister, as if to make up for dismissing her, or for his failure to take fire; and she held him a moment, burying her head on his shoulder. A wave of emotion surged through her; she broke out with a wail:

"Ah, why did she leave us? Why did she leave us?"

"Yes, why indeed?" the young man sighed, disengaging himself with a movement of oppression.

II.

ADELA was so far right as that by the end of the week, though she remained certain, her father had not made the announcement she dreaded. What made her certain was the sense of her changed relations with him — of there being between them something unexpressed, something of which she was as conscious as she would have been of an unhealed wound. When she spoke of this to Godfrey, he said the change was of her own making, that she was cruelly unjust to the governor. She suffered even more from her brother's unexpected perversity; she had had so different a theory about him that her disappointment was almost an humiliation and she needed all her fortitude to pitch her faith lower. She wondered what had happened to him and why he had changed. She would have trusted him to feel right about anything, above all about such a matter as this. Their worship of their mother's memory, their recognition of her sacred place in their past, her exquisite influence in their father's life, his fortunes, his career, in the whole history of the family and welfare of the house — accomplished, clever, gentle, good, beautiful and capable as she had been, a woman whose soft distinction was universally proclaimed, so that on her death one of the Princesses, the most august of her friends, had written Adela such a note about her as princesses were understood very seldom to write : their hushed tenderness over all this was a kind of religion, and also a sort of honour, in falling away from which there was a semblance of treachery. This was not the way people usually felt in London, she knew ; but, strenuous, ardent, observant girl as she was, with secrecies of sentiment and dim originalities of attitude, she had already made up her mind that London was no place to look for delicacies. Remembrance there was hammered thin, and to be faithful was to be a bore. The patient dead were sacrificed ; they had no shrines, for people were literally ashamed of mourning. When they had hustled all sensibility out of their lives, they invented the fiction that they felt too much to utter. Adela said nothing to her sisters ; this reticence was part of the virtue it was her system to exercise for them.

She was to be their mother, a direct deputy and representative.   Before the vision of that other woman parad-
ing in such a character, she felt capable of ingenuities
and subtleties.   The foremost of these was tremulously
to watch her father.   Five days after they had dined together at Mrs. Churchley's he asked her if she had been
to see that lady.

"No indeed, why should I ?"   Adela knew that he
knew she had not been, since Mrs. Churchley would have
told him.

"Don't you call on people after you dine with them?"
said Colonel Chart.

"Yes, in the course of time.   I don't rush off within
the week."

Her father looked at her, and his eyes were colder
than she had ever seen them, which was probably, she
reflected, just the way her own appeared to him.   "Then
you'll please rush off to-morrow.   She's to dine with us
on the 12th, and I shall expect your sisters to come
down."

Adela stared.   "To a dinner party ?"

"It's not to be a dinner party.   I want them to know
Mrs. Churchley."

"Is there to be nobody else ? "

"Godfrey, of course.   A family party."

The girl asked her brother that evening if *that* was not
tantamount to an announcement.   He looked at her
queerly, and then he said, "*I*'ve been to see her."

"What on earth did you do that for ? "

"Father told me he wished it."

"Then he *has* told you ? "

"Told me what ? "   Godfrey asked, while her heart
sank with the sense that he was making difficulties for
her.

"That they're engaged, of course. What else can all this mean?"

"He didn't tell me that, but I like her."

"*Like* her!" the girl shrieked.

"She's very kind, very good."

"To thrust herself upon us when we hate her? Is that what you call kind? Is that what you call decent?"

"Oh, *I* don't hate her," Godfrey rejoined, turning away as if his sister bored him.

She went the next day to see Mrs. Churchley, with a vague plan of breaking out to her, appealing to her, saying, "Oh, spare us! have mercy on us! let him alone! go away!" But that was not easy when they were face to face. Mrs. Churchley had every intention of getting, as she would have said — she was perpetually using the expression — into touch; but her good intentions were as depressing as a tailor's misfits. She could never understand that they had no place for her vulgar charity; that their life was filled with a fragrance of perfection for which she had no sense fine enough. She was as un-domestic as a shop-front and as out of tune as a parrot. She would make them live in the streets, or bring the streets into their lives — it was the same thing. She had evidently never read a book, and she used intona-tions that Adela had never heard, as if she had been an Australian or an American. She understood everything in a vulgar sense; speaking of Godfrey's visit to her and praising him according to her idea, saying horrid things about him — that he was awfully good-looking, a perfect gentleman, the kind she liked. How could her father, who was after all, in everything else, such a dear, listen to a woman, or endure her, who thought she was pleasing when she called the son of his dead wife a perfect gentle-man? What would he have been, pray? Much she

knew about what any of them were! When she told
Adela she wanted her to like her, the girl thought for an
instant her opportunity had come — the chance to plead
with her and beg her off. But she presented such an im-
penetrable surface that it would have been like giving a
message to a varnished door. She wasn't a woman, said
Adela; she was an address.

When she dined in Seymour Street, the "children," as
the girl called the others, including Godfrey, liked her.
Beatrice and Muriel stared shyly and silently at the
wonders of her apparel (she was brutally overdressed!)
without, of course, guessing the danger that tainted the
air. They supposed her, in their innocence, to be amusing, and they didn't know, any more than she did herself,
that she patronised them. When she was upstairs with
them, after dinner, Adela could see her looking round
the room at the things she meant to alter; their mother's
things, not a bit like her own and not good enough for
her. After a quarter of an hour of this, our young
lady felt sure she was deciding that Seymour Street
wouldn't do at all, the dear old home that had done for
their mother for twenty years. Was she plotting to
transport them all to her horrible Prince's Gate? Of
one thing, at any rate, Adela was certain: her father, at
that moment, alone in the dining-room with Godfrey,
pretending to drink another glass of wine to make time,
was coming to the point, was telling the news. When
they came upstairs, they both, to her eyes, looked
strange: the news had been told.

She had it from Godfrey before Mrs. Churchley left
the house, when, after a brief interval, he followed her
out of the drawing-room on her taking her sisters to bed.
She was waiting for him at the door of her room. Her
father was then alone with his *fiancée* (the word was

grotesque to Adela); it was already as if it were her home.

"What did you say to him?" the girl asked, when her brother had told her.

"I said nothing." Then he added, colouring (the expression of her face was such), "There was nothing to say."

"Is that how it strikes you?" said Adela, staring at the lamp.

"He asked me to speak to her," Godfrey went on.

"To speak to her?"

"To tell her I was glad."

"And did you?" Adela panted.

"I don't know. I said something. She kissed me."

"Oh, how *could* you?" shuddered the girl, covering her face with her hands.

"He says she's very rich," said Godfrey simply.

"Is that why you kissed her?"

"I didn't kiss her. Good-night," and the young man, turning his back upon her, went out.

When her brother was gone Adela locked herself in, as if with the fear that she should be overtaken or invaded, and during a sleepless, feverish, memorable night she took counsel of her uncompromising spirit. She saw things as they were, in all the indignity of life. The levity, the mockery, the infidelity, the ugliness, lay as plain as a map before her; it was a world *pour rire*, but she cried about it, all the same. The morning dawned early, or rather it seemed to her that there had been no night, nothing but a sickly, creeping day. But by the time she heard the house stirring again she had determined what to do. When she came down to the breakfast-room her father was already in his place, with newspapers and letters; and she expected the first words he would utter to be a rebuke to her for having disappeared, the night before, without taking leave of Mrs. Churchley. Then she saw that he wished to be intensely kind, to make every allowance, to conciliate and console her. He knew that she knew from Godfrey, and he got up and kissed her. He told her as quickly as possible, to have it over, stammering a little, with an "I've a piece of news for you that will probably shock you," yet looking even exaggeratedly grave and rather pompous, to inspire the respect he didn't deserve. When he kissed her she melted, she burst into tears. He held her against him, kissing her again and again, saying tenderly, "Yes, yes, I know, I know." But he didn't know, or he could never have done it. Beatrice and Muriel came in, frightened when they saw her crying, and still more scared when she turned to them with words and an air that were terrible in their comfortable little lives: "Papa's going to be married; he's going to marry Mrs. Churchley!" After staring a moment and seeing their father look as strange, on his side, as Adela, though in a different way, the children also began to cry, so that when the servants arrived, with tea and boiled eggs, these functionaries were greatly embarrassed with their burden, not knowing whether to come in or hang back. They all scraped together a decorum, and as soon as the things had been put on the table the Colonel banished the men with a glance. Then he made a little affectionate speech to Beatrice and Muriel, in which he assured them that Mrs. Churchley was the kindest, the most delightful, of women, only wanting to make them happy, only wanting to make him happy, and convinced that he would be if they were and that they would be if he was.

"What do such words mean?" Adela asked herself. She declared privately that they meant nothing, but she was silent, and every one was silent, on account of the advent of Miss Flynn, the governess, before whom Colonel Chart preferred not to discuss the situation. Adela recognized on the spot that, if things were to go as he wished, his children would practically never again be alone with him. He would spend all his time with Mrs. Churchley till they were married, and then Mrs. Churchley would spend all her time with him. Adela was ashamed of him, and that was horrible — all the more that every one else would be, all his other friends, every one who had known her mother. But the public dishonour to that high memory should not be enacted; he should not do as he wished.

After breakfast her father told her that it would give him pleasure if, in a day or two, she would take her sisters to see Mrs. Churchley, and she replied that he should be obeyed. He held her hand a moment, looking at her with an appeal in his eyes which presently hardened into sternness. He wanted to know that she forgave him, but he also wanted to say to her that he expected her to mind what she did, to go straight. She turned away her eyes; she was indeed ashamed of him.

She waited three days, and then she took her sisters to see Mrs. Churchley. That lady was surrounded with callers, as Adela knew she would be; it was her "day" and the occasion the girl preferred. Before this she had spent all her time with her sisters, talking to them about their mother, playing upon their memory of her, making them cry and making them laugh, reminding them of certain hours of their early childhood, telling them anecdotes of her own. None the less she assured them that she believed there was no harm at all in Mrs. Churchley, and that when the time should come she would probably take them out immensely. She saw with

G

smothered irritation that they enjoyed their visit in
Prince's Gate; they had never been at anything so
"grown up," nor seen so many smart bonnets and brilliant complexions. Moreover, they were considered with
interest, as if, as features of Mrs. Churchley's new life,
they had been described in advance and were the heroines
of the occasion. There were so many ladies present that
Mrs. Churchley didn't talk to them much; but she called
them her "chicks" and asked them to hand about tea-
cups and bread and butter. All this was highly agreeable and indeed intensely exciting to Beatrice and Muriel,
who had little round red spots in *their* cheeks when they
came away. Adela quivered with the sense that her
mother's children were now Mrs. Churchley's "chicks"
and features of Mrs. Churchley's life.

It was one thing to have made up her mind, however;
it was another thing to make her attempt. It was when
she learned from Godfrey that the day was fixed, the
20th of July, only six weeks removed, that she felt the
importance of prompt action. She learned everything
from Godfrey now, having determined that it would be
hypocrisy to question her father. Even her silence was
hypocritical, but she couldn't weep and wail. Her father
showed extreme tact; taking no notice of her detachment, treating her as if it were a moment of *bouderie*
which he was bound to allow her and which would pout
itself away. She debated much as to whether she should
take Godfrey into her confidence; she would have done
so without hesitation if he had not disappointed her. He
was so strange and so perversely preoccupied that she
could explain it only by the high pressure at which he
was living, his anxiety about his "exam." He was in a
fidget, in a fever, putting on a spurt to come in first;
skeptical moreover about his success and cynical about

everything else. He appeared to agree to the general axiom that they didn't want a strange woman thrust into their home, but he found Mrs. Churchley "very jolly as a person to know." He had been to see her by himself; he had been to see her three times. He said to his sister that he would make the most of her now; he should probably be so little in Seymour Street after these days. What Adela at last determined to say to him was that the marriage would never take place. When he asked her what she meant and who was to prevent it, she replied that the interesting couple would give it up themselves, or that Mrs. Churchley at least would after a week or two back out of it.

"That will be really horrid then," Godfrey rejoined. "The only respectable thing, at the point they've come to, is to put it through. Charming for poor father to have the air of being 'chucked.'"

This made her hesitate two days more, but she found answers more valid than any objections. The many-voiced answer to everything — it was like the autumn wind around the house — was the backward affront to her mother. Her mother was dead, but it killed her again. So one morning, at eleven o'clock, when Adela knew her father was writing letters, she went out quietly and, stopping the first hansom she met, drove to Prince's Gate. Mrs. Churchley was at home, and she was shown into the drawing-room with the request that she would wait five minutes. She waited, without the sense of breaking down at the last, the impulse to run away, which was what she had expected to have. In the cab and at the door her heart had beat terribly, but now, suddenly, with the game really to play, she found herself lucid and calm. It was a joy to her to feel later that this was the way Mrs. Churchley found her; not confused, not stammering nor prevaricating, only a little amazed at her own courage, conscious of the immense responsibility of her step and wonderfully older than her years. Her hostess fixed her at first with the waiting eyes of a cashier, but after a little, to Adela's surprise, she burst into tears. At this the girl cried herself, but with the secret happiness of believing they were saved. Mrs. Churchley said she would think over what she had been told, and she promised Adela, freely enough and very firmly, not to betray the secret of her visit to the Colonel. They were saved — they were saved: the words sung themselves in the girl's soul as she came downstairs. When the door was opened for her she saw her brother on the step, and they looked at each other in surprise, each finding it on the part of the other an odd hour for Prince's Gate. Godfrey remarked that Mrs. Churchley would have enough of the family, and Adela answered that she would perhaps have too much. None the less the young man went in, while his sister took her way home.

III.

Adela Chart saw nothing of her brother for nearly a week; he had more and more his own time and hours, adjusted to his tremendous responsibilities, and he spent whole days at his crammer's. When she knocked at his door, late in the evening, he was not in his room. It was known in the house that he was greatly worried; he was horribly nervous about his ordeal. It was to begin on the 23d of June, and his father was as worried as himself. The wedding had been arranged in relation to this; they wished poor Godfrey's fate settled first, though it was felt that the nuptials would be darkened if it should not be settled right.

Ten days after her morning visit to Mrs. Churchley Adela began to perceive that there was a difference in the air; but as yet she was afraid to exult. It was not a difference for the better, so that there might be still many hours of pain. Her father, since the announcement of his intended marriage, had been visibly pleased with himself, but that pleasure appeared to have undergone a check. Adela had the impression which the passengers on a great steamer receive when, in the middle of the night, they hear the engines stop. As this impression resolves itself into the general sense that something serious has happened, so the girl asked herself what had happened now. She had expected something serious; but it was as if she couldn't keep still in her cabin — she wanted to go up and see. On the 20th, just before breakfast, her maid brought her a message from her brother. Mr. Godfrey would be obliged if she would speak to him in his room. She went straight up to him, dreading to find him ill, broken down on the eve of his formidable week. This was not the case, however, inasmuch as he appeared to be already at work, to have been at work since dawn. But he was very white, and his eyes had a strange and new expression. Her beautiful young brother looked older; he looked haggard and hard. He met her there as if he had been waiting for her, and he said immediately: "Please to tell me this, Adela: what was the purpose of your visit, the other morning, to Mrs. Churchley — the day I met you at her door?"

She stared — she hesitated. "The purpose? What's the matter? Why do you ask?"

"They've put it off — they've put it off a month."

"Ah, thank God!" said Adela.

"Why do you thank God?" Godfrey exclaimed roughly.

His sister gave a strained, intense smile. "You know I think it's all wrong."

He stood looking at her up and down. "What did you do there? How did you interfere?"

"Who told you I interfered?" she asked, flushing.

"You said something — you did something. I knew you had done it when I saw you come out."

"What I did was my own business."

"Damn your own business!" cried the young man.

She had never in her life been so spoken to, and in advance, if she had been given the choice, she would have said that she would rather die than be so spoken to by Godfrey. But her spirit was high, and for a moment she was as angry as if some one had cut at her with a whip. She escaped the blow, but she felt the insult. "And *your* business, then?" she asked. "I wondered what that was when I saw *you*."

He stood a moment longer frowning at her; then, with the exclamation "You've made a pretty mess!" he turned away from her and sat down to his books.

They had put it off, as he said; her father was dry and stiff and official about it. "I suppose I had better let you know that we have thought it best to postpone our marriage till the end of the summer — Mrs. Churchley has so many arrangements to make:" he was not more expansive than that. She neither knew nor greatly cared whether it was her fancy or a reality that he watched her obliquely, to see how she would take these words. She flattered herself that, thanks to Godfrey's preparation, cruel as the form of it had been, she took them very cleverly. She had a perfectly good conscience, for she was now able to judge what odious elements Mrs. Churchley, whom she had not seen since the morning in Prince's Gate, had already introduced into their relations with each other. She was able to infer that her father had not concurred in the postponement, for he was more restless than before, more absent, and distinctly irritable. There was of course still the question of how much of this condition was to be attributed to his solicitude about Godfrey. That young man took occasion to say a horrible thing to his sister: "If I don't pass it will be your fault." These were dreadful days for the girl, and she asked herself how she could have borne them if the hovering spirit of her mother had not been at her side. Fortunately, she always felt it there, sustaining, commending, sanctifying. Suddenly her father announced to her that he wished her to go immediately, with her sisters, down to Overland, where there was always part of a household and where for a few weeks they would be sufficiently comfortable. The only explanation he gave of this desire was that he wanted them out of the way. "Out of the way of what?" she queried, since, for the time, there were to be no preparations in Seymour Street. She was willing to believe that it was out of the way of his nerves.

She never needed urging, however, to go to Overland, the dearest old house in the world, where the happiest days of her young life had been spent and the silent nearness of her mother always seemed greatest. She was happy again, with Beatrice and Muriel and Miss Flynn, and the air of summer, and the haunted rooms, and her mother's garden, and the talking oaks and the nightingales. She wrote briefly to her father, to give him, as he had requested, an account of things; and he wrote back that, since she was so contented (she didn't remember telling him that), she had better not return to town at all. The rest of the season was not important for her, and he was getting on very well. He mentioned that Godfrey had finished his exam; but, as she knew, there would be a tiresome wait before they could learn the result. Godfrey was going abroad for a month with young Sherard — he had earned a little rest and a little fun. He went abroad without a word to Adela, but in his beautiful little hand he took a chaffing leave of Beatrice. The child showed her sister the letter, of which she was very proud and which contained no message for Adela. This was the worst bitterness of the whole crisis for that young lady — that it exhibited so strangely the creature in the world whom, after her mother, she had loved best.

Colonel Chart had said he would "run down" while his children were at Overland, but they heard no more about it. He only wrote two or three times to Miss Flynn, upon matters in regard to which Adela was surprised that he should not have communicated with herself. Muriel accomplished an upright little letter to Mrs. Churchley — her eldest sister neither fostered nor discouraged the performance — to which Mrs. Churchley replied, after a fortnight, in a meagre and, as Adela thought, illiterate fashion, making no allusion to the approach of any closer tie. Evidently the situation had changed; the question of the marriage was dropped, at any rate for the time. This idea gave the girl a singular and almost intoxicating sense of power; she felt as if she were riding a great wave of responsibility. She had chosen and acted, and the greatest could do no more than that. The grand thing was to see one's results, and what else was she doing? These results were in important and opulent lives; the stage was large on which she moved her figures. Such a vision was exciting, and as they had the use of a couple of ponies at Overland she worked off her excitement by a long gallop. A day or two after

this, however, came news of which the effect was to re-
kindle it. Godfrey had come back, the list had been
published, he had passed first. These happy tidings proceeded from the young man himself; he announced them
by a telegram to Beatrice, who had never in her life before received such a missive and was proportionately
inflated. Adela reflected that she herself ought to
have felt snubbed, but she was too happy. They were
free again, they were themselves, the nightmare of the
previous weeks was blown away, the unity and dignity
of her father's life were restored, and, to round off her
sense of success, Godfrey had achieved his first step
toward high distinction. She wrote to him the next day,
as frankly and affectionately as if there had been no es-
trangement between them; and besides telling him that
she rejoiced in his triumph, she begged him in charity to
let them know exactly how the case stood with regard to
Mrs. Churchley.

Late in the summer afternoon she walked through the
park to the village with her letter, posted it and came
back. Suddenly, at one of the turns of the avenue, half-
way to the house, she saw a young man looking toward
her and waiting for her — a young man who proved to
be Godfrey, on his march, on foot, across from the station. He had seen her, as he took his short cut, and if
he had come down to Overland it was not, apparently,
to avoid her. There was none of the joy of his triumph
in his face, however, as he came a very few steps to meet
her; and although, stiffly enough, he let her kiss him and
say, "I'm so glad — I'm so glad!" she felt that this
tolerance was not quite the calmness of the rising diplomatist. He turned toward the house with her and
walked on a short distance, while she uttered the hope
that he had come to stay some days.

"Only till to-morrow morning. They are sending me straight to Madrid. I came down to say good-by; there's a fellow bringing my portmanteau."

"To Madrid? How awfully nice! And it's awfully nice of you to have come," Adela said, passing her hand into his arm.

The movement made him stop, and, stopping, he turned on her, in a flash, a face of something more than suspicion — of passionate reprobation. "What I really came for — you might as well know without more delay — is to ask you a question."

"A question?" Adela repeated with a beating heart.

They stood there, under the old trees, in the lingering light, and, young and fine and fair as they both were, they were in complete superficial accord with the peaceful English scene. A near view, however, would have shown that Godfrey Chart had not come down to Overland to be superficial. He looked deep into his sister's eyes and demanded: "What was it you said that morning to Mrs. Churchley?"

Adela gazed at the ground a moment; then, raising her eyes: "If she has told you, why do you ask?"

"She has told me nothing. I've seen for myself."

"What have you seen?"

"She has broken it off — everything's over — father's in the depths."

"In the depths?" the girl quavered.

"Did you think it would make him jolly?" asked her brother.

"He'll get over it; he'll be glad."

"That remains to be seen. You interfered, you invented something, you got round her. I insist on knowing what you did."

Adela felt that she could be obstinate if she wished,

and that if it should be a question of organizing a defense she should find treasures of perversity under her hand. She stood looking down again a moment, and saying to herself, "I could be dumb and dogged if I chose, but I scorn to be." She was not ashamed of what she had done, but she wanted to be clear. "Are you absolutely certain it's broken off?"

"He is, and she is; so that's as good."

"What reason has she given?"

"None at all — or half a dozen; it's the same thing. She has changed her mind — she mistook her feelings — she can't part with her independence; moreover, he has too many children."

"Did he tell you this?" said Adela.

"Mrs. Churchley told me. She has gone abroad for a year."

"And she didn't tell you what I said to her?"

"Why should I take this trouble if she had?"

"You might have taken it to make me suffer," said Adela. "That appears to be what you want to do."

"No, I leave that to *you;* it's the good turn you've done me!" cried the young man, with hot tears in his eyes.

She stared, aghast with the perception that there was some dreadful thing she didn't know; but he walked on, dropping the question angrily and turning his back to her as if he couldn't trust himself. She read his disgust in his averted face, in the way he squared his shoulders and smote the ground with his stick, and she hurried after him and presently overtook him. She accompanied him for a moment in silence; then she pleaded: "What do you mean? What in the world have I done to you?"

"She would have helped me; she was all ready to do it," said Godfrey.

"Helped you in what?" She wondered what he meant;

if he had made debts that he was afraid to confess to his father and—of all horrible things — had been looking to Mrs. Churchley to pay. She turned red with the mere apprehension of this and, on the heels of her guess, exulted again at having perhaps averted such a shame.

"Can't you see that I'm in trouble? Where are your eyes, your senses, your sympathy, that you talk so much about? Haven't you seen these six months that I've a cursed worry in my life?"

She seized his arm, she made him stop, she stood looking up at him like a frightened little girl. "What's the matter, Godfrey — what *is* the matter?"

"You've vexed me so — I could strangle you!" he growled. This idea added nothing to her dread; her dread was that he had done some wrong, was stained with some guilt. She uttered it to him with clasped hands, begging him to tell her the worst; but, still more passionately, he cut her short with his own cry: "In God's name, satisfy me! What infernal thing did you do?"

"It was not infernal; it was right. I told her mamma had been wretched," said Adela.

"Wretched? You told her such a lie?"

"It was the only way, and she believed me."

"Wretched how — wretched when — wretched where?" the young man stammered.

"I told her papa had made her so, and that *she* ought to know it. I told her the question troubled me unspeakably, but that I had made up my mind it was my duty to initiate her." Adela paused, with the light of bravado in her face, as if, though struck while she phrased it, with the monstrosity of what she had done, she was incapable of abating a jot of it. "I notified her that he had faults and peculiarities that made mamma's life a long worry — a martyrdom that she hid wonderfully from the world, but that we saw and that I had often pitied. I told her what they were, these faults and peculiarities; I put the dots on the *i*'s. I said it wasn't fair to let another person marry him without a warning. I warned her; I satisfied my conscience. She could do as she liked. My responsibility was over."

Godfrey gazed at her; he listened, with parted lips, incredulous and appalled. "You invented such a tissue of falsities and calumnies, and you talk about your conscience? You stand there in your senses and proclaim your crime?"

"I would have committed any crime that would have rescued us."

"You insult and defame your own father?" Godfrey continued.

"He'll never know it; she took a vow she wouldn't tell him."

"I'll be damned if *I* won't tell him!" Godfrey cried.

Adela felt sick at this, but she flamed up to resent the treachery, as it struck her, of such a menace. "I did right — I did right!" she vehemently declared. "I went down on my knees to pray for guidance, and I saved mamma's memory from outrage. But if I hadn't, if I hadn't" — she faltered for an instant — "I'm not worse than you, and I'm not so bad, for you've done something that you're ashamed to tell me."

Godfrey had taken out his watch; he looked at it with quick intensity, as if he were not hearing nor heeding her. Then, glancing up with his calculating eye, he fixed her long enough to exclaim, with unsurpassable horror and contempt: "You raving maniac!" He turned away from her; he bounded down the avenue in the direction from which they had come, and, while she watched him, strode away across the grass, toward the short cut to the station.

IV.

GODFREY's portmanteau, by the time Adela got home, had been brought to the house, but Beatrice and Muriel, who had been informed of this, waited for their brother in vain. Their sister said nothing to them about having seen him, and she accepted, after a little, with a calmness that surprised herself, the idea that he had returned to town to denounce her. She believed that would make no difference now — she had done what she had done. She had somehow a faith in Mrs. Churchley. If Mrs. Churchley had broken off she wouldn't renew. She was a heavy-footed person, incapable of further agility. Adela recognised too that it might well have come over her that there were too many children. Lastly the girl fortified herself with the reflection, grotesque under the circumstances and tending to prove that her sense of humor was not high, that her father, after all, was not a man to be played with. It seemed to her, at any rate, that if she *had* prevented his marriage she could bear anything — bear imprisonment and bread and water, bear lashes and torture, bear even his lifelong reproach. What she could bear least was the wonder of the inconvenience she had inflicted on Godfrey. She had time to turn this over, very vainly, for a succession of days — days more numerous than she had expected, which passed without bringing her from London any summons to come up and take her punishment. She sounded the possible, she compared the degrees of the probable; feeling however that, as a cloistered girl she was poorly equipped for speculation. She tried to imagine the calamitous things young men might do, and could only feel that such things would naturally be connected either with money or with women. She became conscious that after all she knew almost nothing about either subject. Meanwhile there was no reverberation from Seymour Street — only a sultry silence.

At Overland she spent hours in her mother's garden, where she had grown up, where she considered that she was training for old age, for she meant not to depend upon whist. She loved the place as, had she been a good Catholic, she would have loved the smell of her parish church; and indeed there was in her passion for flowers something of the respect of a religion. They seemed to her the only things in the world that really respected themselves, unless one made an exception for Nutkins, who had been in command all through her mother's time, with whom she had had a real friendship, and who had been affected by their pure example. He was the person left in the world with whom, on the whole, she could talk most intimately about her mother. They never had to name her together — they only said "she;" and Nutkins freely conceded that she had taught him everything he knew. When Beatrice and Muriel said "she" they referred to Mrs. Churchley. Adela had reason to believe that she should never marry, and that some day she should have about a thousand a year. This made her see in the far future a little garden of her own, under a hill, full of rare and exquisite things, where she would spend most of her old age on her knees, with an apron and stout gloves, a pair of shears and a trowel, steeped in the comfort of being thought mad.

One morning, ten days after her scene with Godfrey, upon coming back into the house shortly before lunch, she was met by Miss Flynn with the notification that a lady in the drawing-room had been waiting for her for some minutes. "A lady" suggested immediately Mrs. Churchley. It came over Adela that the form in which

her penalty was to descend would be a personal explanation with that misdirected woman. The lady had not
given her name, and Miss Flynn had not seen Mrs.
Churchley; nevertheless the governess was certain that
Adela's surmise was wrong.

"Is she big and dreadful?" the girl asked.

Miss Flynn, who was circumspection itself, hesitated
a moment. "She's dreadful, but she's not big." She
added that she was not sure she ought to let Adela go
in alone; but this young lady felt throughout like a
heroine, and it was not for a heroine to shrink from any
encounter. Was she not, every instant, in transcendent
contact with her mother? The visitor might have no
connection whatever with the drama of her father's
frustrated marriage; but everything, to-day, to Adela,
was a part of that.

Miss Flynn's description had prepared her for a considerable shock, but she was not agitated by her first
glimpse of the person who awaited her. A youngish,
well-dressed woman stood there, and silence was between
them while they looked at each other. Before either
of them had spoken, however, Adela began to see what
Miss Flynn had intended. In the light of the drawing-
room window the lady was five-and-thirty years of age
and had vivid yellow hair. She also had a blue cloth
suit with brass buttons, a stick-up collar like a gentleman's, a necktie arranged in a sailor's knot, with a
golden pin in the shape of a little lawn-tennis racket,
and pearl-grey gloves with big black stitchings. Adela's
second impression was that she was an actress; her third
was that no such person had ever before crossed that
threshold.

"I'll tell you what I've come for," said the apparition.
"I've come to ask you to intercede." She was not an
actress; an actress would have had a nicer voice.

"To intercede?"   Adela was too bewildered to ask her
to sit down.

"With your father, you know.   He doesn't know, but
he'll have to."   Her "have" sounded like "'ave."   She
explained, with many more such sounds, that she was
Mrs. Godfrey, that they had been married seven mortal
months.   If Godfrey was going abroad she must go with
him, and the only way she could go with him would be
for his father to do something.   He was afraid of his
father — that was clear; he was afraid even to tell him.
What she had come down for was to see some other
member of the family face to face ("fice to fice" Mrs.
Godfrey called it), and try if he couldn't be approached
by another side.   If no one else would act, then she
would just have to act herself.   The Colonel would have
to do something — that was the only way out of it.

What really happened Adela never quite understood;
what seemed to be happening was that the room went
round and round.   Through the blur of perception
accompanying this effect the sharp stabs of her visitor's
revelation came to her like the words heard by a patient
"going off" under ether.   She denied passionately,
afterwards, even to herself, that she had done anything
so abject as to faint; but there was a lapse in her consciousness in relation to Miss Flynn's intervention.
This intervention had evidently been active, for when
they talked the matter over, later in the day, with bated
breath and infinite dissimulation for the schoolroom
quarter, the governess had more information, and still
stranger, to impart than to receive.   She was at any
rate under the impression that she had athletically con-
tended, in the drawing-room, with the yellow hair, after
removing Adela from the scene and before inducing Mrs.
Godfrey to withdraw.   Miss Flynn had never known

H

a more thrilling day, for all the rest of it too was
pervaded with agitations and conversations, precautions
and alarms.   It was given out to Beatrice and Muriel
that their sister had been taken suddenly ill, and the
governess ministered to her in her room.   Indeed Adela
had never found herself less at ease; for this time she
had received a blow that she couldn't return.   There
was nothing to do but to take it, to endure the humiliation of her wound.

At first she declined to take it; it was much easier to
consider that her visitor was a monstrous masquerader.
On the face of the matter, moreover, it was not fair to
believe till one heard; and to hear in such a case was to
hear Godfrey himself.   Whatever his sister had tried
to imagine about him she had not arrived at anything so
belittling as an idiotic secret marriage with a dyed and
painted hag.   Adela repeated this last word as if it gave
her some comfort; and indeed where everything was so
bad fifteen years of seniority made the case little worse.
Miss Flynn was portentous, for Miss Flynn had had it
out with the wretch.   She had cross-questioned her and
had not broken her down.   This was the most important
hour of Miss Flynn's life; for whereas she usually had
to content herself with being humbly and gloomily in
the right, she could now be magnanimously and showily
so.   Her only perplexity was as to what she ought to
do — write to Colonel Chart or go up to town to see him.
She bloomed with alternatives, never having known the
like before.   Toward evening Adela was obliged to
recognise that Godfrey's worry, of which he had spoken
to her, had appeared bad enough to consist even of a low
wife, and to remember that, so far from its being in-
conceivable that a young man in his position should
clandestinely take one, she had been present, years be-

fore, during her mother's lifetime, when Lady Molesley
declared gayly, over a cup of tea, that this was precisely
what she expected of her eldest son. The next morning
it was the worst possibilities that seemed the clearest;
the only thing left with a tatter of dusky comfort being
the ambiguity of Godfrey's charge that his sister's action
had "done" for him. That was a matter by itself, and
she racked her brains for a connecting link between Mrs.
Churchley and Mrs. Godfrey. At last she made up her
mind that they were related by blood; very likely,
though differing in fortune, they were cousins or even
sisters. But even then what did her brother mean?

Arrested by the unnatural fascination of opportunity,
Miss Flynn received before lunch a telegram from
Colonel Chart — an order for dinner and a vehicle; he
and Godfrey were to arrive at six o'clock. Adela had
plenty of occupation for the interval, for she was pitying
her father when she was not rejoicing that her mother
had gone too soon to know. She flattered herself she
discerned the providential reason of that cruelty now.
She found time however still to wonder for what purpose, under the circumstances, Godfrey was to be brought
down. She was not unconscious, it is true, that she had
little general knowledge of what usually was done with
young men in that predicament. One talked about the
circumstances, but the circumstances were an abyss. She
felt this still more when she found, on her father's
arrival, that nothing, apparently, was to happen as she
had taken for granted it would. There was a kind of
inviolable hush over the whole affair, but no tragedy, no
publicity, nothing ugly. The tragedy had been in town,
and the faces of the two men spoke of it, in spite of
themselves; so that at present there was only a family
dinner, with Beatrice and Muriel and the governess, and

almost a company tone, the result of the desire to avoid publicity. Adela admired her father; she knew what he was feeling, if Mrs. Godfrey had been at him, and yet she saw him positively gallant. He was very gentle, he never looked at his son, and there were moments when he seemed almost sick with sadness. Godfrey was equally inscrutable and therefore wholly different from what he had been as he stood before her in the park. If he was to start on his career (with such a wife! — wouldn't she utterly blight it?) he was already professional enough to know how to wear a mask.

Before they rose from table the girl was wholly bewildered, so little could she perceive the effects of such large causes. She had nerved herself for a great ordeal, but the air was as sweet as an anodyne. It was constantly plain to her that her father was deadly sad — as pathetic as a creature jilted. He was broken, but he showed no resentment; there was a weight on his heart, but he had lightened it by dressing as immaculately as usual for dinner. She asked herself what immensity of a row there could have been in town to have left his anger so spent. He went through everything, even to sitting with his son after dinner. When they came out together he invited Beatrice and Muriel to the billiard-room; and as Miss Flynn discreetly withdrew Adela was left alone with Godfrey, who was completely changed and not in a rage any more. He was broken, too, but he was not so pathetic as his father. He was only very correct and apologetic; he said to his sister, "I'm awfully sorry *you* were annoyed; it was something I never dreamed of."

She couldn't think immediately what he meant; then she grasped the reference to the yellow hair. She was uncertain, however, what tone to take; perhaps his father had arranged with him that they were to make the best of it. But she spoke her own despair in the way she murmured: "O Godfrey, Godfrey, is it true?"

"I've been the most unutterable donkey — you can say what you like to me. You can't say anything worse than I've said to myself."

"My brother, my brother!" his words made her moan. He hushed her with a movement, and she asked, "What has father said?"

Godfrey looked over her head. "He'll give her six hundred a year."

"Ah, the angel!"

"On condition she never comes near me. She has solemnly promised; and she'll probably leave me alone, to get the money. If she doesn't — in diplomacy — I'm lost." The young man had been turning his eyes vaguely about, this way and that, to avoid meeting hers; but after another instant he gave up the effort, and she had the miserable confession of his glance. "I've been living in hell," he said.

"My brother, my brother!" she repeated.

"I'm not an idiot; yet for her I've behaved like one. Don't ask me — you mustn't know. It was all done in a day, and since then, fancy my condition — fancy my work!"

"Thank God you passed!" cried Adela.

"I would have shot myself if I hadn't. I had an awful day yesterday with father; it was late at night before it was over. I leave England next week. He brought me down here for it to look well — so that the children sha'n't know."

"He's wonderful!" she murmured.

"He's wonderful!" said Godfrey.

"Did *she* tell him?" the girl asked.

"She came straight to Seymour Street from here. She saw him alone first; then he called me in. *That* luxury lasted about an hour."

Adela said, "Poor, poor father!" to this; on which her brother remained silent. Then, after he had remarked that it had been the scene he had lived in terror of all through his cramming, and she had stammered her pity and admiration at such a mixture of anxieties and such a triumph of talent, she demanded: "Have you told him?"

"Told him what?"

"What you said you would — what *I* did."

Godfrey turned away as if at present he had very little interest in that inferior tribulation. "I was angry with you, but I cooled off. I held my tongue."

Adela clasped her hands. "You thought of mamma!"

"Oh, don't speak of mamma," said the young man tenderly.

It was indeed not a happy moment; and she murmured: "No; if you *had* thought of her" —

This made Godfrey turn back at her, with a little flare in his eyes. "Oh, *then* it didn't prevent. I thought that woman was good. I believed in her."

"Is she *very* bad?" his sister inquired.

"I shall never mention her to you again," Godfrey answered, with dignity.

"You may believe that *I* won't speak of her. So father doesn't know?" she added.

"Doesn't know what?"

"That I said that to Mrs. Churchley."

"I don't think so, but you must find out for yourself."

"I shall find out," said Adela. "But what had Mrs. Churchley to do with it?"

"With *my* misery? I told her. I had to tell some one."

"Why didn't you tell me?"

Godfrey hesitated. "Oh, you take things so beastly hard — you make such rows." Adela covered her face with her hands, and he went on: "What I wanted was comfort — not to be lashed up. I thought I should go mad. I wanted Mrs. Churchley to break it to father, to intercede for me and help him to meet it. She was awfully kind to me; she listened and she understood; she could fancy how it had happened. Without her I shouldn't have pulled through. She liked me, you know," Godfrey dropped. "She said she would do what she could for me; she was full of sympathy and resource; I really leaned on her. But when you cut in, of course it spoiled everything. That's why I was so angry with you. She couldn't do anything then."

Adela dropped her hands, staring; she felt that she had walked in darkness. "So that he had to meet it alone?"

"*Dame!*" said Godfrey, who had got up his French tremendously.

Muriel came to the door to say papa wished the two others to join them, and the next day Godfrey returned to town. His father remained at Overland, without an intermission, the rest of the summer and the whole of the autumn, and Adela had a chance to find out, as she had said, whether he knew that she had interfered. But in spite of her chance she never found out. He knew that Mrs. Churchley had thrown him over and he knew that his daughter rejoiced in it, but he appeared not to have divined the relation between the two facts. It was strange that one of the matters he was clearest about — Adela's secret triumph — should have been just the thing which, from this time on, justified less and less such a confidence. She was too sorry for him to be consistently glad. She watched his attempts to wind himself up on

the subject of shorthorns and drainage, and she favoured
to the utmost of her ability his intermittent disposition
to make a figure in orchids. She wondered whether they
mightn't have a few people at Overland; but when she
mentioned the idea her father asked what in the world
there would be to attract them. It was a confoundedly
stupid house, he remarked, with all respect to *her* cleverness. Beatrice and Muriel were mystified; the prospect
of going out immensely had faded so utterly away. They
were apparently not to go out at all. Colonel Chart was
aimless and bored; he paced up and down and went back
to smoking, which was bad for him, and looked drearily
out of windows, as if on the bare chance that something
might arrive. Did he expect Mrs. Churchley to arrive,
to relent? It was Adela's belief that she gave no sign.
But the girl thought it really remarkable of her not
to have betrayed her ingenious young visitor. Adela's
judgment of human nature was perhaps harsh, but she
believed that many women, under the circumstances,
would not have been so forbearing. This lady's conception of the point of honour presented her as rather a
higher type than one might have supposed.

Adela knew her father found the burden of Godfrey's
folly very heavy to bear and was incommoded at having
to pay the horrible woman six hundred a year. Doubtless he was having dreadful letters from her; doubtless
she threatened them all with a hideous exposure. If
the matter should be bruited Godfrey's prospects would
collapse on the spot. He thought Madrid very charming
and curious, but Mrs. Godfrey was in England, so that
his father had to face the music. Adela took a dolorous
comfort in thinking that her mother was out of *that* —
it would have killed her; but this didn't blind her
to the fact that the comfort for her father would perhaps

have been greater if he had had some one to talk to about
his trouble. He never dreamed of doing so to her, and
she felt that she couldn't ask him. In the family life he
wanted utter silence about it. Early in the winter he
went abroad for ten weeks, leaving her with her sisters
in the country, where it was not to be denied that at this
time existence had very little savour. She half expected
that her sister-in-law would descend upon her again; but
the fear was not justified, and the quietude of such a
personage savoured terribly of expense. There were sure
to be extras. Colonel Chart went to Paris and to Monte
Carlo and then to Madrid to see his boy. Adela wondered whether he would meet Mrs. Churchley somewhere,
since, if she had gone for a year, she would still be on
the Continent. If he should meet her perhaps the affair
would come on again: she caught herself musing over
this. Her father brought back no news of her, and
seeing him after an interval, she was struck afresh with
his jilted and wasted air. She didn't like it; she re-
sented it. A little more and she would have said that
that was no way to treat such a man.

They all went up to town in March, and on one of the
first days of April she saw Mrs. Churchley in the park.
She herself remained apparently invisible to that lady —
she herself and Beatrice and Muriel, who sat with her in
their mother's old bottle-green landau. Mrs. Churchley,
perched higher than ever, rode by without a recognition;
but this didn't prevent Adela from going to her before
the month was over. As on her great previous occasion
she went in the morning, and she again had the good
fortune to be admitted. But this time her visit was
shorter, and a week after making it — the week was a
desolation — she addressed to her brother at Madrid a
letter which contained these words:

"I could endure it no longer — I confessed and retracted; I explained to her as well as I could the falsity
of what I said to her ten months ago and the benighted
purity of my motives for saying it. I besought her to
regard it as unsaid, to forgive me, not to despise me too
much, to take pity on poor *perfect* papa and come back
to him. She was more good-natured than you might
have expected; indeed, she laughed extravagantly. She
had never believed me — it was too absurd; she had
only, at the time, disliked me. She found me utterly
false (she was very frank with me about this), and she
told papa that she thought I was horrid. She said she
could never live with such a girl, and as I would certainly never marry I must be sent away; in short she
quite loathed me. Papa defended me, he refused to
sacrifice me, and this led practically to their rupture.
Papa gave her up, as it were, for me. Fancy the angel,
and fancy what I must try to be to him for the rest of
his life! Mrs. Churchley can never come back — she's
going to marry Lord Dovedale."

THE PUPIL.[1]

I.

THE poor young man hesitated and procrastinated: it cost him such an effort to broach the subject of terms, to speak of money to a person who spoke only of feelings and, as it were, of the aristocracy. Yet he was unwilling to take leave, treating his engagement as settled, without some more conventional glance in that direction than he could find an opening for in the manner of the large, affable lady who sat there drawing a pair of soiled *gants de Suède* through a fat, jewelled hand and, at once pressing and gliding, repeated over and over everything but the thing he would have liked to hear. He would have liked to hear the figure of his salary; but just as he was nervously about to sound that note the little boy came back — the little boy Mrs. Moreen had sent out of the room to fetch her fan. He came back without the fan, only with the casual observation that he couldn't find it. As he dropped this cynical confession he looked straight and hard at the candidate for the honour of taking his education in hand. This personage reflected, somewhat grimly, that the first thing he should have to teach his little charge would be to appear to address himself to his mother

123

when he spoke to her — especially not to make her such an improper answer as that.

When Mrs. Moreen bethought herself of this pretext for getting rid of their companion, Pemberton supposed it was precisely to approach the delicate subject of his remuneration. But it had been only to say some things about her son which it was better that a boy of eleven shouldn't catch. They were extravagantly to his advantage, save when she lowered her voice to sigh, tapping her left side familiarly: "And all overclouded by *this*, you know — all at the mercy of a weakness —!" Pemberton gathered that the weakness was in the region of the heart. He had known the poor child was not robust: this was the basis on which he had been invited to treat, through an English lady, an Oxford acquaintance, then at Nice, who happened to know both his needs and those of the amiable American family looking out for something really superior in the way of a resident tutor.

The young man's impression of his prospective pupil, who had first come into the room, as if to see for himself, as soon as Pemberton was admitted, was not quite the soft solicitation the visitor had taken for granted. Morgan Moreen was, somehow, sickly without being delicate, and that he looked intelligent (it is true Pemberton wouldn't have enjoyed his being stupid), only added to the suggestion that, as with his big mouth and big ears he really couldn't be called pretty, he might be unpleasant. Pemberton was modest — he was even timid; and the chance that his small scholar might prove cleverer than himself had quite figured, to his nervousness, among the dangers of an untried experiment. He reflected, however, that these were risks one had to run when one accepted a position, as it was called, in a private family; when as yet one's University honours had, pecuniarily speaking, remained barren. At any rate, when Mrs. Moreen got up as if to intimate that, since it was understood he would enter upon his duties within the week she would let him off now, he succeeded, in spite of the presence of the child, in squeezing out a phrase about the rate of payment. It was not the fault of the conscious smile which seemed a reference to the lady's expensive identity, if the allusion did not sound rather vulgar. This was exactly because she became still more gracious to reply: "Oh! I can assure you that all that will be quite regular."

Pemberton only wondered, while he took up his hat, what "all that" was to amount to — people had such different ideas. Mrs. Moreen's words, however, seemed to commit the family to a pledge definite enough to elicit from the child a strange little comment, in the shape of the mocking, foreign ejaculation, "Oh, là-là!"

Pemberton, in some confusion, glanced at him as he walked slowly to the window with his back turned, his hands in his pockets and the air in his elderly shoulders of a boy who didn't play. The young man wondered if he could teach him to play, though his mother had said it would never do and that this was why school was impossible. Mrs. Moreen exhibited no discomfiture; she only continued blandly: "Mr. Moreen will be delighted to meet your wishes. As I told you, he has been called to London for a week. As soon as he comes back you shall have it out with him."

This was so frank and friendly that the young man could only reply, laughing as his hostess laughed: "Oh! I don't imagine we shall have much of a battle."

"They'll give you anything you like," the boy remarked unexpectedly, returning from the window. "We don't mind what anything costs — we live awfully well."

"My darling, you're too quaint!" his mother exclaimed, putting out to caress him a practiced but ineffectual hand. He slipped out of it, but looked with intelligent, innocent eyes at Pemberton, who had already had time to notice that from one moment to the other his small satiric face seemed to change its time of life. At this moment it was infantine; yet it appeared also to be under the influence of curious intuitions and knowledges. Pemberton rather disliked precocity, and he was disappointed to find gleams of it in a disciple not yet in his teens. Nevertheless he divined on the spot that Morgan wouldn't prove a bore. He would prove on the contrary a kind of excitement. This idea held the young man, in spite of a certain repulsion.

"You pompous little person! We're not extravagant!" Mrs. Moreen gayly protested, making another unsuccessful attempt to draw the boy to her side. "You must know what to expect," she went on to Pemberton.

"The less you expect the better!" her companion interposed. "But we *are* people of fashion."

"Only so far as *you* make us so!" Mrs. Moreen mocked, tenderly. "Well, then, on Friday — don't tell me you're superstitious — and mind you don't fail us. Then you'll see us all. I'm so sorry the girls are out. I guess you'll like the girls. And, you know, I've another son, quite different from this one."

"He tries to imitate me," said Morgan to Pemberton.

"He tries? Why, he's twenty years old!" cried Mrs. Moreen.

"You're very witty," Pemberton remarked to the child — a proposition that his mother echoed with enthusiasm, declaring that Morgan's sallies were the delight of the house. The boy paid no heed to this; he only inquired abruptly of the visitor, who was surprised after-

wards that he hadn't struck him as offensively forward:
"Do you *want* very much to come?"

"Can you doubt it, after such a description of what I
shall hear?" Pemberton replied.   Yet he didn't want to
come at all; he was coming because he had to go somewhere, thanks to the collapse of his fortune at the end
of a year abroad, spent on the system of putting his tiny
patrimony into a single full wave of experience.   He
had had his full wave, but he couldn't pay his hotel bill.
Moreover, he had caught in the boy's eyes the glimpse
of a far-off appeal.

"Well, I'll do the best I can for you," said Morgan;
with which he turned away again.   He passed out of
one of the long windows; Pemberton saw him go and
lean on the parapet of the terrace.   He remained there
while the young man took leave of his mother, who, on
Pemberton's looking as if he expected a farewell from
him, interposed with: "Leave him, leave him; he's so
strange!"   Pemberton suspected she was afraid of something he might say.   "He's a genius — you'll love him,"
she added.   "He's much the most interesting person in
the family."   And before he could invent some civility
to oppose to this, she wound up with: "But we're all
good, you know!"

"He's a genius — you'll love him!" were words that
recurred to Pemberton before the Friday, suggesting,
among other things that geniuses were not invariably
lovable.   However, it was all the better if there was an
element that would make tutorship absorbing: he had
perhaps taken too much for granted that it would be
dreary.   As he left the villa after his interview, he looked
up at the balcony and saw the child leaning over it.
"We shall have great larks!" he called up.

Morgan hesitated a moment; then he answered, laugh-

ing: "By the time you come back I shall have thought
of something witty!"

This made Pemberton say to himself: "After all he's
rather nice."

II.

On the Friday he saw them all, as Mrs. Moreen had
promised, for her husband had come back and the girls
and the other son were at home. Mr. Moreen had a white
moustache, a confiding manner and, in his buttonhole,
the ribbon of a foreign order — bestowed, as Pemberton
eventually learned, for services. For what services he
never clearly ascertained: this was a point — one of a
large number — that Mr. Moreen's manner never confided. What it emphatically did confide was that he
was a man of the world. Ulick, the firstborn, was in
visible training for the same profession — under the
disadvantage as yet, however, of a buttonhole only
feebly floral and a moustache with no pretensions to type.
The girls had hair and figures and manners and small fat
feet, but had never been out alone. As for Mrs. Moreen,
Pemberton saw on a nearer view that her elegance was
intermittent and her parts didn't always match. Her
husband, as she had promised, met with enthusiasm
Pemberton's ideas in regard to a salary. The young
man had endeavoured to make them modest, and Mr.
Moreen confided to him that *he* found them positively
meagre. He further assured him that he aspired to be
intimate with his children, to be their best friend, and
that he was always looking out for them. That was
what he went off for, to London and other places — to
look out; and this vigilance was the theory of life, as
well as the real occupation, of the whole family. They
all looked out, for they were very frank on the subject

of its being necessary. They desired it to be understood that they were earnest people, and also that their fortune, though quite adequate for earnest people, required the most careful administration. Mr. Moreen, as the parent bird, sought sustenance for the nest. Ulick found sustenance mainly at the club, where Pemberton guessed that it was usually served on green cloth. The girls used to do up their hair and their frocks themselves, and our young man felt appealed to to be glad, in regard to Morgan's education, that, though it must naturally be of the best, it didn't cost too much. After a little he *was* glad, forgetting at times his own needs in the interest inspired by the child's nature and education and the pleasure of making easy terms for him.

During the first weeks of their acquaintance Morgan had been as puzzling as a page in an unknown language — altogether different from the obvious little Anglo-Saxons who had misrepresented childhood to Pemberton. Indeed the whole mystic volume in which the boy had been bound demanded some practice in translation. To-day, after a considerable interval, there is something phantasmagoric, like a prismatic reflection or a serial novel, in Pemberton's memory of the queerness of the Moreens. If it were not for a few tangible tokens — a lock of Morgan's hair, cut by his own hand, and the half-dozen letters he got from him when they were separated — the whole episode and the figures peopling it would seem too inconsequent for anything but dreamland. The queerest thing about them was their success (as it appeared to him for a while at the time), for he had never seen a family so brilliantly equipped for failure. Wasn't it success to have kept him so hatefully long? Wasn't it success to have drawn him in that first morning at *déjeuner*, the Friday he came — it was enough to

I

make one superstitious — so that he utterly committed himself, and this not by calculation or a *mot d'ordre*, but by a happy instinct which made them, like a band of gipsies, work so neatly together ? They amused him as much as if they had really been a band of gipsies. He was still young and had not seen much of the world — his English years had been intensely usual; therefore the reversed conventions of the Moreens (for they had their standards), struck him as topsyturvy. He had encountered nothing like them at Oxford; still less had any such note been struck to his younger American ear during the four years at Yale in which he had richly supposed himself to be reacting against Puritanism. The reaction of the Moreens, at any rate, went ever so much further. He had thought himself very clever that first day in hitting them all off in his mind with the term " cosmopolite." Later, it seemed feeble and colourless enough — confessedly, helplessly provisional.

However, when he first applied it to them he had a degree of joy — for an instructor he was still empirical — as if from the apprehension that to live with them would really be to see life. Their sociable strangeness was an intimation of that — their chatter of tongues, their gaiety and good humour, their infinite dawdling (they were always getting themselves up, but it took forever, and Pemberton had once found Mr. Moreen shaving in the drawing-room), their French, their Italian and, in the spiced fluency, their cold, tough slices of American. They lived on macaroni and coffee (they had these articles prepared in perfection), but they knew recipes for a hundred other dishes. They overflowed with music and song, were always humming and catching each other up, and had a kind of professional acquaintance with continental cities. They talked of " good places " as if they had been strolling players. They had at Nice a villa, a carriage, a piano and a banjo, and they went to official parties. They were a perfect calendar of the "days" of their friends, which Pemberton knew them, when they were indisposed, to get out of bed to go to, and which made the week larger than life when Mrs. Moreen talked of them with Paula and Amy. Their romantic initiations gave their new inmate at first an almost dazzling sense of culture. Mrs. Moreen had translated something, at some former period — an author whom it made Pemberton feel *borné* never to have heard of. They could imitate Venetian and sing Neapolitan, and when they wanted to say something very particular they communicated with each other in an ingenious dialect of their own — a sort of spoken cipher, which Pemberton at first took for Volapuk, but which he learned to understand as he would not have understood Volapuk.

"It's the family language — Ultramoreen," Morgan explained to him drolly enough; but the boy rarely condescended to use it himself, though he attempted colloquial Latin as if he had been a little prelate.

Among all the "days" with which Mrs. Moreen's memory was taxed she managed to squeeze in one of her own, which her friends sometimes forgot. But the house derived a frequented air from the number of fine people who were freely named there and from several mysterious men with foreign titles and English clothes whom Morgan called the princes and who, on sofas with the girls, talked French very loud, as if to show they were saying nothing improper. Pemberton wondered how the princes could ever propose in that tone and so publicly: he took for granted cynically that this was what was desired of them. Then he acknowledged that even for the chance of such an advantage Mrs. Moreen would never allow

Paula and Amy to receive alone. These young ladies were not at all timid, but it was just the safeguards that made them so graceful. It was a houseful of Bohemians who wanted tremendously to be Philistines.

In one respect, however, certainly, they achieved no rigour — they were wonderfully amiable and ecstatic about Morgan. It was a genuine tenderness, an artless admiration, equally strong in each. They even praised his beauty, which was small, and were rather afraid of him, as if they recognised that he was of a finer clay. They called him a little angel and a little prodigy and pitied his want of health effusively. Pemberton feared at first that their extravagance would make him hate the boy, but before this happened he had become extravagant himself. Later, when he had grown rather to hate the others, it was a bribe to patience for him that they were at any rate nice about Morgan, going on tiptoe if they fancied he was showing symptoms, and even giving up somebody's "day" to procure him a pleasure. But mixed with this was the oddest wish to make him independent, as if they felt that they were not good enough for him. They passed him over to Pemberton very much as if they wished to force a constructive adoption on the obliging bachelor and shirk altogether a responsibility. They were delighted when they perceived that Morgan liked his preceptor, and could think of no higher praise for the young man. It was strange how they contrived to reconcile the appearance, and indeed the essential fact, of adoring the child with their eagerness to wash their hands of him. Did they want to get rid of him before he should find them out ? Pemberton was finding them out month by month. At any rate, the boy's relations turned their backs with exaggerated delicacy, as if to escape the charge of interfering. See-

ing in time how little he had in common with them (it
was by *them* he first observed it — they proclaimed it
with complete humility), his preceptor was moved to
speculate on the mysteries of transmission, the far jumps
of heredity. Where his detachment from most of the
things they represented had come from was more than
an observer could say — it certainly had burrowed under
two or three generations.

As for Pemberton's own estimate of his pupil, it was
a good while before he got the point of view, so little
had he been prepared for it by the smug young barbarians
to whom the tradition of tutorship, as hitherto revealed
to him, had been adjusted. Morgan was scrappy and
surprising, deficient in many properties supposed common to the *genus* and abounding in others that were the
portion only of the supernaturally clever. One day
Pemberton made a great stride: it cleared up the question to perceive that Morgan *was* supernaturally clever
and that, though the formula was temporarily meagre,
this would be the only assumption on which one could
successfully deal with him. He had the general quality
of a child for whom life had not been simplified by
school, a kind of homebred sensibility which might have
been bad for himself but was charming for others, and
a whole range of refinement and perception — little
musical vibrations as taking as picked-up airs — begot-
ten by wandering about Europe at the tail of his migra-
tory tribe. This might not have been an education to
recommend in advance, but its results with Morgan
were as palpable as a fine texture. At the same time
he had in his composition a sharp spice of stoicism,
doubtless the fruit of having had to begin early to bear
pain, which produced the impression of pluck and made
it of less consequence that he might have been thought

at school rather a polyglot little beast.   Pemberton
indeed quickly found himself rejoicing that school was
out of the question: in any million of boys it was probably good for all but one, and Morgan was that millionth.
It would have made him comparative and superior — it
might have made him priggish.   Pemberton would try
to be school himself — a bigger seminary than five
hundred grazing donkeys; so that, winning no prizes,
the boy would remain unconscious and irresponsible and
amusing — amusing, because, though life was already intense in his childish nature, freshness still made there
a strong draught for jokes.   It turned out that even
in the still air of Morgan's various disabilities jokes
flourished greatly.   He was a pale, lean, acute, unde-
veloped little cosmopolite, who liked intellectual gym-
nastics and who, also, as regards the behaviour of
mankind, had noticed more things than you might suppose, but who nevertheless had his proper playroom of
superstitions, where he smashed a dozen toys a day.

III.

At Nice once, towards evening, as the pair sat resting
in the open air after a walk, looking over the sea at the
pink western lights, Morgan said suddenly to his companion: "Do you like it — you know, being with us all in
this intimate way?"

"My dear fellow, why should I stay if I didn't?"

"How do I know you will stay?   I'm almost sure you
won't, very long."

"I hope you don't mean to dismiss me," said Pemberton.

Morgan considered a moment, looking at the sunset.
"I think if I did right I ought to."

"Well, I know I'm supposed to instruct you in virtue; but in that case don't do right."

"You're very young — fortunately," Morgan went on, turning to him again.

"Oh yes, compared with you!"

"Therefore, it won't matter so much if you do lose a lot of time."

"That's the way to look at it," said Pemberton accommodatingly.

They were silent a minute; after which the boy asked: "Do you like my father and mother very much?"

"Dear me, yes. They're charming people."

Morgan received this with another silence; then, unexpectedly, familiarly, but at the same time affectionately, he remarked: "You're a jolly old humbug!"

For a particular reason the words made Pemberton change colour. The boy noticed in an instant that he had turned red, whereupon he turned red himself and the pupil and the master exchanged a longish glance in which there was a consciousness of many more things than are usually touched upon, even tacitly, in such a relation. It produced for Pemberton an embarrassment; it raised, in a shadowy form, a question (this was the first glimpse of it), which was destined to play as singular and, as he imagined, owing to the altogether peculiar conditions, an unprecedented part in his intercourse with his little companion. Later, when he found himself talking with this small boy in a way in which few small boys could ever have been talked with, he thought of that clumsy moment on the bench at Nice as the dawn of an understanding that had broadened. What had added to the clumsiness then was that he thought it his duty to declare to Morgan that he might abuse him (Pemberton) as much as he liked, but must never abuse his parents. To this Morgan had the easy reply that he hadn't dreamed of abusing them; which appeared to be true: it put Pemberton in the wrong.

"Then why am I a humbug for saying *I* think them charming?" the young man asked, conscious of a certain rashness.

"Well — they're not *your* parents."

"They love you better than anything in the world — never forget that," said Pemberton.

"Is that why you like them so much?"

"They're very kind to me," Pemberton replied, evasively.

"You *are* a humbug!" laughed Morgan, passing an arm into his tutor's. He leaned against him, looking off at the sea again and swinging his long, thin legs.

"Don't kick my shins," said Pemberton, while he reflected: "Hang it, I can't complain of them to the child!"

"There's another reason, too," Morgan went on, keeping his legs still.

"Another reason for what?"

"Besides their not being your parents."

"I don't understand you," said Pemberton.

"Well, you will before long. All right!"

Pemberton did understand, fully, before long; but he made a fight even with himself before he confessed it. He thought it the oddest thing to have a struggle with the child about. He wondered he didn't detest the child for launching him in such a struggle. But by the time it began the resource of detesting the child was closed to him. Morgan was a special case, but to know him was to accept him on his own odd terms. Pemberton had spent his aversion to special cases before arriving at knowledge. When at last he did arrive he felt that he was in an extreme predicament. Against every interest he had attached himself. They would have to meet things together. Before they went home that evening, at Nice, the boy had said, clinging to his arm:

"Well, at any rate you'll hang on to the last."

"To the last?"

"Till you're fairly beaten."

"*You* ought to be fairly beaten!" cried the young man, drawing him closer.

IV.

A YEAR after Pemberton had come to live with them Mr. and Mrs. Moreen suddenly gave up the villa at Nice. Pemberton had got used to suddenness, having seen it practiced on a considerable scale during two jerky little tours — one in Switzerland the first summer, and the other late in the winter, when they all ran down to Florence and then, at the end of ten days, liking it much less than they had intended, straggled back in mysterious depression. They had returned to Nice "for ever," as they said; but this didn't prevent them from squeezing, one rainy, muggy May night, into a second-class railway-carriage — you could never tell by which class they would travel — where Pemberton helped them to stow away a wonderful collection of bundles and bags. The explanation of this manœuvre was that they had determined to spend the summer "in some bracing place;" but in Paris they dropped into a small furnished apartment — a fourth floor in a third-rate avenue, where there was a smell on the staircase and the *portier* was hateful — and passed the next four months in blank in-digence.

The better part of this baffled sojourn was for the pre-

ceptor and his pupil, who, visiting the Invalides and
Notre Dame, the Conciergerie and all the museums, took
a hundred remunerative rambles. They learned to know
their Paris, which was useful, for they came back another year for a longer stay, the general character of
which in Pemberton's memory to-day mixes pitiably and
confusedly with that of the first. He sees Morgan's
shabby knickerbockers — the everlasting pair that didn't
match his blouse and that as he grew longer could only
grow faded. He remembers the particular holes in his
three or four pair of coloured stockings.

Morgan was dear to his mother, but he never was better dressed than was absolutely necessary — partly, no
doubt, by his own fault, for he was as indifferent to his
appearance as a German philosopher. "My dear fellow,
you *are* coming to pieces," Pemberton would say to him
in sceptical remonstrance; to which the child would
reply, looking at him serenely up and down: "My dear
fellow, so are you! I don't want to cast you in the
shade." Pemberton could have no rejoinder for this —
the assertion so closely represented the fact. If however the deficiencies of his own wardrobe were a chapter
by themselves he didn't like his little charge to look
too poor. Later he used to say: "Well, if we are poor,
why, after all, shouldn't we look it?" and he consoled
himself with thinking there was something rather elderly
and gentlemanly in Morgan's seediness — it differed from
the untidiness of the urchin who plays and spoils his
things. He could trace perfectly the degrees by which,
in proportion as her little son confined himself to his
tutor for society, Mrs. Moreen shrewdly forbore to renew his garments. She did nothing that didn't show,
neglected him because he escaped notice, and then, as
he illustrated this clever policy, discouraged at home his

public appearances. Her position was logical enough —
those members of her family who did show had to be
showy.

During this period and several others Pemberton was
quite aware of how he and his comrade might strike people; wandering languidly through the Jardin des Plantes
as if they had nowhere to go, sitting, on the winter days,
in the galleries of the Louvre, so splendidly ironical to
the homeless, as if for the advantage of the *calorifère*.
They joked about it sometimes: it was the sort of joke
that was perfectly within the boy's compass. They
figured themselves as part of the vast, vague, hand-to-
mouth multitude of the enormous city and pretended they
were proud of their position in it — it showed them such
a lot of life and made them conscious of a sort of demo-
cratic brotherhood. If Pemberton could not feel a sympathy in destitution with his small companion (for after
all Morgan's fond parents would never have let him
really suffer), the boy would at least feel it with him,
so it came to the same thing. He used sometimes to
wonder what people would think they were — fancy they
were looked askance at, as if it might be a suspected case
of kidnapping. Morgan wouldn't be taken for a young
patrician with a preceptor — he wasn't smart enough;
though he might pass for his companion's sickly little
brother. Now and then he had a five-franc piece, and
except once, when they bought a couple of lovely neckties,
one of which he made Pemberton accept, they laid it out
scientifically in old books. It was a great day, always
spent on the quays, rummaging among the dusty boxes
that garnish the parapets. These were occasions that
helped them to live, for their books ran low very soon
after the beginning of their acquaintance. Pemberton
had a good many in England, but he was obliged to write

to a friend and ask him kindly to get some fellow to give him something for them.

If the bracing climate was untasted that summer the young man had an idea that at the moment they were about to make a push the cup had been dashed from their lips by a movement of his own. It had been his first blow-out, as he called it, with his patrons; his first successful attempt (though there was little other success about it), to bring them to a consideration of his impossible position. As the ostensible eve of a costly journey the moment struck him as a good one to put in a signal protest — to present an ultimatum. Ridiculous as it sounded he had never yet been able to compass an uninterrupted private interview with the elder pair or with either of them singly. They were always flanked by their elder children, and poor Pemberton usually had his own little charge at his side. He was conscious of its being a house in which the surface of one's delicacy got rather smudged; nevertheless he had kept the bloom of his scruple against announcing to Mr. and Mrs. Moreen with publicity that he couldn't go on longer without a little money. He was still simple enough to suppose Ulick and Paula and Amy might not know that since his arrival he had only had a hundred and forty francs; and he was magnanimous enough to wish not to compromise their parents in their eyes. Mr. Moreen now listened to him, as he listened to every one and to everything, like a man of the world, and seemed to appeal to him — though not of course too grossly — to try and be a little more of one himself. Pemberton recognised the importance of the character from the advantage it gave Mr. Moreen. He was not even confused, whereas poor Pemberton was more so than there was any reason for. Neither was he surprised — at least any more than a gentleman had to be who freely confessed himself a little shocked, though not, strictly, at Pemberton.

"We must go into this, mustn't we, dear?" he said to his wife. He assured his young friend that the matter should have his very best attention; and he melted into space as elusively as if, at the door, he were taking an inevitable but deprecatory precedence. When, the next moment, Pemberton found himself alone with Mrs. Moreen it was to hear her say: "I see, I see," stroking the roundness of her chin and looking as if she were only hesitating between a dozen easy remedies. If they didn't make their push Mr. Moreen could at least disappear for several days. During his absence his wife took up the subject again spontaneously, but her contribution to it was merely that she had thought all the while they were getting on so beautifully. Pemberton's reply to this revelation was that unless they immediately handed him a substantial sum he would leave them for ever. He knew she would wonder how he would get away, and for a moment expected her to inquire. She didn't, for which he was almost grateful to her, so little was he in a position to tell.

"You won't, you know you won't — you're too interested," she said. "You *are* interested, you know you are, you dear, kind man!" She laughed, with almost condemnatory archness, as if it were a reproach (but she wouldn't insist), while she flirted a soiled pockethandkerchief at him.

Pemberton's mind was fully made up to quit the house the following week. This would give him time to get an answer to a letter he had despatched to England. If he did nothing of the sort — that is, if he stayed another year and then went away only for three months — it was not merely because before the answer to his letter came

(most unsatisfactory when it did arrive), Mr. Moreen
generously presented him — again with all the precautions of a man of the world — three hundred francs. He
was exasperated to find that Mrs. Moreen was right, that
he couldn't bear to leave the child. This stood out
clearer for the very reason that, the night of his desperate appeal to his patrons, he had seen fully for the
first time where he was. Wasn't it another proof of
the success with which those patrons practiced their arts
that they had managed to avert for so long the illumi-
nating flash? It descended upon Pemberton with a lurid-
ness which perhaps would have struck a spectator as
comically excessive, after he had returned to his little
servile room, which looked into a close court where a
bare, dirty opposite wall took, with the sound of shrill
clatter, the reflection of lighted back-windows. He had
simply given himself away to a band of adventurers.
The idea, the word itself, had a sort of romantic horror
for him — he had always lived on such safe lines. Later
it assumed a more interesting, almost a soothing, sense:
it pointed a moral, and Pemberton could enjoy a moral.
The Moreens were adventurers not merely because they
didn't pay their debts, because they lived on society,
but because their whole view of life, dim and confused
and instinctive, like that of clever colour-blind animals,
was speculative and rapacious and mean. Oh! they
were "respectable," and that only made them more *im-
mondes*. The young man's analysis of them put it at
last very simply — they were adventurers because they
were abject snobs. That was the completest account of
them — it was the law of their being. Even when this
truth became vivid to their ingenious inmate he remained unconscious of how much his mind had been
prepared for it by the extraordinary little boy who had

now become such a complication in his life. Much less could he then calculate on the information he was still to owe to the extraordinary little boy.

V.

But it was during the ensuing time that the real problem came up — the problem of how far it was excusable to discuss the turpitude of parents with a child of twelve, of thirteen, of fourteen. Absolutely inexcusable and quite impossible it of course at first appeared; and indeed the question didn't press for a while after Pemberton had received his three hundred francs. They produced a sort of lull, a relief from the sharpest pressure. Pemberton frugally amended his wardrobe and even had a few francs in his pocket. He thought the Moreens looked at him as if he were almost too smart, as if they ought to take care not to spoil him. If Mr. Moreen hadn't been such a man of the world he would perhaps have said something to him about his neckties. But Mr. Moreen was always enough a man of the world to let things pass — he had certainly shown that. It was singular how Pemberton guessed that Morgan, though saying nothing about it, knew something had happened. But three hundred francs, especially when one owed money, couldn't last for ever; and when they were gone — the boy knew when they were gone — Morgan did say something. The party had returned to Nice at the beginning of the winter, but not to the charming villa. They went to an hotel, where they stayed three months, and then they went to another hotel, explaining that they had left the first because they had waited and waited and couldn't get the rooms they wanted. These apartments, the rooms they wanted, were generally very

splendid; but fortunately they never *could* get them —
fortunately, I mean, for Pemberton, who reflected always
that if they had got them there would have been still
less for educational expenses.   What Morgan said at
last was said suddenly, irrelevantly, when the moment
came, in the middle of a lesson, and consisted of the
apparently unfeeling words: "You ought to *filer*, you
know — you really ought."

Pemberton stared.   He had learnt enough French
slang from Morgan to know that to *filer* meant to go
away.   "Ah, my dear fellow, don't turn me off!"

Morgan pulled a Greek lexicon toward him (he used a
Greek-German), to look out a word, instead of asking it
of Pemberton.   "You can't go on like this, you know."

"Like what, my boy?"

"You know they don't pay you up," said Morgan,
blushing and turning his leaves.

"Don't pay me?"   Pemberton stared again and feigned
amazement.   "What on earth put that into your head?"

"It has been there a long time," the boy replied, con-
tinuing his search.

Pemberton was silent, then he went on: "I say, what
are you hunting for?   They pay me beautifully."

"I'm hunting for the Greek for transparent fiction,"
Morgan dropped.

"Find that rather for gross impertinence, and disabuse
your mind.   What do I want of money?"

"Oh, that's another question!"

Pemberton hesitated — he was drawn in different ways.
The severely correct thing would have been to tell the
boy that such a matter was none of his business and bid
him go on with his lines.   But they were really too
intimate for that; it was not the way he was in the habit
of treating him; there had been no reason it should be.

On the other hand Morgan had quite lighted on the truth — he really shouldn't be able to keep it up much longer; therefore why not let him know one's real motive for forsaking him? At the same time it wasn't decent to abuse to one's pupil the family of one's pupil; it was better to misrepresent than to do that. So in reply to Morgan's last exclamation he just declared, to dismiss the subject, that he had received several payments.

"I say — I say!" the boy ejaculated, laughing.

"That's all right," Pemberton insisted. "Give me your written rendering."

Morgan pushed a copybook across the table, and his companion began to read the page, but with something running in his head that made it no sense. Looking up after a minute or two he found the child's eyes fixed on him, and he saw something strange in them. Then Morgan said: "I'm not afraid of the reality."

"I haven't yet seen the thing that you *are* afraid of — I'll do you that justice!"

This came out with a jump (it was perfectly true), and evidently gave Morgan pleasure. "I've thought of it a long time," he presently resumed.

"Well, don't think of it any more."

The child appeared to comply, and they had a comfortable and even an amusing hour. They had a theory that they were very thorough, and yet they seemed always to be in the amusing part of lessons, the intervals between the tunnels, where there were waysides and views. Yet the morning was brought to a violent end by Morgan's suddenly leaning his arms on the table, burying his head in them and bursting into tears. Pemberton would have been startled at any rate; but he was doubly startled because, as it then occurred to him, it was the first time he had ever seen the boy cry. It was rather awful.

K

The next day, after much thought, he took a decision and, believing it to be just, immediately acted upon it. He cornered Mr. and Mrs. Moreen again and informed them that if, on the spot, they didn't pay him all they owed him, he would not only leave their house, but would tell Morgan exactly what had brought him to it.

"Oh, you *haven't* told him?" cried Mrs. Moreen, with a pacifying hand on her well-dressed bosom.

"Without warning you? For what do you take me?"

Mr. and Mrs. Moreen looked at each other, and Pemberton could see both that they were relieved and that there was a certain alarm in their relief. "My dear fellow," Mr. Moreen demanded, "what use *can* you have, leading the quiet life we all do, for such a lot of money?" — an inquiry to which Pemberton made no answer, occupied as he was in perceiving that what passed in the mind of his patrons was something like: "Oh, then, if we've felt that the child, dear little angel, has judged us and how he regards us, and we haven't been betrayed, he must have guessed — and, in short, it's *general!*" an idea that rather stirred up Mr. and Mrs. Moreen, as Pemberton had desired that it should. At the same time, if he had thought that his threat would do something towards bringing them round, he was disappointed to find they had taken for granted (how little they appreciated his delicacy!) that he had already given them away to his pupil. There was a mystic uneasiness in their parental breasts, and that was the way they had accounted for it. None the less his threat did touch them; for if they had escaped it was only to meet a new danger. Mr. Moreen appealed to Pemberton, as usual, as a man of the world; but his wife had recourse, for the first time since the arrival of their inmate, to a fine *hauteur*, reminding him that a devoted mother, with

her child, had arts that protected her against gross mis-
representation.

"I should misrepresent you grossly if I accused you
of common honesty!" the young man replied; but as he
closed the door behind him sharply, thinking he had not
done himself much good, while Mr. Moreen lighted
another cigarette, he heard Mrs. Moreen shout after
him, more touchingly:

"Oh, you do, you *do*, put the knife to one's throat!"

The next morning, very early, she came to his room.
He recognised her knock, but he had no hope that she
brought him money; as to which he was wrong, for she
had fifty francs in her hand. She squeezed forward in
her dressing-gown, and he received her in his own, between his bath-tub and his bed. He had been tolerably
schooled by this time to the "foreign ways" of his hosts.
Mrs. Moreen was zealous, and when she was zealous she
didn't care what she did; so she now sat down on his
bed, his clothes being on the chairs, and, in her preoccu-
pation, forgot, as she glanced round, to be ashamed of
giving him such a nasty room. What Mrs. Moreen was
zealous about on this occasion was to persuade him that
in the first place she was very good-natured to bring him
fifty francs, and, in the second, if he would only see it,
he was really too absurd to expect to be *paid*. Wasn't
he paid enough, without perpetual money — wasn't he
paid by the comfortable, luxurious home that he enjoyed
with them all, without a care, an anxiety, a solitary
want? Wasn't he sure of his position, and wasn't that
everything to a young man like him, quite unknown,
with singularly little to show, the ground of whose
exorbitant pretensions it was not easy to discover?
Wasn't he paid, above all, by the delightful relation he
had established with Morgan — quite ideal, as from

master to pupil — and by the simple privilege of knowing and living with so amazingly gifted a child, than
whom really — she meant literally what she said — there
was no better company in Europe? Mrs Moreen herself
took to appealing to him as a man of the world; she
said "Voyons, mon cher," and "My dear sir, look here
now;" and urged him to be reasonable, putting it before
him that it was really a chance for him. She spoke as
if, according as he *should* be reasonable, he would prove
himself worthy to be her son's tutor and of the extraordinary confidence they had placed in him.

After all, Pemberton reflected, it was only a difference
of theory, and the theory didn't matter much. They
had hitherto gone on that of remunerated, as now they
would go on that of gratuitous, service; but why should
they have so many words about it? Mrs. Moreen, however, continued to be convincing; sitting there with her
fifty francs she talked and repeated, as women repeat,
and bored and irritated him, while he leaned against the
wall with his hands in the pockets of his wrapper,
drawing it together round his legs and looking over the
head of his visitor at the grey negations of his window.
She wound up with saying: "You see I bring you a
definite proposal."

"A definite proposal?"

"To make our relations regular, as it were — to put
them on a comfortable footing."

"I see — it's a system," said Pemberton. "A kind of
blackmail."

Mrs. Moreen bounded up, which was what the young
man wanted.

"What do you mean by that?"

"You practice on one's fears — one's fears about the
child if one should go away."

"And, pray, what would happen to him in that event?" demanded Mrs. Moreen, with majesty.

"Why, he'd be alone with *you*."

"And pray, with whom *should* a child be but with those whom he loves most?"

"If you think that, why don't you dismiss me?"

"Do you pretend that he loves you more than he loves *us?*" cried Mrs. Moreen.

"I think he ought to. I make sacrifices for him. Though I've heard of those *you* make, I don't see them."

Mrs. Moreen stared a moment; then, with emotion, she grasped Pemberton's hand. "*Will* you make it — the sacrifice?"

Pemberton burst out laughing. "I'll see — I'll do what I can — I'll stay a little longer. Your calculation is just — I *do* hate intensely to give him up; I'm fond of him and he interests me deeply, in spite of the inconvenience I suffer. You know my situation perfectly; I haven't a penny in the world, and, occupied as I am with Morgan, I'm unable to earn money."

Mrs. Moreen tapped her undressed arm with her folded bank-note. "Can't you write articles? Can't you translate, as *I* do?"

"I don't know about translating; it's wretchedly paid."

"I am glad to earn what I can," said Mrs. Moreen virtuously, with her head high.

"You ought to tell me who you do it for." Pemberton paused a moment, and she said nothing; so he added: "I've tried to turn off some little sketches, but the magazines won't have them — they're declined with thanks."

"You see then you're not such a phœnix — to have such pretensions," smiled his interlocutress.

"I haven't time to do things properly," Pemberton went on. Then as it came over him that he was almost abjectly good-natured to give these explanations he added: "If I stay on longer it must be on one condition — that Morgan shall know distinctly on what footing I am."

Mrs. Moreen hesitated. "Surely you don't want to show off to a child?"

"To show *you* off, do you mean?"

Again Mrs. Moreen hesitated, but this time it was to produce a still finer flower. "And *you* talk of blackmail!"

"You can easily prevent it," said Pemberton.

"And *you* talk of practicing on fears," Mrs. Moreen continued.

"Yes, there's no doubt I'm a great scoundrel."

His visitor looked at him a moment — it was evident that she was sorely bothered. Then she thrust out her money àt him. "Mr. Moreen desired me to give you this on account."

"I'm much obliged to Mr. Moreen; but we have no account."

"You won't take it?"

"That leaves me more free," said Pemberton.

"To poison my darling's mind?" groaned Mrs. Moreen.

"Oh, your darling's mind!" laughed the young man.

She fixed him a moment, and he thought she was going to break out tormentedly, pleadingly: "For God's sake, tell me what *is* in it!" But she checked this impulse — another was stronger. She pocketed the money — the crudity of the alternative was comical — and swept out of the room with the desperate concession: "You may tell him any horror you like!"

VI.

A couple of days after this, during which Pemberton had delayed to profit by Mrs. Moreen's permission to tell her son any horror, the two had been for a quarter of an hour walking together in silence when the boy became sociable again with the remark: "I'll tell you how I know it; I know it through Zénobie."

"Zénobie? Who in the world is *she?*"

"A nurse I used to have — ever so many years ago. A charming woman. I liked her awfully, and she liked me."

"There's no accounting for tastes. What is it you know through her?"

"Why, what their idea is. She went away because they didn't pay her. She did like me awfully, and she stayed two years. She told me all about it — that at last she could never get her wages. As soon as they saw how much she liked me they stopped giving her anything. They thought she'd stay for nothing, out of devotion. And she did stay ever so long — as long as she could. She was only a poor girl. She used to send money to her mother. At last she couldn't afford it any longer, and she went away in a fearful rage one night — I mean of course in a rage against *them*. She cried over me tremendously, she hugged me nearly to death. She told me all about it," Morgan repeated. "She told me it was their idea. So I guessed, ever so long ago, that they have had the same idea with you."

"Zénobie was very shrewd," said Pemberton. "And she made you so."

"Oh, that wasn't Zénobie; that was nature. And experience!" Morgan laughed.

"Well, Zénobie was a part of your experience."

"Certainly I was a part of hers, poor dear!" the boy exclaimed. "And I'm a part of yours."

"A very important part. But I don't see how you know that I've been treated like Zénobie."

"Do you take me for an idiot?" Morgan asked. "Haven't I been conscious of what we've been through together?"

"What we've been through?"

"Our privations — our dark days."

"Oh, our days have been bright enough."

Morgan went on in silence for a moment. Then he said: "My dear fellow, you're a hero!"

"Well, you're another!" Pemberton retorted.

"No, I'm not; but I'm not a baby. I won't stand it any longer. You must get some occupation that pays. I'm ashamed, I'm ashamed!" quavered the boy in a little passionate voice that was very touching to Pemberton.

"We ought to go off and live somewhere together," said the young man.

"I'll go like a shot if you'll take me."

"I'd get some work that would keep us both afloat," Pemberton continued.

"So would I. Why shouldn't *I* work? I ain't such a *crétin!*"

"The difficulty is that your parents wouldn't hear of it," said Pemberton. "They would never part with you; they worship the ground you tread on. Don't you see the proof of it? They don't dislike me; they wish me no harm; they're very amiable people; but they're perfectly ready to treat me badly for your sake."

The silence in which Morgan received this graceful sophistry struck Pemberton somehow as expressive. After a moment Morgan repeated: "You *are* a hero!"

Then he added: "They leave me with you altogether. You've all the responsibility. They put me off on you from morning till night. Why, then, should they object to my taking up with you completely? I'd help you."

"They're not particularly keen about my being helped, and they delight in thinking of you as *theirs*. They're tremendously proud of you."

"I'm not proud of them. But you know *that*," Morgan returned.

"Except for the little matter we speak of they're charming people," said Pemberton, not taking up the imputation of lucidity, but wondering greatly at the child's own, and especially at this fresh reminder of something he had been conscious of from the first — the strangest thing in the boy's large little composition, a temper, a sensibility, even a sort of ideal, which made him privately resent the general quality of his kinsfolk. Morgan had in secret a small loftiness which begot an element of reflection, a domestic scorn not imperceptible to his companion (though they never had any talk about it), and absolutely anomalous in a juvenile nature, especially when one noted that it had not made this nature "old-fashioned," as the word is of children — quaint or wizened or offensive. It was as if he had been a little gentleman and had paid the penalty by discovering that he was the only such person in the family. This comparison didn't make him vain; but it could make him melancholy and a trifle austere. When Pemberton guessed at these young dimnesses he saw him serious and gallant, and was partly drawn on and partly checked, as if with a scruple, by the charm of attempting to sound the little cool shallows which were quickly growing deeper. When he tried to figure to himself the morning twilight of childhood, so as to deal with it safely, he perceived that it was never fixed, never arrested, that ignorance, at the instant one touched it, was already flushing faintly into knowledge, that there was nothing that at a given moment you could say a clever child didn't know. It seemed to him that *he* both knew too much to imagine Morgan's simplicity and too little to disembroil his tangle.

The boy paid no heed to his last remark; he only went on: "I should have spoken to them about their idea, as I call it, long ago, if I hadn't been sure what they would say."

"And what would they say?"

"Just what they said about what poor Zénobie told me — that it was a horrid, dreadful story, that they had paid her every penny they owed her."

"Well, perhaps they had," said Pemberton.

"Perhaps they've paid you!"

"Let us pretend they have, and *n'en parlons plus.*"

"They accused her of lying and cheating," Morgan insisted perversely. "That's why I don't want to speak to them."

"Lest they should accuse me, too?"

To this Morgan made no answer, and his companion, looking down at him (the boy turned his eyes, which had filled, away), saw that he couldn't have trusted himself to utter.

"You're right. Don't squeeze them," Pemberton pursued. "Except for that, they *are* charming people."

"Except for *their* lying and *their* cheating?"

"I say — I say!" cried Pemberton, imitating a little tone of the lad's which was itself an imitation.

"We must be frank, at the last; we *must* come to an understanding," said Morgan, with the importance of the small boy who lets himself think he is arranging great affairs — almost playing at shipwreck or at Indians. "I know all about everything," he added.

"I daresay your father has his reasons," Pemberton observed, too vaguely, as he was aware.

"For lying and cheating?"

"For saving and managing and turning his means to the best account. He has plenty to do with his money. You're an expensive family."

"Yes, I'm very expensive," Morgan rejoined, in a manner which made his preceptor burst out laughing.

"He's saving for *you*," said Pemberton. "They think of you in everything they do."

"He might save a little —— " The boy paused. Pemberton waited to hear what. Then Morgan brought out oddly: "A little reputation."

"Oh, there's plenty of that. That's all right!"

"Enough of it for the people they know, no doubt. The people they know are awful."

"Do you mean the princes? We mustn't abuse the princes."

"Why not? They haven't married Paula — they haven't married Amy. They only clean out Ulick."

"You *do* know everything!" Pemberton exclaimed.

"No, I don't, after all. I don't know what they live on, or how they live, or *why* they live! What have they got and how did they get it? Are they rich, are they poor, or have they a *modeste aisance?* Why are they always chiveying about — living one year like ambassadors and the next like paupers? Who are they, any way, and what are they? I've thought of all that — I've thought of a lot of things. They're so beastly worldly. That's what I hate most — oh, I've *seen* it! All they care about is to make an appearance and to pass for something or other. What do they want to pass for? What *do* they, Mr. Pemberton?"

"You pause for a reply," said Pemberton, treating the inquiry as a joke, yet wondering too, and greatly struck with the boy's intense, if imperfect, vision. "I haven't the least idea."

"And what good does it do? Haven't I seen the way people treat them — the "nice" people, the ones they want to know? They'll take anything from them — they'll lie down and be trampled on. The nice ones hate that — they just sicken them. You're the only really nice person we know."

"Are you sure? They don't lie down for me!"

"Well, you shan't lie down for them. You've got to go — that's what you've got to do," said Morgan.

"And what will become of you?"

"Oh, I'm growing up. I shall get off before long. I'll see you later."

"You had better let me finish you," Pemberton urged, lending himself to the child's extraordinarily competent attitude.

Morgan stopped in their walk, looking up at him. He had to look up much less than a couple of years before — he had grown, in his loose leanness, so long and high. "Finish me?" he echoed.

"There are such a lot of jolly things we can do together yet. I want to turn you out — I want you to do me credit."

Morgan continued to look at him. "To give you credit — do you mean?"

"My dear fellow, you're too clever to live."

"That's just what I'm afraid you think. No, no; it isn't fair — I can't endure it. We'll part next week. The sooner it's over the sooner to sleep."

"If I hear of anything — any other chance, I promise to go," said Pemberton.

Morgan consented to consider this. "But you'll be honest," he demanded; "you won't pretend you haven't heard?"

"I'm much more likely to pretend I have."

"But what can you hear of, this way, stuck in a hole with us? You ought to be on the spot, to go to England — you ought to go to America."

"One would think you were *my* tutor!" said Pemberton.

Morgan walked on, and after a moment he began again: "Well, now that you know that I know and that we look at the facts and keep nothing back — it's much more comfortable, isn't it?"

"My dear boy, it's so amusing, so interesting, that it surely will be quite impossible for me to forego such hours as these."

This made Morgan stop once more. "You *do* keep something back. Oh, you're not straight — *I* am!"

"Why am I not straight?"

"Oh, you've got your idea!"

"My idea?"

"Why, that I probably sha'n't live, and that you can stick it out till I'm removed."

"You *are* too clever to live!" Pemberton repeated.

"I call it a mean idea," Morgan pursued. "But I shall punish you by the way I hang on."

"Look out or I'll poison you!" Pemberton laughed.

"I'm stronger and better every year. Haven't you noticed that there hasn't been a doctor near me since you came?"

"*I'm* your doctor," said the young man, taking his arm and drawing him on again.

Morgan proceeded, and after a few steps he gave a sigh of mingled weariness and relief. "Ah, now that we look at the facts, it's all right!"

VII.

THEY looked at the facts a good deal after this; and
one of the first consequences of their doing so was that
Pemberton stuck it out, as it were, for the purpose.
Morgan made the facts so vivid and so droll, and at the
same time so bald and so ugly, that there was fascination in talking them over with him, just as there would
have been heartlessness in leaving him alone with them.
Now that they had such a number of perceptions in common it was useless for the pair to pretend that they
didn't judge such people; but the very judgment, and the
exchange of perceptions, created another tie.   Morgan
had never been so interesting as now that he himself
was made plainer by the sidelight of these confidences.
What came out in it most was the soreness of his characteristic pride.   He had plenty of that, Pemberton felt
— so much that it was perhaps well it should have had
to take some early bruises.   He would have liked his
people to be gallant, and he had waked up too soon to
the sense that they were perpetually swallowing humble-
pie.   His mother would consume any amount, and his
father would consume even more than his mother.   He
had a theory that Ulick had wriggled out of an "affair"
at Nice : there had once been a flurry at home, a regular
panic, after which they all went to bed and took medi-
cine, not to be accounted for on any other supposition.
Morgan had a romantic imagination, fed by poetry and
history, and he would have liked those who "bore his
name" (as he used to say to Pemberton with the humour
that made his sensitiveness manly), to have a proper
spirit.   But their one idea was to get in with people
who didn't want them and to take snubs as if they were
honourable scars.   Why people didn't want them more

he didn't know — that was people's own affair; after all
they were not superficially repulsive — they were a
hundred times cleverer than most of the dreary grandees,
the "poor swells" they rushed about Europe to catch up
with.   "After all, they *are* amusing — they are!" Morgan used to say, with the wisdom of the ages.   To
which Pemberton always replied: "Amusing — the great
Moreen troupe?   Why, they're altogether delightful;
and if it were not for the hitch that you and I (feeble
performers!) make in the *ensemble*, they would carry
everything before them."

What the boy couldn't get over was that this particular blight seemed, in a tradition of self-respect, so unde-
served and so arbitrary.   No doubt people had a right
to take the line they liked; but why should *his* people
have liked the line of pushing and toadying and lying
and cheating?   What had their forefathers — all decent
folk, so far as he knew — done to them, or what had *he*
done to them?   Who had poisoned their blood with the
fifth-rate social ideal, the fixed idea of making smart
acquaintances and getting into the *monde chic*, especially
when it was foredoomed to failure and exposure?   They
showed so what they were after; that was what made
the people they wanted not want *them*.   And never a
movement of dignity, never a throb of shame at looking
each other in the face, never any independence or resentment or disgust.   If his father or his brother would only
knock some one down once or twice a year!   Clever as
they were they never guessed how they appeared.   They
were good-natured, yes — as good-natured as Jews at the
doors of clothing-shops!   But was that the model one
wanted one's family to follow?   Morgan had dim memories of an old grandfather, the maternal, in New York,
whom he had been taken across the ocean to see, at the

age of five: a gentleman with a high neckcloth and a good deal of pronunciation, who wore a dress-coat in the morning, which made one wonder what he wore in the evening, and had, or was supposed to have, "property" and something to do with the Bible Society. It couldn't have been but that *he* was a good type. Pemberton himself remembered Mrs. Clancy, a widowed sister of Mr. Moreen's, who was as irritating as a moral tale and had paid a fortnight's visit to the family at Nice shortly after he came to live with them. She was "pure and refined," as Amy said, over the banjo, and had the air of not knowing what they meant and of keeping something back. Pemberton judged that what she kept back was an approval of many of their ways; therefore it was to be supposed that she too was of a good type, and that Mr. and Mrs. Moreen and Ulick and Paula and Amy might easily have been better if they would.

But that they wouldn't was more and more perceptible from day to day. They continued to "chivey," as Morgan called it, and in due time became aware of a variety of reasons for proceeding to Venice. They mentioned a great many of them — they were always strikingly frank, and had the brightest friendly chatter, at the late foreign breakfast in especial, before the ladies had made up their faces, when they leaned their arms on the table, had something to follow the *demi-tasse*, and, in the heat of familiar discussion as to what they "really ought" to do, fell inevitably into the languages in which they could *tutoyer*. Even Pemberton liked them, then; he could endure even Ulick when he heard him give his little flat voice for the "sweet sea-city." That was what made him have a sneaking kindness for them — that they were so out of the workaday world and kept him so out of it. The summer had waned when, with cries of ecstasy, they

all passed out on the balcony that overhung the Grand
Canal; the sunsets were splendid — the Dorringtons had
arrived. The Dorringtons were the only reason they
had not talked of at breakfast; but the reasons that they
didn't talk of at breakfast always came out in the end.
The Dorringtons, on the other hand, came out very little; or else, when they did, they stayed — as was natural
— for hours, during which periods Mrs. Moreen and the
girls sometimes called at their hotel (to see if they had
returned) as many as three times running. The gondola
was for the ladies; for in Venice too there were "days,"
which Mrs. Moreen knew in their order an hour after
she arrived. She immediately took one herself, to which
the Dorringtons never came, though on a certain occasion
when Pemberton and his pupil were together at St. Mark's
— where, taking the best walks they had ever had and
haunting a hundred churches, they spent a great deal of
time — they saw the old lord turn up with Mr. Moreen
and Ulick, who showed him the dim basilica as if it belonged to them. Pemberton noted how much less,
among its curiosities, Lord Dorrington carried himself
as a man of the world; wondering too whether, for such
services, his companions took a fee from him. The
autumn, at any rate, waned, the Dorringtons departed,
and Lord Verschoyle, the eldest son, had proposed
neither for Amy nor for Paula.

One sad November day, while the wind roared round
the old palace and the rain lashed the lagoon, Pemberton,
for exercise and even somewhat for warmth (the Moreens
were horribly frugal about fires — it was a cause of suffering to their inmate), walked up and down the big bare
sala with his pupil. The scagliola floor was cold, the
high battered casements shook in the storm, and the
stately decay of the place was unrelieved by a particle

L

of furniture. Pemberton's spirits were low, and it came
over him that the fortune of the Moreens was now even
lower. A blast of desolation, a prophecy of disaster
and disgrace, seemed to draw through the comfortless
hall. Mr. Moreen and Ulick were in the Piazza, looking
out for something, strolling drearily, in mackintoshes,
under the arcades; but still, in spite of mackintoshes,
unmistakable men of the world. Paula and Amy were
in bed — it might have been thought they were staying
there to keep warm. Pemberton looked askance at the
boy at his side, to see to what extent he was conscious
of these portents. But Morgan, luckily for him, was
now mainly conscious of growing taller and stronger
and indeed of being in his fifteenth year. This fact was
intensely interesting to him — it was the basis of a private theory (which, however, he had imparted to his
tutor) that in a little while he should stand on his own
feet. He considered that the situation would change —
that, in short, he should be "finished," grown up, produ-
cible in the world of affairs and ready to prove himself
of sterling ability. Sharply as he was capable, at times,
of questioning his circumstances, there were happy hours
when he was as superficial as a child; the proof of
which was his fundamental assumption that he should
presently go to Oxford, to Pemberton's college, and,
aided and abetted by Pemberton, do the most wonderful
things. It vexed Pemberton to see how little, in such a
project, he took account of ways and means: on other
matters he was so sceptical about them. Pemberton tried
to imagine the Moreens at Oxford, and fortunately failed;
yet unless they were to remove there as a family there
would be no *modus vivendi* for Morgan. How could he
live without an allowance, and where was the allowance
to come from? He (Pemberton) might live on Morgan;

but how could Morgan live on him? What was to become of him anyhow? Somehow, the fact that he was a big boy now, with better prospects of health, made the question of his future more difficult. So long as he was frail the consideration that he inspired seemed enough of an answer to it. But at the bottom of Pemberton's heart was the recognition of his probably being strong enough to live and not strong enough to thrive. He himself, at any rate, was in a period of natural, boyish rosiness about all this, so that the beating of the tempest seemed to him only the voice of life and the challenge of fate. He had on his shabby little overcoat, with the collar up, but he was enjoying his walk.

It was interrupted at last by the appearance of his mother at the end of the *sala*. She beckoned to Morgan to come to her, and while Pemberton saw him, complacent, pass down the long vista, over the damp false marble, he wondered what was in the air. Mrs. Moreen said a word to the boy and made him go into the room she had quitted. Then, having closed the door after him, she directed her steps swiftly to Pemberton. There *was* something in the air, but his wildest flight of fancy wouldn't have suggested what it proved to be. She signified that she had made a pretext to get Morgan out of the way, and then she inquired — without hesitation — if the young man could lend her sixty francs. While, before bursting into a laugh, he stared at her with surprise, she declared that she was awfully pressed for the money; she was desperate for it — it would save her life.

"Dear lady, *c'est trop fort!*" Pemberton laughed. "Where in the world do you suppose I should get sixty francs, *du train dont vous allez?*"

"I thought you worked — wrote things; don't they pay you?"

"Not a penny."

"Are you such a fool as to work for nothing?"

"You ought surely to know that."

Mrs. Moreen stared an instant, then she coloured a little.   Pemberton saw she had quite forgotten the terms — if "terms" they could be called — that he had ended by accepting from herself; they had burdened her memory as little as her conscience. "Oh, yes, I see what you mean — you have been very nice about that; but why go back to it so often?"   She had been perfectly urbane with him ever since the rough scene of explanation in his room, the morning he made her accept *his* "terms" — the necessity of his making his case known to Morgan. She had felt no resentment, after seeing that there was no danger of Morgan's taking the matter up with her.   Indeed, attributing this immunity to the good taste of his influence with the boy, she had once said to Pemberton: "My dear fellow; it's an immense comfort you're a gentleman."   She repeated this, in substance, now. "Of course you're a gentleman — that's a bother the less!"   Pemberton reminded her that he had not "gone back" to anything; and she also repeated her prayer that, somewhere and somehow, he would find her sixty francs.   He took the liberty of declaring that if he could find them it wouldn't be to lend them to *her* — as to which he consciously did himself injustice, knowing that if he had them he would certainly place them in her hand.   He accused himself, at bottom and with some truth, of a fantastic, demoralised sympathy with her.   If misery made strange bedfellows it also made strange sentiments.   It was moreover a part of the demoralisation and of the general bad effect of living with such people that one had to make rough retorts, quite out of the tradition of good manners.

"Morgan, Morgan, to what pass have I come for you?" he privately exclaimed, while Mrs. Moreen floated voluminously down the *sala* again, to liberate the boy; groaning, as she went, that everything was too odious.

Before the boy was liberated there came a thump at the door communicating with the staircase, followed by the apparition of a dripping youth who poked in his head. Pemberton recognised him as the bearer of a telegram and recognised the telegram as addressed to himself. Morgan came back as, after glancing at the signature (that of a friend in London), he was reading the words: "Found jolly job for you — engagement to coach opulent youth on own terms. Come immediately." The answer, happily, was paid, and the messenger waited. Morgan, who had drawn near, waited too, and looked hard at Pemberton; and Pemberton, after a moment, having met his look, handed him the telegram. It was really by wise looks (they knew each other so well), that, while the telegraph-boy, in his waterproof cape, made a great puddle on the floor, the thing was settled between them. Pemberton wrote the answer with a pencil against the frescoed wall, and the messenger departed. When he had gone Pemberton said to Morgan:

"I'll make a tremendous charge; I'll earn a lot of money in a short time, and we'll live on it."

"Well, I hope the opulent youth will be stupid — he probably will — " Morgan parenthesised, "and keep you a long time."

"Of course, the longer he keeps me the more we shall have for our old age."

"But suppose *they* don't pay you!" Morgan awfully suggested.

"Oh, there are not two such — !" Pemberton paused,

he was on the point of using an invidious term. Instead of this he said "two such chances."

Morgan flushed — the tears came to his eyes. "*Dites toujours,* two such rascally crews!" Then, in a different tone, he added: "Happy opulent youth!"

"Not if he's stupid!"

"Oh, they're happier then. But you can't have everything, can you?" the boy smiled.

Pemberton held him, his hands on his shoulders. "What will become of *you*, what will you do?" He thought of Mrs. Moreen, desperate for sixty francs.

"I shall turn into a man." And then, as if he recognised all the bearings of Pemberton's allusion: "I shall get on with them better when you're not here."

"Ah, don't say that — it sounds as if I set you against them!"

"You do — the sight of you. It's all right; you know what I mean. I shall be beautiful. I'll take their affairs in hand; I'll marry my sisters."

"You'll marry yourself!" joked Pemberton; as high, rather tense pleasantry would evidently be the right, or the safest, tone for their separation.

It was, however, not purely in this strain that Morgan suddenly asked: "But I say — how will you get to your jolly job? You'll have to telegraph to the opulent youth for money to come on."

Pemberton bethought himself. "They won't like that, will they?"

"Oh, look out for them!"

Then Pemberton brought out his remedy. "I'll go to the American Consul; I'll borrow some money of him — just for the few days, on the strength of the telegram."

Morgan was hilarious. "Show him the telegram — then stay and keep the money!"

Pemberton entered into the joke enough to reply that, for Morgan, he was really capable of that; but the boy, growing more serious, and to prove that he hadn't meant what he said, not only hurried him off to the Consulate (since he was to start that evening, as he had wired to his friend), but insisted on going with him. They splashed through the tortuous perforations and over the humpbacked bridges, and they passed through the Piazza, where they saw Mr. Moreen and Ulick go into a jeweller's shop. The Consul proved accommodating (Pemberton said it wasn't the letter, but Morgan's grand air), and on their way back they went into St. Mark's for a hushed ten minutes. Later they took up and kept up the fun of it to the very end; and it seemed to Pemberton a part of that fun that Mrs. Moreen, who was very angry when he had announced to her his intention, should charge him, grotesquely and vulgarly, and in reference to the loan she had vainly endeavoured to effect, with bolting lest they should "get something out" of him. On the other hand he had to do Mr. Moreen and Ulick the justice to recognise that when, on coming in, *they* heard the cruel news, they took it like perfect men of the world.

VIII.

WHEN Pemberton got at work with the opulent youth, who was to be taken in hand for Balliol, he found himself unable to say whether he was really an idiot or it was only, on his own part, the long association with an intensely living little mind that made him seem so. From Morgan he heard half-a-dozen times: the boy wrote charming young letters, a patchwork of tongues, with indulgent postscripts in the family Volapuk and, in little squares and rounds and crannies of the text, the drollest illustrations — letters that he was divided between the impulse to show his present disciple, as a kind of wasted incentive, and the sense of something in them that was profanable by publicity. The opulent youth went up, in due course, and failed to pass; but it seemed to add to the presumption that brilliancy was not expected of him all at once that his parents, condoning the lapse, which they good-naturedly treated as little as possible as if were Pemberton's, should have sounded the rally again, begged the young coach to keep his pupil in hand another year.

The young coach was now in a position to lend Mrs. Moreen sixty francs, and he sent her a post-office order for the amount. In return for this favour he received a frantic, scribbled line from her: "Implore you to come back instantly — Morgan dreadfully ill." They were on the rebound, once more in Paris — often as Pemberton had seen them depressed he had never seen them crushed — and communication was therefore rapid. He wrote to the boy to ascertain the state of his health, but he received no answer to his letter. Accordingly he took an abrupt leave of the opulent youth and, crossing the Channel, alighted at the small hotel, in the quarter of the Champs Elysées, of which Mrs. Moreen had given him the address. A deep if dumb dissatisfaction with this lady and her companions bore him company: they couldn't be vulgarly honest, but they could live at hotels, in velvety *entresols*, amid a smell of burnt pastilles, in the most expensive city in Europe. When he had left them, in Venice, it was with an irrepressible suspicion that something was going to happen; but the only thing that had happened was that they succeeded in getting away. "How is he? where is he?" he asked of Mrs. Moreen; but before she could speak, these questions were answered by the pressure round his neck of a pair of arms, in shrunken sleeves, which were perfectly capable of an effusive young foreign squeeze.

"Dreadfully ill — I don't see it!" the young man cried. And then, to Morgan: "Why on earth didn't you relieve me?   Why didn't you answer my letter?"

Mrs. Moreen declared that when she wrote he was very bad, and Pemberton learned at the same time from the boy that he had answered every letter he had received. This led to the demonstration that Pemberton's note had been intercepted.   Mrs. Moreen was prepared to see the fact exposed, as Pemberton perceived, the moment he faced her, that she was prepared for a good many other things.   She was prepared above all to maintain that she had acted from a sense of duty, that she was enchanted she had got him over, whatever they might say; and that it was useless of him to pretend that he didn't *know*, in all his bones, that his place at such a time was with Morgan.   He had taken the boy away from them, and now he had no right to abandon him.   He had created for himself the gravest responsibilities; he must at least abide by what he had done.

"Taken him away from you?" Pemberton exclaimed indignantly.

"Do it — do it, for pity's sake; that's just what I want. I can't stand *this* — and such scenes.   They're treacherous!"   These words broke from Morgan, who had intermitted his embrace, in a key which made Pemberton turn quickly to him, to see that he had suddenly seated himself, was breathing with evident difficulty and was very pale.

"*Now* do you say he's not ill — my precious pet?" shouted his mother, dropping on her knees before him with clasped hands, but touching him no more than if he had been a gilded idol. "It will pass — it's only for an instant; but don't say such dreadful things!"

"I'm all right — all right," Morgan panted to Pemberton, whom he sat looking up at with a strange smile, his hands resting on either side on the sofa.

"Now do you pretend I've been treacherous — that I've deceived?" Mrs. Moreen flashed at Pemberton as she got up.

"It isn't *he* says it, it's I!" the boy returned, apparently easier, but sinking back against the wall; while Pemberton, who had sat down beside him, taking his hand, bent over him.

"Darling child, one does what one can; there are so many things to consider," urged Mrs. Moreen. "It's his *place* — his only place. You see *you* think it is now."

"Take me away — take me away," Morgan went on, smiling to Pemberton from his white face.

"Where shall I take you, and how — oh, *how*, my boy?" the young man stammered, thinking of the rude way in which his friends in London held that, for his convenience, and without a pledge of instantaneous return, he had thrown them over; of the just resentment with which they would already have called in a successor, and of the little help as regarded finding fresh employment that resided for him in the flatness of his having failed to pass his pupil.

"Oh, we'll settle that. You used to talk about it," said Morgan. "If we can only go, all the rest's a detail."

"Talk about it as much as you like, but don't think you can attempt it. Mr. Moreen would never consent — it would be so precarious," Pemberton's hostess explained to him. Then to Morgan she explained: "It would destroy our peace, it would break our hearts. Now that

he's back it will be all the same again. You'll have
your life, your work and your freedom, and we'll all be
happy as we used to be. You'll bloom and grow perfectly well, and we won't have any more silly experi-
ments, will we? They're too absurd. It's Mr. Pemberton's place — every one in his place. You in yours,
your papa in his, me in mine — *n'est-ce pas, chéri?* We'll
all forget how foolish we've been, and we'll have lovely
times."

She continued to talk and to surge vaguely about the
little draped, stuffy *salon*, while Pemberton sat with
the boy, whose colour gradually came back; and she
mixed up her reasons, dropping that there were going to
be changes, that the other children might scatter (who
knew? — Paula had her ideas), and that then it might be
fancied how much the poor old parent-birds would want
the little nestling. Morgan looked at Pemberton, who
wouldn't let him move; and Pemberton knew exactly
how he felt at hearing himself called a little nestling.
He admitted that he had had one or two bad days, but
he protested afresh against the iniquity of his mother's
having made them the ground of an appeal to poor Pemberton. Poor Pemberton could laugh now, apart from
the comicality of Mrs. Moreen's producing so much
philosophy for her defence (she seeemd to shake it out
of her agitated petticoats, which knocked over the light
gilt chairs), so little did the sick boy strike him as qualified to repudiate any advantage.

He himself was in for it, at any rate. He should
have Morgan on his hands again indefinitely; though
indeed he saw the lad had a private theory to produce
which would be intended to smooth this down. He was
obliged to him for it in advance; but the suggested
amendment didn't keep his heart from sinking a little,

any more than it prevented him from accepting the prospect on the spot, with some confidence moreover that he would do so even better if he could have a little supper. Mrs. Moreen threw out more hints about the changes that were to be looked for, but she was such a mixture of smiles and shudders (she confessed she was very nervous), that he couldn't tell whether she were in high feather or only in hysterics. If the family were really at last going to pieces why shouldn't she recognise the necessity of pitching Morgan into some sort of lifeboat? This presumption was fostered by the fact that they were established in luxurious quarters in the capital of pleasure; that was exactly where they naturally *would* be established in view of going to pieces. Moreover didn't she mention that Mr. Moreen and the others were enjoying themselves at the opera with Mr. Granger, and wasn't *that* also precisely where one would look for them on the eve of a smash? Pemberton gathered that Mr. Granger was a rich, vacant American — a big bill with a flourishy heading and no items; so that one of Paula's "ideas" was probably that this time she had really done it, which was indeed an unprecedented blow to the general cohesion. And if the cohesion was to terminate what was to become of poor Pemberton? He felt quite enough bound up with them to figure, to his alarm, as a floating spar in case of a wreck.

It was Morgan who eventually asked if no supper had been ordered for him; sitting with him below, later, at the dim, delayed meal, in the presence of a great deal of corded green plush, a plate of ornamental biscuit and a languor marked on the part of the waiter. Mrs. Moreen had explained that they had been obliged to secure a room for the visitor out of the house; and Morgan's consolation (he offered it while Pemberton reflected on the nastiness of lukewarm sauces), proved to be, largely, that this circumstance would facilitate their escape. He talked of their escape (recurring to it often afterwards), as if they were making up a "boy's book" together. But he likewise expressed his sense that there was something in the air, that the Moreens couldn't keep it up much longer. In point of fact, as Pemberton was to see, they kept it up for five or six months. All the while, however, Morgan's contention was designed to cheer him. Mr. Moreen and Ulick, whom he had met the day after his return, accepted that return like perfect men of the world. If Paula and Amy treated it even with less formality an allowance was to be made for them, inasmuch as Mr. Granger had not come to the opera after all. He had only placed his box at their service, with a bouquet for each of the party; there was even one apiece, embittering the thought of his profusion, for Mr. Moreen and Ulick. "They're all like that," was Morgan's comment; "at the very last, just when we think we've got them fast, we're chucked!"

Morgan's comments, in these days, were more and more free; they even included a large recognition of the extraordinary tenderness with which he had been treated while Pemberton was away. Oh, yes, they couldn't do enough to be nice to him, to show him they had him on their mind and make up for his loss. That was just what made the whole thing so sad, and him so glad, after all, of Pemberton's return — he had to keep thinking of their affection less, had less sense of obligation. Pemberton laughed out at this last reason, and Morgan blushed and said: "You know what I mean." Pemberton knew perfectly what he meant; but there were a good many things it didn't make any clearer. This episode of his second sojourn in Paris stretched itself out wearily, with their resumed readings and wanderings and maunderings, their potterings on the quays, their hauntings of the museums, their occasional lingerings in the Palais Royal, when the first sharp weather came on and there was a comfort in warm emanations, before Chevet's wonderful succulent window. Morgan wanted to hear a great deal about the opulent youth — he took an immense interest in him. Some of the details of his opulence — Pemberton could spare him none of them — evidently intensified the boy's appreciation of all his friend had given up to come back to him; but in addition to the greater reciprocity established by such a renunciation he had always his little brooding theory, in which there was a frivolous gaiety too, that their long probation was drawing to a close. Morgan's conviction that the Moreens couldn't go on much longer kept pace with the unexpended impetus with which, from month to month, they did go on. Three weeks after Pemberton had rejoined them they went on to another hotel, a dingier one than the first; but Morgan rejoiced that his tutor had at least still not sacrificed the advantage of a room outside. He clung to the romantic utility of this when the day, or rather the night, should arrive for their escape.

For the first time, in this complicated connection, Pemberton felt sore and exasperated. It was, as he had said to Mrs. Moreen in Venice, *trop fort* — everything was *trop fort*. He could neither really throw off his blighting burden nor find in it the benefit of a pacified conscience or of a rewarded affection. He had spent all the money that he had earned in England, and he felt that his youth was going and that he was getting nothing back for it. It was all very well for Morgan to seem to consider that he would make up to him for all inconveniences by settling himself upon him permanently — there was an irritating flaw in such a view. He saw what the boy had in his mind; the conception that as his friend had had the generosity to come back to him he must show his gratitude by giving him his life. But the poor friend didn't desire the gift — what could he do with Morgan's life? Of course at the same time that Pemberton was irritated he remembered the reason, which was very honourable to Morgan and which consisted simply of the fact that he was perpetually making one forget that he was after all only a child. If one dealt with him on a different basis one's misadventures were one's own fault. So Pemberton waited in a queer confusion of yearning and alarm for the catastrophe which was held to hang over the house of Moreen, of which he certainly at moments felt the symptoms brush his cheek and as to which he wondered much in what form it would come.

Perhaps it would take the form of dispersal — a frightened *sauve qui peut*, a scuttling into selfish corners. Certainly they were less elastic than of yore; they were evidently looking for something they didn't find. The Dorringtons hadn't reappeared, the princes had scattered; wasn't that the beginning of the end? Mrs. Moreen had lost her reckoning of the famous "days;" her social calendar was blurred — it had turned its face to the wall. Pemberton suspected that the great, the cruel, discomfiture had been the extraordinary behaviour of Mr. Granger, who seemed not to know what he wanted, or, what was much worse, what *they* wanted. He kept sending flowers, as if to bestrew the path of his retreat, which was never the path of return. Flowers were all very well, but — Pemberton could complete the proposition. It was now positively conspicuous that in the long run the Moreens were a failure; so that the young

man was almost grateful the run had not been short.
Mr. Moreen, indeed, was still occasionally able to get
away on business, and, what was more surprising, he
was also able to get back. Ulick had no club, but you
could not have discovered it from his appearance, which
was as much as ever that of a person looking at life
from the window of such an institution; therefore Pemberton was doubly astonished at an answer he once heard
him make to his mother, in the desperate tone of a man
familiar with the worst privations. Her question Pemberton had not quite caught; it appeared to be an appeal
for a suggestion as to whom they could get to take Amy.
"Let the devil take her!" Ulick snapped; so that Pemberton could see that not only they had lost their amia-
bility, but had ceased to believe in themselves. He
could also see that if Mrs. Moreen was trying to get
people to take her children she might be regarded as
closing the hatches for the storm. But Morgan would
be the last she would part with.

One winter afternoon — it was a Sunday — he and the
boy walked far together in the Bois de Boulogne. The
evening was so splendid, the cold lemon-coloured sunset
so clear, the stream of carriages and pedestrians so
amusing and the fascination of Paris so great, that they
stayed out later than usual and became aware that they
would have to hurry home to arrive in time for dinner.
They hurried accordingly, arm-in-arm, good-humoured
and hungry, agreeing that there was nothing like Paris
after all and that after all, too, that had come and gone
they were not yet sated with innocent pleasures. When
they reached the hotel they found that, though scanda-
lously late, they were in time for all the dinner they
were likely to sit down to. Confusion reigned in the
apartments of the Moreens (very shabby ones this

time, but the best in the house), and before the interrupted service of the table (with objects displaced almost
as if there had been a scuffle, and a great wine stain
from an overturned bottle), Pemberton could not blink
the fact that there had been a scene of proprietary mu-
tiny.   The storm had come — they were all seeking
refuge.   The hatches were down — Paula and Amy were
invisible (they had never tried the most casual art upon
Pemberton, but he felt that they had enough of an eye
to him not to wish to meet him as young ladies whose
frocks had been confiscated), and Ulick appeared to have
jumped overboard.   In a word, the host and his staff
had ceased to "go on" at the pace of their guests, and
the air of embarrassed detention, thanks to a pile of gaping trunks in the passage, was strangely commingled
with the air of indignant withdrawal.

When Morgan took in all this — and he took it in very
quickly — he blushed to the roots of his hair.   He had
walked, from his infancy, among difficulties and dangers,
but he had never seen a public exposure.   Pemberton
noticed, in a second glance at him, that the tears had
rushed into his eyes and that they were tears of bitter
shame.   He wondered for an instant, for the boy's sake,
whether he might successfully pretend not to understand.
Not successfully, he felt, as Mr. and Mrs. Moreen,
dinnerless by their extinguished hearth, rose before him
in their little dishonoured *salon*, considering apparently
with much intensity what lively capital would be next
on their list.   They were not prostrate, but they were
very pale, and Mrs. Moreen had evidently been crying.
Pemberton quickly learned however that her grief was
not for the loss of her dinner, much as she usually enjoyed it, but on account of a necessity much more tragic.
She lost no time in laying this necessity bare, in telling

M

him how the change had come, the bolt had fallen, and how they would all have to turn themselves about. Therefore cruel as it was to them to part with their darling she must look to him to carry a little further the influence he had so fortunately acquired with the boy — to induce his young charge to follow him into some modest retreat. They depended upon him, in a word, to take their delightful child temporarily under his protection — it would leave Mr. Moreen and herself so much more free to give the proper attention (too little, alas! had been given), to the readjustment of their affairs.

"We trust you — we feel that we can," said Mrs. Moreen, slowly rubbing her plump white hands and looking, with compunction, hard at Morgan, whose chin, not to take liberties, her husband stroked with a tentative paternal forefinger.

"Oh, yes; we feel that we can. We trust Mr. Pemberton fully, Morgan," Mr. Moreen conceded.

Pemberton wondered again if he might pretend not to understand; but the idea was painfully complicated by the immediate perception that Morgan had understood.

"Do you mean that he may take me to live with him — for ever and ever?" cried the boy. "Away, away, anywhere he likes?"

"For ever and ever? *Comme vous-y-allez!*" Mr. Moreen laughed indulgently. "For as long as Mr. Pemberton may be so good."

"We've struggled, we've suffered," his wife went on; "but you've made him so your own that we've already been through the worst of the sacrifice."

Morgan had turned away from his father — he stood looking at Pemberton with a light in his face. His blush had died out, but something had come that was brighter and more vivid. He had a moment of boyish joy,

scarcely mitigated by the reflection that, with this unexpected consecration of his hope — too sudden and too
violent; the thing was a good deal less like a boy's book
— the "escape" was left on their hands. The boyish
joy was there for an instant, and Pemberton was almost
frightened at the revelation of gratitude and affection
that shone through his humiliation. When Morgan
stammered "My dear fellow, what do you say to *that?*"
he felt that he should say something enthusiastic. But
he was still more frightened at something else that immediately followed and that made the lad sit down
quickly on the nearest chair. He had turned very white
and had raised his hand to his left side. They were all
three looking at him, but Mrs. Moreen was the first to
bound forward. "Ah, his darling little heart!" she
broke out; and this time, on her knees before him and
without respect for the idol, she caught him ardently in
her arms. "You walked him too far, you hurried him
too fast!" she tossed over her shoulder at Pemberton. The boy made no protest, and the next instant his
mother, still holding him, sprang up with her face con-
vulsed and with the terrified cry "Help, help! he's
going, he's gone!" Pemberton saw, with equal horror,
by Morgan's own stricken face, that he *was* gone. He
pulled him half out of his mother's hands, and for a
moment, while they held him together, they looked, in
their dismay, into each other's eyes. "He couldn't stand
it, with his infirmity," said Pemberton — "the shock,
the whole scene, the violent emotion."

"But I thought he *wanted* to go to you!" wailed Mrs.
Moreen.

"I *told* you he didn't, my dear," argued Mr. Moreen.
He was trembling all over, and he was, in his way, as
deeply affected as his wife. But, after the first, he took
his bereavement like a man of the world.

BROOKSMITH.[1]

WE are scattered now, the friends of the late Mr. Oliver Offord; but whenever we chance to meet I think we are conscious of a certain esoteric respect for each other. "Yes, you too have been in Arcadia," we seem not too grumpily to allow. When I pass the house in Mansfield Street I remember that Arcadia was there. I don't know who has it now, and I don't want to know; its enough to be so sure that if I should ring the bell there would be no such luck for me as that Brooksmith should open the door. Mr. Offord, the most agreeable, the most lovable of bachelors, was a retired diplomatist, living on his pension, confined by his infirmities to his fireside and delighted to be found there any afternoon in the year by such visitors as Brooksmith allowed to come up. Brooksmith was his butler and his most intimate friend, to whom we all stood, or I should say sat, in the same relation in which the subject of the sovereign finds himself to the prime minister. By having been for years, in foreign lands, the most delightful Englishman any one had ever known, Mr. Offord had, in my opinion, rendered signal service to his country. But I suppose he had been too much liked — liked even by those who didn't like *it* — so that as people of that sort never get

[1] *Copyright, 1891, by Macmillan & Co.*

titles or dotations for the horrid things they have *not* done, his principal reward was simply that we went to see him.

Oh, we went perpetually, and it was not our fault if he was not overwelmed with this particular honour. Any visitor who came once came again — to come merely once was a slight which nobody, I am sure, had ever put upon him. His circle, therefore, was essentially composed of *habitués*, who were *habitués* for each other as well as for him, as those of a happy *salon* should be. I remember vividly every element of the place, down to the intensely Londonish look of the grey opposite houses, in the gap of the white curtains of the high windows, and the exact spot where, on a particular afternoon, I put down my tea-cup for Brooksmith, lingering an instant, to gather it up as if he were plucking a flower. Mr. Offord's drawing-room was indeed Brooksmith's garden, his pruned and tended human *parterre*, and if we all flourished there and grew well in our places it was largely owing to his supervision.

Many persons have heard much, though most have doubtless seen little, of the famous institution of the *salon*, and many are born to the depression of knowing that this finest flower of social life refuses to bloom where the English tongue is spoken. The explanation is usually that our women have not the skill to cultivate it — the art to direct, between suggestive shores, the course of the stream of talk. My affectionate, my pious memory of Mr. Offord contradicts this induction only, I fear, more insidiously to confirm it. The very sallow and slightly smoked drawing-room in which he spent so large a portion of the last years of his life certainly deserved the distinguished name; but on the other hand it could not be said at all to owe its stamp to the soft pressure of the

indispensable sex. The dear man had indeed been
capable of one of those sacrifices to which women are
deemed peculiarly apt; he had recognised (under the
influence, in some degree, it is true, of physical infirmity), that if you wished people to find you at home you
must manage not to be out. He had in short accepted
the fact which many dabblers in the social art are slow
to learn, that you must really, as they say, take a line
and that the only way to be at home is to stay at home.
Finally his own fireside had become a summary of his
habits. Why should he ever have left it? — since this
would have been leaving what was notoriously pleasantest
in London, the compact charmed cluster (thinning away
indeed into casual couples), round the fine old last century chimney-piece which, with the exception of the
remarkable collection of miniatures, was the best thing
the place contained. Mr. Offord was not rich; he had
nothing but his pension and the use for life of the somewhat superannuated house.

When I am reminded by some uncomfortable contrast
of to-day how perfectly we were all handled there I ask
myself once more what had been the secret of such
perfection. One had taken it for granted at the time,
for anything that is supremely good produces more acceptance than surprise. I felt we were all happy, but I
didn't consider how our happiness was managed. And
yet there were questions to be asked, questions that
strike me as singularly obvious now that there is nobody
to answer them. Mr. Offord had solved the insoluble;
he had, without feminine help (save in the sense that
ladies were dying to come to him and he saved the lives
of several), established a *salon ;* but I might have guessed
that there was a method in his madness — a law in his
success. He had not hit it off by a mere fluke. There

was an art in it all, and how was the art so hidden?
Who, indeed, if it came to that, was the occult artist?
Launching this inquiry the other day, I had already got
hold of the tail of my reply. I was helped by the very
wonder of some of the conditions that came back to me
— those that used to seem as natural as sunshine in a fine
climate.

How was it, for instance, that we never were a crowd,
never either too many or too few, always the right people *with* the right people (there must really have been no
wrong people at all), always coming and going, never
sticking fast nor overstaying, yet never popping in or
out with an indecorous familiarity? How was it that
we all sat where we wanted and moved when we wanted
and met whom we wanted and escaped whom we wanted;
joining, according to the accident of inclination, the
general circle or falling in with a single talker on a convenient sofa? Why were all the sofas so convenient,
the accidents so happy, the talkers so ready, the listeners
so willing, the subjects presented to you in a rotation
as quickly fore-ordained as the courses at dinner? A
dearth of topics would have been as unheard of as a lapse
in the service. These speculations couldn't fail to lead
me to the fundamental truth that Brooksmith had been
somehow at the bottom of the mystery. If he had not
established the *salon* at least he had carried it on.
Brooksmith, in short, was the artist!

We felt this, covertly, at the time, without formulat-
ing it, and were conscious, as an ordered and prosperous
community, of his evenhanded justice, untainted with
flunkeyism. He had none of that vulgarity — his touch
was infinitely fine. The delicacy of it was clear to me
on the first occasion my eyes rested, as they were so
often to rest again, on the domestic revealed, in the

turbid light of the street, by the opening of the house-
door.   I saw on the spot that though he had plenty of
school he carried it without arrogance — he had remained
articulate and human.   *L'Ecole Anglaise,* Mr. Offord
used to call him, laughing, when, later, it happened
more than once that we had some conversation about
him.   But I remember accusing Mr. Offord of not doing
him quite ideal justice.   That he was not one of the
giants of the school, however, my old friend, who really
understood him perfectly and was devoted to him, as I
shall show, quite admitted; which doubtless poor Brooksmith had himself felt, to his cost, when his value in the
market was originally determined.   The utility of his
class in general is estimated by the foot and the inch,
and poor Brooksmith had only about five feet two to put
into circulation.   He acknowledged the inadequacy of
this provision, and I am sure was penetrated with the
everlasting fitness of the relation between service and
stature.   If *he* had been Mr. Offord he certainly would
have found Brooksmith wanting, and indeed the laxity
of his employer on this score was one of many things
which he had had to condone and to which he had at last
indulgently adapted himself.

I remember the old man's saying to me: "Oh, my servants, if they can live with me a fortnight they can live
with me for ever.   But it's the first fortnight that tries
'em."   It was in the first fortnight, for instance, that
Brooksmith had had to learn that he was exposed to
being addressed as "my dear fellow" and "my poor
child."   Strange and deep must such a probation have
been to him, and he doubtless emerged from it tempered
and purified.   This was written to a certain extent in
his appearance; in his spare, brisk little person, in his
cloistered white face and extraordinarily polished hair,

which told of responsibility, looked as if it were kept up to the same high standard as the plate; in his small, clear, anxious eyes, even in the permitted, though not exactly encouraged tuft on his chin. "He thinks me rather mad, but I've broken him in, and now he likes the place, he likes the company," said the old man. I embraced this fully after I had become aware that Brooksmith's main characteristic was a deep and shy refinement, though I remember I was rather puzzled when, on another occasion, Mr. Offord remarked: "What he likes is the talk — mingling in the conversation." I was conscious that I had never seen Brooksmith permit himself this freedom, but I guessed in a moment that what Mr. Offord alluded to was a participation more intense than any speech could have represented — that of being perpetually present on a hundred legitimate pretexts, errands, necessities, and breathing the very atmosphere of criticism, the famous criticism of life. "Quite an education, sir, isn't it, sir?" he said to me one day at the foot of the stairs, when he was letting me out; and I have always remembered the words and the tone as the first sign of the quickening drama of poor Brooksmith's fate. It was indeed an education, but to what was this sensitive young man of thirty-five, of the servile class, being educated?

Practically and inevitably, for the time, to companionship, to the perpetual, the even exaggerated reference and appeal of a person brought to dependence by his time of life and his infirmities and always addicted moreover (this was the exaggeration) to the art of giving you pleasure by letting you do things for him. There were certain things Mr. Offord was capable of pretending he liked you to do, even when he didn't, if he thought *you* liked them. If it happened that you didn't either (this was rare, but it might be), of course there were cross-purposes; but Brooksmith was there to prevent their going very far. This was precisely the way he acted as moderator: he averted misunderstandings or cleared them up. He had been capable, strange as it may appear, of acquiring for this purpose an insight into the French tongue, which was often used at Mr. Offord's; for besides being habitual to most of the foreigners, and they were many, who haunted the place or arrived with letters (letters often requiring a little worried consideration, of which Brooksmith always had cognisance), it had really become the primary language of the master of the house. I don't know if all the *malentendus* were in French, but almost all the explanations were, and this didn't a bit prevent Brooksmith from following them. I know Mr. Offord used to read passages to him from Montaigne and Saint-Simon, for he read perpetually when he was alone — when they were alone, I should say — and Brooksmith was always about. Perhaps you'll say no wonder Mr. Offord's butler regarded him as "rather mad." However, if I'm not sure what he thought about Montaigne I'm convinced he admired Saint-Simon. A certain feeling for letters must have rubbed off on him from the mere handling of his master's books, which he was always carrying to and fro and putting back in their places.

I often noticed that if an anecdote or a quotation, much more a lively discussion, was going forward, he would, if busy with the fire or the curtains, the lamp or the tea, find a pretext for remaining in the room till the point should be reached. If his purpose was to catch it you were not discreet to call him off, and I shall never forget a look, a hard, stony stare (I caught it in its passage), which, one day when there were a good many people in the room, he fastened upon the footman who was helping him in the service and who, in an undertone, had asked him some irrelevant question. It was the only manifestation of harshness that I ever observed on Brooksmith's part, and at first I wondered what was the matter. Then I became conscious that Mr. Offord was relating a very curious anecdote, never before perhaps made so public, and imparted to the narrator by an eye-witness of the fact, bearing upon Lord Byron's life in Italy. Nothing would induce me to reproduce it here; but Brooksmith had been in danger of losing it. If I ever should venture to reproduce it I shall feel how much I lose in not having my fellow-auditor to refer to.

The first day Mr. Offord's door was closed was therefore a dark date in contemporary history. It was raining hard and my umbrella was wet, but Brooksmith took it from me exactly as if this were a preliminary for going upstairs. I observed however that instead of putting it away he held it poised and trickling over the rug, and then I became aware that he was looking at me with deep, acknowledging eyes — his air of universal responsibility. I immediately understood; there was scarcely need of the question and the answer that passed between us. When I did understand that the old man had given up, for the first time, though only for the occasion, I exclaimed dolefully: "What a difference it will make — and to how many people!"

"I shall be one of them, sir!" said Brooksmith; and that was the beginning of the end.

Mr. Offord came down again, but the spell was broken, and the great sign of it was that the conversation was, for the first time, not directed. It wandered and stumbled, a little frightened, like a lost child — it had let go the nurse's hand.   "The worst of it is that now we shall talk about my health — *c'est la fin de tout*," Mr. Offord said, when he reappeared; and then I recognised what a sign of change that would be — for he had never tolerated anything so provincial. The talk became ours, in a word — not his; and as ours, even when *he* talked, it could only be inferior.   In this form it was a distress to Brooksmith, whose attention now wandered from it altogether: he had so much closer a vision of his master's intimate conditions than our superficialities represented. There were better hours, and he was more in and out of the room, but I could see that he was conscious that the great institution was falling to pieces. He seemed to wish to take counsel with me about it, to feel responsible for its going on in some form or other.   When for the second period — the first had lasted several days — he had to tell me that our old friend didn't receive, I half expected to hear him say after a moment: "Do you think I ought to, sir, in his place?" — as he might have asked me, with the return of autumn, if I thought he had better light the drawing-room fire.

He had a resigned philosophic sense of what his guests — our guests, as I came to regard them in our colloquies — would expect.   His feeling was that he wouldn't absolutely have approved of himself as a substitute for the host; but he was so saturated with the religion of habit that he would have made, for our friends, the necessary sacrifice to the divinity.   He would take them on a little further, till they could look about them.   I think I saw him also mentally confronted with the opportunity to deal — for once in his life — with some of his own dumb preferences, his limitations of sympathy, *weeding* a little, in prospect, and returning to a purer tradition. It was not unknown to me that he considered that toward the end of Mr. Offord's career a certain laxity of selection had crept in.

At last it came to be the case that we all found the closed door more often than the open one; but even when it was closed Brooksmith managed a crack for me to squeeze through; so that practically I never turned away without having paid a visit. The difference simply came to be that the visit was to Brooksmith. It took place in the hall, at the familiar foot of the stairs, and we didn't sit down — at least Brooksmith didn't; moreover it was devoted wholly to one topic and always had the air of being already over — beginning, as it were, at the end. But it was always interesting — it always gave me something to think about. It is true that the subject of my meditation was ever the same — ever "It's all very well, but what *will* become of Brooksmith?" Even my private answer to this question left me still unsatisfied. No doubt Mr. Offord would provide for him, but *what* would he provide? that was the great point. He couldn't provide society; and society had become a necessity of Brooksmith's nature. I must add that he never showed a symptom of what I may call sordid solicitude — anxiety on his own account. He was rather livid and intensely grave, as befitted a man before whose eyes the "shade of that which once was great" was passing away. He had the solemnity of a person winding up, under depressing circumstances, a long established and celebrated business; he was a kind of social executor or liquidator. But his manner seemed to testify exclusively to the uncertainty of *our* future. I couldn't in those days have afforded it — I lived in two rooms in Jermyn Street and didn't "keep a man;" but even if my income had permitted I shouldn't have ventured to say to Brooksmith (emulating Mr. Offord), "My dear

fellow, I'll take you on." The whole tone of our intercourse was so much more an implication that it was *I*
who should now want a lift. Indeed there was a tacit
assurance in Brooksmith's whole attitude that he would
have me on his mind.

One of the most assiduous members of our circle had
been Lady Kenyon, and I remember his telling me one
day that her ladyship had, in spite of her own infirmities, lately much aggravated, been in person to inquire.
In answer to this I remarked that she would feel it more
than any one. Brooksmith was silent a moment; at the
end of which he said, in a certain tone (there is no re-
producing some of his tones), "I'll go and see her." I
went to see her myself, and I learned that he had waited
upon her; but when I said to her, in the form of a joke
but with a core of earnest, that when all was over some
of us ought to combine, to club together to set Brooksmith up on his own account, she replied a trifle disap-
pointingly: "Do you mean in a public-house?" I looked
at her in a way that I think Brooksmith himself would
have approved, and then I answered: "Yes, the Offord
Arms." What I had meant, of course, was that, for the
love of art itself, we ought to look to it that such a
peculiar faculty and so much acquired experience should
not be wasted. I really think that if we had caused a
few black-edged cards to be struck off and circulated —
"Mr. Brooksmith will continue to receive on the old
premises from four to seven; business carried on as usual
during the alterations" — the majority of us would have
rallied.

Several times he took me upstairs — always by his own
proposal — and our dear old friend, in bed, in a curious
flowered and brocaded *casaque* which made him, especially as his head was tied up in a handkerchief to

match, look, to my imagination, like the dying Voltaire, held for ten minutes a sadly shrunken little *salon*. I felt indeed each time, as if I were attending the last *coucher* of some social sovereign. He was royally whimsical about his sufferings and not at all concerned — quite as if the Constitution provided for the case — about his successor. He glided over *our* sufferings charmingly, and none of his jokes — it was a gallant abstention, some of them would have been so easy — were at our expense. Now and again, I confess, there was one at Brooksmith's, but so pathetically sociable as to make the excellent man look at me in a way that seemed to say: "Do exchange a glance with me, or I sha'n't be able to stand it." What he was not able to stand was not what Mr. Offord said about him, but what he wasn't able to say in return. His notion of conversation, for himself, was giving you the convenience of speaking to him; and when he went to "see" Lady Kenyon, for instance, it was to carry her the tribute of his receptive silence. Where would the speech of his betters have been if proper service had been a manifestation of sound? In that case the fundamental difference would have had to be shown by *their* dumbness, and many of them, poor things, were dumb enough without that provision. Brooksmith took an unfailing interest in the preservation of the fundamental difference; it was the thing he had most on his conscience.

What had become of it, however, when Mr. Offord passed away like any inferior person — was relegated to eternal stillness like a butler upstairs? His aspect for several days after the expected event may be imagined, and the multiplication by funereal observance of the things he didn't say. When everything was over — it was late the same day — I knocked at the door of the house of mourning as I so often had done before. I could never call on Mr. Offord again, but I had come, literally, to call on Brooksmith. I wanted to ask him if there was anything I could do for him, tainted with vagueness as this inquiry could only be. My wild dream of taking him into my own service had died away: my service was not worth his being taken into. My offer to him could only be to help him to find another place, and yet there was an indelicacy, as it were, in taking for granted that his thoughts would immediately be fixed on another. I had a hope that he would be able to give his life a different form — though certainly not the form, the frequent result of such bereavements, of his setting up a little shop. That would have been dreadful; for I should have wished to further any enterprise that he might embark in, yet how could I have brought myself to go and pay him shillings and take back coppers over a counter? My visit then was simply an intended compliment. He took it as such, gratefully and with all the tact in the world. He knew I really couldn't help him and that I knew he knew I couldn't; but we discussed the situation — with a good deal of elegant generality — at the foot of the stairs, in the hall already dismantled, where I had so often discussed other situations with him. The executors were in possession, as was still more apparent when he made me pass for a few minutes into the dining-room, where various objects were muffled up for removal.

Two definite facts, however, he had to communicate; one being that he was to leave the house for ever that night (servants, for some mysterious reason, seem always to depart by night), and the other — he mentioned it only at the last, with hesitation — that he had already been informed his late master had left him a legacy of eighty pounds. "I'm very glad," I said, and Brooksmith rejoined: "It was so like him to think of me." This was all that passed between us on the subject, and I know nothing of his judgment of Mr. Offord's memento. Eighty pounds are always eighty pounds, and no one has ever left *me* an equal sum; but, all the same, for Brooksmith, I was disappointed. I don't know what I had expected — in short I was disappointed. Eighty pounds might stock a little shop — a *very* little shop; but, I repeat, I couldn't bear to think of that. I asked my friend if he had been able to save a little, and he replied: "No, sir; I have had to do things." I didn't inquire what things he had had to do; they were his own affair, and I took his word for them as assentingly as if he had had the greatness of an ancient house to keep up; especially as there was something in his manner that seemed to convey a prospect of further sacrifice.

"I shall have to turn round a bit, sir — I shall have to look about me," he said; and then he added, indulgently, magnanimously: "If you should happen to hear of anything for me —— "

I couldn't let him finish; this was, in its essence, too much in the really grand manner. It would be a help to my getting him off my mind to be able to pretend I *could* find the right place, and that help he wished to give me, for it was doubtless painful to him to see me in so false a position. I interposed with a few words to the effect that I was well aware that wherever he should go, whatever he should do, he would miss our old friend terribly — miss him even more than I should, having been with him so much more. This led him to make the speech that I have always remembered as the very text of the whole episode.

"Oh, sir, it's sad for *you*, very sad, indeed, and for a
N

great many gentlemen and ladies; that it is, sir. But for me, sir, it is, if I may say so, still graver even than that: it's just the loss of something that was everything. For me, sir," he went on, with rising tears, "he was just *all*, if you know what I mean, sir. You have others, sir, I daresay — not that I would have you understand me to speak of them as in any way tantamount. But you have the pleasures of society, sir; if it's only in talking about him, sir, as I daresay you do freely — for all his blessed memory has to fear from it — with gentlemen and ladies who have had the same honour. That's not for me, sir, and I have to keep my associations to myself. Mr. Offord was *my* society, and now I have no more. You go back to conversation, sir, after all, and I go back to my place," Brooksmith stammered, without exaggerated irony or dramatic bitterness, but with a flat, unstudied veracity and his hand on the knob of the street-door. He turned it to let me out and then he added: "I just go downstairs, sir, again, and I stay there."

"My poor child," I replied, in my emotion, quite as Mr. Offord used to speak, "my dear fellow, leave it to me; we'll look after you, we'll all do something for you."

"Ah, if you could give me some one *like* him! But there ain't two in the world," said Brooksmith as we parted.

He had given me his address — the place where he would be to be heard of. For a long time I had no occasion to make use of the information; for he proved indeed, on trial, a very difficult case. In a word the people who knew him and had known Mr. Offord, didn't want to take him, and yet I couldn't bear to try to thrust him among people who didn't know him. I spoke to many of our old friends about him, and I found them all governed by the odd mixture of feelings of which I myself was conscious, and disposed, further, to entertain a suspicion that he was "spoiled," with which I then would have nothing to do. In plain terms a certain embarrassment, a sensible awkwardness, when they thought of it, attached to the idea of using him as a menial: they had met him so often in society. Many of them would have asked him, and did ask him, or rather did ask me to ask him, to come and see them; but a mere visiting-list was not what I wanted for him. He was too short for people who were very particular; nevertheless I heard of an opening in a diplomatic household which led me to write him a note, though I was looking much less for something grand than for something human. Five days later I heard from him. The secretary's wife had decided, after keeping him waiting till then, that she couldn't take a servant out of a house in which there had not been a lady. The note had a P.S. : "It's a good job there wasn't, sir, such a lady as some."

A week later he came to see me and told me he was "suited" — committed to some highly respectable people (they were something very large in the City), who lived on the Bayswater side of the Park. "I daresay it will be rather poor, sir," he admitted; "but I've seen the fireworks, haven't I, sir? — it can't be fireworks *every* night. After Mansfield Street there ain't much choice." There was a certain amount, however, it seemed; for the following year, going one day to call on a country cousin, a lady of a certain age who was spending a fortnight in town with some friends of her own, a family unknown to me and resident in Chester Square, the door of the house was opened, to my surprise and gratification, by Brooksmith in person. When I came out I had some conversation with him, from which I gathered that he had found the large City people too dull for endurance, and I guessed, though he didn't say it, that he had found them vulgar as well. I don't know what judgment he would have passed on his actual patrons if my relative had not been their friend; but under the circumstances he abstained from comment.

None was necessary, however, for before the lady in question brought her visit to a close they honoured me with an invitation to dinner, which I accepted. There was a largeish party on the occasion, but I confess I thought of Brooksmith rather more than of the seated company. They required no depth of attention — they were all referable to usual, irredeemable, inevitable types. It was the world of cheerful commonplace and conscious gentility and prosperous density, a full-fed, material, insular world, a world of hideous florid plate and ponderous order and thin conversation. There was not a word said about Byron. Nothing would have induced me to look at Brooksmith in the course of the repast, and I felt sure that not even my overturning the wine would have induced him to meet my eye. We were in intellectual sympathy — we felt, as regards each other, a kind of social responsibility. In short we had been in Arcadia together, and we had both come to *this!* No wonder we were ashamed to be confronted. When he helped on my overcoat, as I was going away, we parted, for the first time since the earliest days in Mansfield Street, in silence. I thought he looked lean and wasted, and I guessed that his new place was not more "human" than his previous one. There was plenty of beef and beer, but there was no reciprocity. The question for him to have asked before accepting the position would have been not "How many footmen are kept?" but "How much imagination?"

The next time I went to the house — I confess it was not very soon — I encountered his successor, a personage who evidently enjoyed the good fortune of never having quitted his natural level. Could any be higher? he seemed to ask — over the heads of three footmen and even of some visitors. He made me feel as if Brooksmith were dead; but I didn't dare to inquire — I couldn't have borne his "I haven't the least idea, sir." I despatched a note to the address Brooksmith had given me after Mr. Offord's death, but I received no answer. Six months later, however, I was favoured with a visit from an elderly, dreary, dingy person, who introduced herself to me as Mr. Brooksmith's aunt and from whom I learned that he was out of place and out of health and had allowed her to come and say to me that if I could spare half-an-hour to look in at him he would take it as a rare honour.

I went the next day — his messenger had given me a new address — and found my friend lodged in a short sordid street in Marylebone, one of those corners of London that wear the last expression of sickly meanness. The room into which I was shown was above the small establishment of a dyer and cleaner who had inflated kid gloves and discoloured shawls in his shop-front. There was a great deal of grimy infant life up and down the place, and there was a hot, moist smell within, as of the "boiling" of dirty linen. Brooksmith sat with a blanket over his legs at a clean little window, where, from behind stiff bluish-white curtains, he could look across at a huckster's and a tinsmith's and a small greasy public-house. He had passed through an illness and was convalescent, and his mother, as well as his aunt, was in attendance on him. I liked the mother, who was bland and intensely humble, but I didn't much fancy the aunt, whom I connected, perhaps unjustly, with the opposite public-house (she seemed somehow to be greasy with the same grease), and whose furtive eye followed every movement of my hand, as if to see if it were not going into my pocket. It didn't take this direction — I couldn't, unsolicited, put myself at that sort of ease with Brooksmith. Several times the door of the room opened, and mysterious old women peeped in and shuffled back again. I don't know who they were; poor Brooksmith seemed encompassed with vague, prying, beery females.

He was vague himself, and evidently weak, and much embarrassed, and not an allusion was made between us to Mansfield Street. The vision of the *salon* of which he had been an ornament hovered before me, however, by contrast, sufficiently. He assured me that he was really getting better, and his mother remarked that he would come round if he could only get his spirits up. The aunt echoed this opinion, and I became more sure that in her own case she knew where to go for such a purpose. I'm afraid I was rather weak with my old friend, for I neglected the opportunity, so exceptionally good, to rebuke the levity which had led him to throw up honourable positions — fine, stiff, steady berths, with morning prayers, as I knew, attached to one of them — in Bayswater and Belgravia. Very likely his reasons had been profane and sentimental; he didn't want morning prayers, he wanted to be somebody's dear fellow; but I couldn't be the person to rebuke him. He shuffled these episodes out of sight — I saw that he had no wish to discuss them. I perceived further, strangely enough, that it would probably be a questionable pleasure for him to see me again: he doubted now even of my power to condone his aberrations. He didn't wish to have to explain; and his behaviour, in future, was likely to need explanation. When I bade him farewell he looked at me a moment with eyes that said everything: "How can I talk about those exquisite years in this place, before these people, with the old women poking their heads in? It was very good of you to come to see me — it wasn't my idea; *she* brought you. We've said everything; it's over; you'll lose all patience with me, and I'd rather you shouldn't see the rest." I sent him some money, in a letter, the next day, but I saw the rest only in the light of a barren sequel.

A whole year after my visit to him I became aware once, in dining out, that Brooksmith was one of the several servants who hovered behind our chairs. He had not opened the door of the house to me, and I had not recognised him in the cluster of retainers in the hall. This time I tried to catch his eye, but he never gave me a chance, and when he handed me a dish I could only be careful to thank him audibly. Indeed I partook of two *entrées* of which I had my doubts, subsequently converted into certainties, in order not to snub him. He looked well enough in health, but much older, and wore, in an exceptionally marked degree, the glazed and expressionless mask of the British domestic *de race*. I saw with dismay that if I had not known him I should have taken him, on the showing of his countenance, for an extravagant illustration of irresponsive servile gloom. I said to myself that he had become a reactionary, gone over to the Philistines, thrown himself into religion, the religion of his "place," like a foreign lady *sur le retour*. I divined moreover that he was only engaged for the evening — he had become a mere waiter, had joined the band of the white-waistcoated who "go out." There was something pathetic in this fact, and it was a terrible vulgarisation of Brooksmith. It was the mercenary prose of butlerhood; he had given up the struggle for the poetry. If reciprocity was what he had missed, where was the reciprocity now? Only in the bottoms of the wine-glasses and the five shillings (or whatever they get), clapped into his hand by the permanent man. However, I supposed he had taken up a precarious branch of his profession because after all it sent him less downstairs. His relations with London society were more superficial, but they were of course more various. As I went away, on this occasion, I looked out for him eagerly among the four or five attendants whose perpendicular persons, fluting the walls of London passages, are supposed to lubricate the process of departure; but he was not on duty. I asked one of the others if he were not in the house, and received the prompt answer: "Just left, sir. Anything I can do for you, sir?" I wanted to say "Please give him my kind regards;" but I abstained; I didn't want to compromise him, and I never came across him again.

Often and often, in dining out, I looked for him, sometimes accepting invitations on purpose to multiply the chances of my meeting him. But always in vain; so that as I met many other members of the casual class over and over again, I at last adopted the theory that he always procured a list of expected guests beforehand and kept away from the banquets which he thus learned I was to grace. At last I gave up hope, and one day, at the end of three years, I received another visit from his aunt. She was drearier and dingier, almost squalid, and she was in great tribulation and want. Her sister, Mrs. Brooksmith, had been dead a year, and three months later her nephew had disappeared. He had always looked after her a bit — since her troubles; I never knew what her troubles had been — and now she hadn't so much as a petticoat to pawn. She had also a niece, to whom she had been everything, before her troubles, but the niece had treated her most shameful. These were details; the great and romantic fact was Brooksmith's final evasion of his fate. He had gone out to wait one evening, as usual, in a white waistcoat she had done up for him with her own hands, being due at a large party up Kensington way. But he had never come home again, and had never arrived at the large party, or at any party that any one could make out. No trace of him had come to light — no gleam of the white waistcoat had pierced the obscurity of his doom. This news was a sharp shock to me, for I had my ideas about his real destination. His aged relative had promptly, as she said, guessed the worst. Somehow and somewhere he had got out of the way altogether, and now I trust that, with characteristic deliberation, he is changing the plates of the immortal gods. As my depressing visitant also said, he never *had* got his spirits up. I was fortunately able to dismiss her with her own somewhat improved. But the dim ghost of poor Brooksmith is one of those that I see. He had indeed been spoiled.

THE SOLUTION.[1]

"OH yes, you may write it down — every one's dead."
I profited by my old friend's permission and made a note
of the story, which, at the time he told it to me, seemed
curious and interesting. Will it strike you in the same
light? Perhaps not, but I will run the risk and copy it
out for you as I reported it, with just a little amplifica-
tion from memory. Though every one *is* dead, perhaps
you had better not let it go further. My old friend is
dead himself, and how can I say how I miss him? He
had many merits, and not the least of them was that he
was always at home. The infirmities of the last years
of his life confined him to London and to his own house,
and of an afternoon, between five and six o'clock, I
often knocked at his door. He is before me now, as
he leans back in his chair, with his eyes wandering round
the top of his room as if a thousand ghostly pictures
were suspended there. Following his profession in
many countries, he had seen much of life and knew
much of men. This thing dropped from him piece by
piece (one wet, windy spring afternoon, when we happened to be uninterrupted), like a painless belated confession. I have only given it continuity.

202

I.

It was in Rome, a hundred years ago, or as nearly so as it must have been to be an episode of my extreme youth. I was just twenty-three, and attached to our diplomatic agency there; the other secretaries were all my seniors. Is it because I was twenty-three, or because the time and the place were really better, that this period glows in my memory with all sorts of poetic, romantic lights? It seems to me to have consisted of five winters of sunshine without a cloud; of long excursions on the Campagna and in the Alban and Sabine hills; of joyous artists' feasts, spread upon the warm stones of ruined temples and tombs; of splendid Catholic processions and ceremonies; of friendly, familiar evenings, prolonged very late, in the great painted and tapestried saloons of historic palaces. It was the slumberous, pictorial Rome of the Popes, before the Italians had arrived or the local colour departed, and though I have been back there in recent years it is always the early impression that is evoked for me by the name. The yellow steps, where models and beggars lounged in the sun, had a golden tone, and the models and beggars themselves a magnificent brown one, which it looked easy to paint showily. The excavations, in those days, were comparatively few, but the "subjects" — I was an incorrigible sketcher — were many. The carnival lasted a month, the flowers (and even the flower-girls) lasted for ever, and the old statues in the villas and the galleries became one's personal friends.

Of course we had other friends than these, and that is what I am coming to. I have lived in places where the society was perhaps better, but I have lived in none where I liked it better, in spite of the fact that it was considerably pervaded by Mrs. Goldie. Mrs. Goldie was an English lady, a widow with three daughters, and her name, accompanied not rarely, I fear, with an irreverent objurgation, was inevitably on our lips. She had a house on the Pincian Hill, from winter to winter; she came early in the season and stayed late, and she formed, with her daughters — Rosina, Veronica and Augusta — an uncompromising feature of every entertainment. As the principal object in any view of Rome is the dome of St. Peter's, so the most prominent figure in the social prospect was always the Honourable Blanche. She was a daughter of Lord Bolitho, and there were several elderly persons among us who remembered her in the years before her marriage, when her maiden designation was jocosely — I forget what the original joke had been — in people's mouths. They reintroduced it, and it became common in speaking of her. There must have been some public occasion when, as a spinster, she had done battle for her precedence and had roared out her luckless title. She was capable of that.

I was so fond of the place that it appeared to be natural every one else should love it, but I afterwards wondered what could have been the source of Mrs. Goldie's interest in it. She didn't know a Raphael from a Caravaggio, and even after many years could not have told you the names of the seven hills. She used to drive her daughters out to sketch, but she would never have done that if she had cared for the dear old ruins. However, it has always been a part of the magic of Rome that the most dissimilar breasts feel its influence; and though it is, or rather it was, the most exquisite place in the world, uncultivated minds have been known to enjoy it as much as students and poets. It has always touched alike the *raffiné* and the barbarian. Mrs. Goldie was a good deal

of a barbarian, and she had her reasons for liking the
Papal city.   Her mind was fixed on tea-parties and
the "right people to know."   She valued the easy soci-
iability, the picnics, the functions, the frequent opportunities for producing her girls.   These opportunities
indeed were largely of her own making; for she was
highly hospitable, in the simple Roman fashion, and
held incessant receptions and *conversazioni*.   Dinners
she never gave, and when she invited you to lunch, *al
fresco*, in the shadow of the aqueducts that stride across
the plain, she expected you to bring with you a cold
chicken and a bottle of wine.   No one, however, in those
patriarchal times, was thought the worse of in Rome for
being frugal.   That was another reason why Mrs. Goldie
had elected to live there; it was the capital in Europe
where the least money — and she had but little — would
go furthest in the way of grandeur.   It cost her nothing
to produce her girls, in proportion to the impressiveness
of the spectacle.

I don't know what we should have done without her
house, for the young men of the diplomatic body, as well
as many others, treated it almost as a club.   It was
largely for our benefit that the Misses Goldie were produced.   I sometimes wondered, even in those days, if
our sense of honour was quite as fine as it might have
been, to have permitted us to amuse ourselves at the
expense of this innocent and hospitable group.   The
jokes we made about them were almost as numerous as
the cups of tea that we received from the hands of the
young ladies; and though I have never thought that
youth is delicate (delicacy is an acquired virtue and
comes later), there was this excuse for our esoteric
mirth, that it was simply contagious.   We laughed at
the airs of greatness the Honourable Blanche gave her-

self and at the rough-and-ready usage to which she subjected the foreign tongues. It even seemed to us droll,
in a crowd, to see her push and press and make play
with her elbows, followed by the compact wedge of
Rosina, Veronica and Augusta, whom she had trained to
follow up her advantages. We noted the boldness with
which she asked for favours when they were not offered
and snatched them when they were refused, and we
almost admired the perpetual manœuvres and conspira-
cies, all of the most public and transparent kind, which
did not prevent her from honestly believing that she
was the most shrinking and disinterested of women.
She was always in a front seat, always flushed with the
achievement of getting there, and always looking round
and grimacing, signalling and telegraphing, pointing to
other places for other people, waving her parasol and
fan and marshalling and ordering the girls. She was
tall and angular, and held her head very high; it was
surmounted with wonderful turbans and plumages, and
indeed the four ladies were caparisoned altogether in a
manner of their own.

The oddest thing in the mother was that she bragged
about the fine people and the fine things she had left
behind her in England; she protested too much, and
if you had listened to her you would have had the gravest doubts of her origin and breeding. They were
genuinely "good," however, and her vulgarity was as
incontestable as her connections. It is a mistake to suppose it is only the people who would like to be what
they are not who are snobs. That class includes equally
many of those who are what the others would like to be.
I used to think, of old, that Thackeray overdid his ridi-
cule of certain types; but I always did him justice when
I remembered Mrs. Goldie. I don't want to finish her

off by saying she was good-natured; but she certainly never abused people, and if she was very worldly she was not the only one. She never even thought of the people she didn't like, much less did she speak of them, for all her time was given to talking about her favourites, as she called them, who were usually of princely name (princes in Rome are numerous and *d'un commerce facile*), and her regard for whom was not chilled by the scant pains they sometimes took to encourage it. What was original in her was the candour and, to a certain extent, the brutality with which she played her game.

The girls were not pretty, but they might have been less plain if they had felt less oppressively the responsibility of their looks. You could not say exactly whether they were ugly or only afraid, on every occasion, that their mother would think them so. This expression was naturally the reverse of ornamental. They were good creatures, though they generally had the air of having slept in their clothes in order to be ready in time. Rosina and Augusta were better than Veronica: we had a theory that Veronica had a temper and sometimes "stood up" to her mother. She was the beauty, she had handsome hair, she sang, alas — she quavered out English ditties beneath the Roman *lambris*. She had pretensions individually, in short; the others had not even those that their mother had for them. In general, however, they were bullied and overpowered by their stern parent; all they could do was to follow her like frightened sheep, and they lived with their eyes fixed on her, so as to execute, at a glance from her, the evolutions in which they had been drilled. We were sorry for them, for we were sure that she secretly felt, with rage, that they were not brilliant and sat upon them for it with all her weight, which of course didn't tend to wake them up. None the less we talked of them profanely, and especially of Veronica, who had the habit of addressing us indiscriminately, though so many of us were English, in incomprehensible strange languages.

When I say "we" I must immediately except the young American secretary, with whom we lived much (at least I did, for I liked him, little as the trick I played him may have shown it), and who never was profane about anything: a circumstance to be noticed the more as the conversation of his chief, the representative of the United States *près du Saint-Père* at that time, was apt (though this ancient worthy was not "bearded like the pard," but clean-shaven — once or twice a week) to be full of strange oaths. His name was Henry Wilmerding, he came from some northern State (I am speaking now of the secretary, not of the minister), and he was as fresh and sociable a young fellow as you could wish to see. The minister was the drollest possible type, but we all delighted in him; indeed I think that among his colleagues he was the most popular man in the diplomatic body. He was a product of the Carolinas and always wore a dress-coat and a faded, superannuated neckcloth; his hat and boots were also of a fashion of his own. He talked very slowly, as if he were delivering a public address, used innumerable "sirs," of the forensic, not in the least of the social kind, and always made me feel as if I were the Speaker of the American Congress, though indeed I never should have ventured to call him to order. The curious part of his conversation was that, though it was rich in expletives, it was also extremely sententious: he uttered them with a solemnity which made them patriarchal and scriptural. He used to remind me of the busts of some of the old dry-faced, powerful Roman lawgivers and administrators.

He spoke no language but that of his native State, but
that mattered little, as we all learned it and practiced it
for our amusement.   We ended by making constant use
of it among ourselves: we talked it to each other in his
presence and under his nose.   It seems to me, as I look
back, that we must have been rare young brutes; but he
was an unsuspecting diplomatist.   Indeed they were a
pair, for I think Wilmerding never knew — he had such
a western bloom of his own.

Wilmerding was a gentleman and he was not a fool,
but he was not in the least a man of the world.   I
couldn't fancy in what society he had grown up; I could
only see it was something very different from any of our
milieux.   If he had been turned out by one of ours he
couldn't have been so innocent without being stupid or
so unworldly without being underbred.   He was full
of natural delicacy, worse luck: if he hadn't been I
shouldn't be telling you this little story of my own
shame.   He once mentioned to me that his ancestors
had been Quakers, and though he was not at all what
you call a muff (he was a capital rider, and in the exaltation of his ideas of what was due to women a very
knight of romance), there was something rather dove-
like in his nature, suggestive of drab tints and the smell
of lavender.   All the Quakers, or people of Quaker
origin, of whom I ever heard have been rich, and Wilmerding, happy dog, was not an exception to the rule.   I
think this was partly the reason why we succumbed to
temptation: we should have handled him more tenderly
if he had had the same short allowance as ourselves.
He never talked of money (I have noticed Americans
rarely do — it's a part of their prudery), but he was free-
handed and extravagant and evidently had a long purse
to draw upon.   He used to buy shocking daubs from

O

those of his compatriots who then cultivated "arrt" (they pronounced the word so oddly), in Rome, and I knew a case where he let a fellow have his picture back (it was certainly a small loss), to sell it over again. His family were proprietors of large cotton-mills from which banknotes appeared to flow in inexhaustible streams. They sent him the handsomest remittances and let him know that the question of supplies was the last he need trouble himself about. There was something so enviable, so ideal in such a situation as this that I daresay it aggravated us a little, in spite of our really having such a kindness for him.

It had that effect especially upon one of our little band — a young French attaché, Guy de Montaut, one of the most delightful creatures I have ever known and certainly the Frenchman I have met in the world whom I have liked best. He had all the qualities of his nation and none of its defects — he was born for human intercourse. He loved a joke as well as I, but his jokes as a general thing were better than mine. It is true that this one I am speaking of, in which he had an equal hand, was bad enough. We were united by a community of debt — we owed money at the same places. Montaut's family was so old that they had long ago spent their substance and were not in the habit of pressing unsolicited drafts upon his acceptance. Neither of us quite understood why the diplomatic career should be open to a young Quaker, or the next thing to it, who was a cotton-spinner into the bargain. At the British establishment, at least, no form of dissent less fashionable than the Catholic was recognised, and altogether it was very clear to me that the ways of the Americans were not as our ways. Montaut, as you may believe, was as little as possible of a Quaker; and if he was considerate

of women it was in a very different manner from poor
Wilmerding. I don't think he respected them much,
but he would have insisted that he sometimes spared
them. I wondered often how Wilmerding had ever
come to be a secretary of legation, as at that period, in
America (I don't know how much they have changed it),
such posts were obtained by being begged for and
"worked" for in various crooked ways. It was impossible to go in less for haughtiness; yet with all Wilmerding's mildness, and his being the model of the nice
young man, I couldn't have imagined his asking a
favour.

He went to Mrs. Goldie's as much as the rest of us, but
really no more, I think — no more, certainly, until the
summer we all spent at Frascati. During that happy September we were constantly in and out of her house, and
it is possible that when the others were out he was sometimes in. I mean that he played backgammon in the
loggia of the villa with Rosy and Gussie, and even
strolled, or sat, in the dear old Roman garden with
them, looking over Veronica's shoulder while her pencil
vainly attempted a perspective or a perpendicular. It
was a charming, sociable, promiscuous time, and these
poor girls were more or less gilded, for all of us, by it.
The long, hot Roman summer had driven the strangers
away, and the native society had gone into *villeggiatura*.
My chief had crossed the Alps, on his annual leave, and
the affairs of our house — they were very simple matters,
no great international questions — were in the hands of
a responsible underling. I forget what had become of
Montaut's people; he himself, at any rate, was not to
have his holiday till later. We were in the same situation, he and I, save that I had been able to take several
bare rooms, for a couple of months, in a rambling old

palace in a fold of the Alban hills. The few survivors
of our Roman circle were my neighbours there, and I
offered hospitality to Montaut, who, as often as he was
free, drove out along the Appian Way to stay with me
for a day or two at a time. I think he had a little personal tie in Rome which took up a good deal of his time.

The American minister and his lady — she was easily
shocked but still more easily reassured — had fled to
Switzerland, so that Wilmerding was left to watch over
the interests of the United States. He took a furnished
villa at Frascati (you could have one for a few *scudi* a
month), and gave very pleasant and innocent bachelor
parties. If he was often at Mrs. Goldie's she returned
his visits with her daughters, and I can live over
lovely evenings (oh youth, oh memory!) when tables
were set for supper in the garden and lighted by the
fireflies, when some of the villagers — such voices as one
heard there and such natural art! — came in to sing for
us, and when we all walked home in the moonlight with
the ladies, singing, ourselves, along the road. I am not
sure that Mrs. Goldie herself didn't warble to the
southern night. This is a proof of the humanising,
poetising conditions in which we lived. Mrs. Goldie
had remained near Rome to save money; there was also
a social economy in it, as she kept her eye on some of
her princesses. Several of these high dames were in
residence in our neighbourhood, and we were a happy
family together.

I don't quite know why we went to see Mrs. Goldie
so much if we didn't like her better, unless it be that my
immediate colleagues and I inevitably felt a certain
loyalty to the principal English house. Moreover we
did like the poor lady better in fact than we did in
theory and than the irreverent tone we took about her

might have indicated. Wilmerding, all the same, remained her best listener, when she poured forth the ex-
ploits and alliances of her family. He listened with
exaggerated interest — he held it unpardonable to let
one's attention wander from a lady, however great a
bore she might be. Mrs. Goldie thought very well of
him, on these and other grounds, though as a general
thing she and her daughters didn't like strangers unless
they were very great people. In that case they recognised their greatness, but thought they would have been
much greater if they had been English. Of the greatness of Americans they had but a limited sense, and they
never compared them with the English, the French or
even the Romans. The most they did was to compare
them with each other; and in this respect they had a
sort of measure. They thought the rich ones much less
small than the others.

The summer I particularly speak of, Mrs. Goldie's
was not simply the principal English house but really
the only one — that is for the world in general. I knew
of another that I had a very different attachment to and
was even presumptuous enough to consider that I had an
exclusive interest in. It was not exactly a house, however; it was only a big, cool, shabby, frescoed sitting-
room in the inn at Albano, a huge, melancholy mansion
that had come down in the world. It formed for the
time the habitation of a charming woman whom I fondly
believed to be more to me than any other human being.
This part of my tale is rather fatuous, or it would be if
it didn't refer to a hundred years ago. Not that my
devotion was of the same order as my friend Montaut's,
for the object of it was the most honourable of women,
an accomplished English lady. Her name was Mrs.
Rushbrook, and I should be capable at this hour of tell-

ing you a great deal about her. The description that would be most to the purpose, I confess (it puts the matter in a word), is that I was very far gone about her. I was really very bad, and she was some five years my elder, which, given my age, only made my condition more natural. She had been in Rome, for short visits, three or four times during my period there: her little girl was delicate, and her idea was to make a long stay in a southern climate.

She was the widow of an officer in the navy; she spoke of herself as very poor, but I knew enough of her relations in England to be sure that she would suffer no real inconvenience. Moreover she was extravagant, careless, even slightly capricious. If the "Bohemian" had been invented in those days she might possibly have been one — a very small, fresh, dainty one. She was so pretty that she has remained in my mind *the* pretty woman among those I have known, who, thank heaven, have not been few. She had a lovely head, and her chestnut hair was of a shade I have never seen since. And her figure had such grace and her voice such a charm; she was in short the woman a fellow loves. She was natural and clever and kind, and though she was five years older than I she always struck me as an embodiment of youth — of the golden morning of life. We made such happy discoveries together when first I knew her: we liked the same things, we disliked the same people, we had the same favourite statues in the Vatican, the same secret preferences in regard to views on the Campagna. We loved Italy in the same way and in the same degree; that is with the difference that I cared less for it after I knew her, because I cared so much more for her than for anything else. She painted, she studied Italian, she collected and noted the songs of the people, and she had the wit to pick up certain *bibelots* and curiosities — lucky woman — before other people had thought of them. It was long ago that she passed out of my ken, and yet I feel that she was very modern.

Partly as a new-comer (she had been at Sorrento to give her little girl sea-baths), and partly because she had her own occupations and lived to herself, she was rather out of our circle at Frascati. Mrs. Goldie had gone to see her, however, and she had come over to two or three of our parties. Several times I drove to Albano to fetch her, but I confess that my quest usually ended in my remaining with her. She joined more than one of our picnics (it is ridiculous how many we had), and she was notably present on an important occasion, the last general meeting before our little colony dispersed. This was neither more nor less than a tea-party — a regular five o'clock tea, though the fashion hadn't yet come in — on the summit of Monte Cavo. It sounds very vulgar, but I assure you it was delightful. We went up on foot, on ponies, or donkeys: the animals were for the convenience of the ladies, and our provisions and utensils were easily carried. The great heat had abated; besides, it was late in the day. The Campagna lay beneath us like a haunted sea (if you can imagine that — the ghosts of dead sentries walking on the deep) and the glow of the afternoon was divine. You know it all — the way the Alban mount slopes into the plain and the dome of St. Peter's rises out of it, the colour of the Sabines, which look so near, the old grey villages, the ruins of cities, of nations, that are scattered on the hills.

Wilmerding was of our party, as a matter of course, and Mrs. Goldie and the three girls and Montaut, confound him, with his communicative sense that everything was droll. He hadn't in his composition a grain of respect. Fortunately he didn't need it to make him happy. We had our tea, we looked at the view, we chattered in groups or strolled about in couples: no doubt we desecrated sufficiently a sublime historic spot. We lingered late, but late as it was we perceived, when we gathered ourselves together to descend the little mountain, that Veronica Goldie was missing. So was Henry Wilmerding, it presently appeared; and then it came out that they had been seen moving away together. We looked for them a little; we called for them; we waited for them. We were all there and we talked about them, Mrs. Goldie of course rather more loudly than the rest. She qualified their absence, I remember, as a "most extraordinary performance." Montaut said to me, in a lowered voice: "Diable, diable, diable!" I remember his saying also: "You others are very lucky. What would have been thought if it was I?" We waited in a small, a very small, embarrassment, and before long the young lady turned up with her companion. I forget where they had been; they told us, without confusion: they had apparently a perfectly good conscience. They had not really been away long; but it so happened that we all noticed it and that for a quarter of an hour we thought of it. Besides, the dusk had considerably deepened. As soon as they joined us we started homeward. A little later we all separated, and Montaut and I betook ourselves to our own quarters. He said to me that evening, in relation to this little incident: "In my country, you know, he would have to marry her."

"I don't believe it," I answered.

"Well, *he* would believe it, I'm sure."

"I don't believe that."

"Try him and you'll see. He'll believe anything."

The idea of trying him — such is the levity of youth —

took possession of me; but at the time I said nothing. Montaut returned to Rome the next day, and a few days later I followed him — my *villeggiatura* was over. Our afternoon at Monte Cavo had had no consequences that I perceived. When I saw Montaut again in Rome one of the first things he said to me was:

"Well, has Wilmerding proposed?"

"Not that I know of."

"Didn't you tell him he ought?"

"My dear fellow, he'd knock me down."

"Never in the world. He'd thank you for the hint — he's so candid." I burst out laughing at this, and he asked if our friend had come back. When I said I had left him at Frascati he exclaimed: "Why, he's compromising her more!"

I didn't quite understand, and I remember asking: "Do you think he really ought to offer her marriage, as a gentleman?"

"Beyond all doubt, in any civilised society."

"What a queer thing, then, is civilisation! Because I'm sure he has done her no harm."

"How can you be sure? However, call it good if you like. It's a benefit one is supposed to pay for the privilege of conferring."

"He won't see it."

"He will if you open his eyes."

"That's not my business. And there's no one to make him see it," I replied.

"Couldn't the Honourable Blanche make him? It seems to me I would trust her."

"Trust her then and be quiet."

"You're afraid of his knocking you down," Montaut said.

I suppose I replied to this remark with another equally

derisive, but I remember saying a moment later: "I'm rather curious to see if he would take such a representation seriously."

"I bet you a louis he will!" Montaut declared; and there was something in his tone that led me to accept the bet.

II.

In Rome, of a Sunday afternoon, every one went over to St. Peter's; I don't know whether the agreeably frivolous habit still prevails: it had little to do, I fear, with the spirit of worship. We went to hear the music — the famous vesper-service of the Papal choir, and also to learn the news, to stroll about and talk and look at each other. If we treated the great church as a public promenade, or rather as a splendid international *salon,* the fault was not wholly our own, and indeed practically there was little profanity in such an attitude. One's attitude was insignificant, and the bright immensity of the place protected conversation and even gossip. It struck one not as a particular temple, but as formed by the very walls of the faith that has no small pruderies to enforce. One early autumn day, in especial, we crossed the Tiber and lifted the ponderous leather curtain of the door to get a general view of the return of our friends to Rome. Half an hour's wandering lighted up the question of who had arrived, as every one, in his degree, went there for a solution of it. At the end of ten minutes I came upon Henry Wilmerding; he was standing still, with his head thrown back and his eyes raised to the far-arching dome as if he had felt its spell for the first time. The body of the church was almost clear of people; the visitors were collected in the chapel where service was held and just outside of it; the splendid

chant and the strange high voices of some of the choris-
ters came to us from a great distance. Before Wilmerding saw me I had time to say to him: "I thought you
intended to remain at Frascati till the end of the week."

"I did, but I changed my mind."

"You came away suddenly, then?"

"Yes, it was rather sudden."

"Are you going back?" I presently asked.

"There's nothing particular to go back for."

I hesitated a moment. "Was there anything particular
to come away for?"

"My dear fellow, not that I know of," he replied,
with a slight flush in his cheek — an intimation (not
that I needed it), that I had a little the air of challeng-
ing his right to go and come as he chose.

"Not in relation to those ladies?"

"Those ladies?"

"Don't be so unnaturally blank. Your dearest
friends."

"Do you mean the Goldies?"

"Don't overdo it. Whom on earth should I mean?"

It is difficult to explain, but there was something
youthfully bland in poor Wilmerding which operated
as a provocation: it made him seem imperturbable,
which he really was not. My little discussion with
Montaut about the success with which he might be made
to take a joke seriously had not, till this moment, borne
any fruit in my imagination, but the idea became prolific,
or at least it became amusing, as I stood face to face
with him on those solemn fields of marble. There was
a temptation to see how much he would swallow. He
was candid, and his candour was like a rather foolish
blank page, the gaping, gilt-edged page of an album,
presenting itself for the receipt of a quotation or a

thought. Why shouldn't one write something on it, to see how it would look? In this case the inscription could only be a covert pleasantry — an impromptu containing a surprise. If Wilmerding was innocent, that, no doubt, ought to have made one kind, and I had not the faintest intention of being cruel. His blandness might have operated to conciliate, and it was only the turn of a hair that it had the other effect. That hair, let me suppose, was simply the intrinsic brutality — or call it the high animal-spirits — of youth. If after the little experiment suggested by Montaut had fixed itself in my fancy I let him off, it would be because I pitied him. But it was absurd to pity Wilmerding — we envied him, as I have hinted, too much. If he was the white album-page seductive to pointed doggerel he was unmistakably gilt-edged.

"Oh, the Goldies," he said in a moment — "I wouldn't have stayed any longer for *them*. I came back because I wanted to — I don't see that it requires so much explanation."

"No more do I!" I laughed. "Come and listen to the singing." I passed my hand into his arm and we strolled toward the choir and the concourse of people assembled before the high doorway. We lingered there a little: till this hour I never can recall without an ache for the old days the way the afternoon light, taking the heavenly music and diffusing it, slants through the golden recesses of the white windows, set obliquely in the walls. Presently we saw Guy de Montaut in the crowd, and he came toward us after having greeted us with a gesture. He looked hard at me, with a smile, as if the sight of us together reminded him of his wager and he wanted to know whether he had lost or won. I let him know with a glance that he was to be quiet or he would spoil everything, and he was as quiet as he knew how to be. This is not saying much, for he always had an itch to play with fire. It was really the desire to keep his hands off Wilmerding that led me to deal with our friend in my own manner. I remember that as we stood there together Montaut made several humorous attempts to treat him as a great conqueror, of which I think Wilmerding honestly failed to perceive the drift. It was Montaut's saying " You ought to bring them back — we miss them too much," that made me prepare to draw our amiable victim away.

"They're not my property," Wilmerding replied, accepting the allusion this time as to the four English ladies.

"Ah, *all* of them, *mon cher* — I never supposed!" the Frenchman cried, with great merriment, as I broke up our colloquy. I laughed, too — the image he presented seemed comical then — and judged that we had better leave the church. I proposed we should take a turn on the Pincian, crossing the Tiber by the primitive ferry which in those days still plied at the marble steps of the Ripetta, just under the back-windows of the Borghese palace.

"Montaut was talking nonsense just then, but *have* they refused you?" I asked as we took our way along the rustic lane that used to wander behind the castle of St. Angelo, skirting the old grassy fortifications and coming down to the Tiber between market-gardens, vineyards and dusty little trellised suburban drinking-shops which had a withered bush over the gate.

"Have *who* refused me?"

"Ah, you keep it up too long!" I answered; and I was silent a little.

"What's the matter with you this afternoon?" he asked. "Why can't you leave the poor Goldies alone?"

"Why can't *you*, my dear fellow — that seems to me the natural inquiry. Excuse my having caught Montaut's tone just now. I don't suppose you proposed for all of them."

"Proposed? — I've proposed for none of them!"

"Do you mean that Mrs. Goldie hasn't seemed to expect it?"

"I don't know what she has seemed to expect."

"Can't you imagine what she would naturally look for? If you can't, it's only another proof of the different way you people see things. Of course you have a right to your own way."

"I don't think I know what you are talking about," said poor Wilmerding.

"My dear fellow, I don't want to be offensive, dotting my i's so. You can so easily tell me it's none of my business."

"It isn't your being plain that would be offensive — it's your kicking up such a dust."

"You're very right," I said; "I've taken a liberty and I beg your pardon. We'll talk about something else."

We talked about nothing, however; we went our way in silence and reached the bank of the river. We waited for the ferryman without further speech, but I was conscious that a bewilderment was working in my companion. As I relate my behaviour to you it strikes me, at this distance of time, as that of a very demon. All I can say is that it seemed to me innocent then: youth and gaiety and reciprocity, and something in the sophisticating Roman air which converted all life into a pleasant comedy, apologised for me as I went. Besides, I had no vision of consequences: my part was to prove, as against the too mocking Montaut, that there would be no consequences at all. I remember the way Wilmerding, as we crossed, sat on the edge of the big flat boat, looking down at the yellow swirl of the Tiber. He didn't meet my eye, and he was serious; which struck me as a promise of further entertainment. From the Ripetta we strolled to the Piazza del Popolo, and then began to mount one of the winding ways that diversify the slope of the Pincian. Before we got to the top Wilmerding said to me: "What do you mean by the different way 'we people' see things? Whom do you mean by us people?"

"You innocent children of the west, most unsophisti-cated of Yankees. Your ideas, your standards, your measures, your manners are different."

"The ideas and the manners of gentlemen are the same all the world over."

"Yes — I fear I can't gainsay you there," I replied.

"I don't ask for the least allowance on the score of being a child of the west. I don't propose to be a bar-barian anywhere."

"You're the best fellow in the world," I continued; "but it's nevertheless true — I have been impressed with it on various occasions — that your countrypeople have, in perfect good faith, a different attitude toward women. They think certain things possible that we Europeans, cynical and corrupt, look at with a suspicious eye."

"What things do you mean?"

"Oh, don't you know them? You have more freedom than we."

"Ah, never!" my companion cried, in a tone of con-viction that still rings in my ears.

"What I mean is that you have less," I said, laugh-ing. "Evidently women, *chez vous*, are not so easily compromised. You must live, over there, in a state of Arcadian, or rather of much more than Arcadian innocence. You can do all sorts of things without committing yourselves. With a quarter of them, in this uncomfortable hemisphere, one is up to one's neck in engagements."

"In engagements?"

"One has given pledges that have in honour to be redeemed — unless a fellow chooses to wriggle out of them. There is the question of intentions, and the question of how far, in the eyes of the world, people have really gone. Here it's the fashion to assume, if there is the least colour for it, that they have gone pretty far. I daresay often they haven't. But they get the credit of it. That's what makes them often ask themselves — or each other — why they mayn't as well die for sheep as for lambs."

"I know perfectly well what you mean: that's precisely what makes me so careful," said Wilmerding.

I burst into mirth at this — I liked him even better when he was subtile than when he was simple. "You're a dear fellow and a gentleman to the core, and it's all right, and you have only to trust your instincts. There goes the Boccarossa," I said, as we entered the gardens which crown the hill and which used to be as pleasantly neglected of old as they are regulated and cockneyfied to-day. The lovely afternoon was waning and the good-humoured, *blasé* crowd (it has seen so much, in its time) formed a public to admire the heavy Roman coaches, laden with yellow principessas, which rumbled round the contracted circle. The old statues in the shrubbery, the colour of the sunset, the view of St. Peter's, the pines against the sky on Monte Mario, and all the roofs and towers of Rome between — these things are doubtless a still fresher remembrance with you than with me. I leaned with Wilmerding against the balustrade of one of the terraces and we gave the usual tribute of a gaze to the dome of Michael Angelo. Then my companion broke out, with perfect irrelevance:

"Don't you think I've been careful enough?"

It's needless — it would be odious — to tell you in detail what advantage I took of this. I hated (I told him) the slang of the subject, but I was bound to say he would be generally judged — in any English, in any French circle — to have shown what was called marked interest.

"Marked interest in what? Marked interest in whom? You can't appear to have been attentive to four women at once."

"Certainly not. But isn't there one whom you may be held particularly to have distinguished?"

"One?" Wilmerding stared. "You don't mean the old lady?"

"*Commediante!* Does your conscience say absolutely nothing to you?"

"My conscience? What has that got to do with it?"

"Call it then your sense of the way that — to effete prejudice — the affair may have looked."

"The affair — what affair?"

"Honestly, can't you guess? Surely there is one of the young ladies to whom the proprieties point with a tolerably straight finger."

He hesitated; then he cried: "Heaven help me — you don't mean Veronica?"

The pleading wail with which he uttered this question was almost tragic, and for a moment his fate trembled in the balance. I was on the point of letting him off, as I may say, if he disliked the girl so much as that. It was a revelation — I didn't know how much he did dislike her. But at this moment a carriage stopped near

P

the place where we had rested, and, turning round, I saw it contained two ladies whom I knew. They greeted me and prepared to get out, so that I had to go and help them. But before I did this I said to my companion: "Don't worry, after all. It will all blow over."

"Upon my word, it will have to!" I heard him ejaculate as I left him. He turned back to the view of St. Peter's. My ladies alighted and wished to walk a little, and I spent five minutes with them; after which, when I looked for Wilmerding, he had disappeared. The last words he had spoken had had such a sharp note of impatience that I was reassured. I had ruffled him, but I had won my bet of Montaut.

Late that night (I had just come in — I was never at home in the evening) there was a tinkle of my bell, and my servant informed me that the signorino of the "American embassy" wished to speak to me. Wilmerding was ushered in, very pale, so pale that I thought he had come to demand satisfaction of me for having tried to make a fool of him. But he hadn't, it soon appeared; he hadn't in the least: he wanted explanations, but they were quite of another kind. He only wished to arrive at the truth — to ask me two or three earnest questions. I ought of course to have told him on the spot that I had only been making use of him for a slight psychological experiment. But I didn't, and this omission was my great fault. I can only declare, in extenuation of it, that I had scruples about betraying Montaut. Besides, I did cling a little to my experiment. There was something that fascinated me in the idea of the supreme sacrifice he was ready to make if it should become patent to him that he had put upon an innocent girl, or upon a confiding mother, a slight, a disappointment even purely conventional. I urged him to let me lay the ghost I had too inconsiderately raised, but at the same time I was curious to see what he would do if the idea of reparation should take possession of him. He would be consistent, and it would be strange to see that. I remember saying to him before he went away: "Have you really a very great objection to Veronica Goldie?" I thought he was going to reply "I loathe her!" But he answered:

"A great objection? I pity her, if I've deceived her."

"Women must have an easy time in your country," I said; and I had an idea the remark would contribute to soothe him.

Nevertheless, the next day, early in the afternoon, being still uneasy, I went to his lodgings. I had had, by a rare chance, a busy morning, and this was the first moment I could spare. Wilmerding had delightful quarters in an old palace with a garden — an old palace with old busts ranged round an old loggia and an old porter in an old cocked hat and a coat that reached to his heels leaning against the *portone*. From this functionary I learned that the signorino had quitted Rome in a two-horse carriage an hour before: he had gone back to Frascati — he had taken a servant and a portmanteau. This news did not confirm my tranquillity in exactly the degree I could have wished, and I stood there looking, and I suppose feeling, rather blank while I considered it. A moment later I was surprised in this attitude by Guy de Montaut, who turned into the court with the step of a man bent on the same errand as myself. We looked at each other — he with a laugh, I with a frown — and then I said: "I don't like it — he's gone."

"Gone? — to America?"

"On the contrary — back to the hills."

Montaut's laugh rang out, and he exclaimed: "Of

course you don't like it! Please to hand me over the sum of money that I have had the honour of winning from you."

"Not so fast. What proves to you that you've won it?"

"Why, his going like this — after the talk I had with him this morning."

"What talk had you with him this morning?"

Montaut looked at the old porter, who of course couldn't understand us, but, as if he scented the drift of things, was turning his perceptive Italian eye from one of us to the other. "Come and walk with me, and I'll tell you. The drollest thing!" he went on, as we passed back to the street. "The poor child has been to see me."

"To propose to you a meeting?"

"Not a bit — to ask my advice."

"Your advice?"

"As to how to act in the premises. *Il est impayable.*"

"And what did you say to him?"

"I said Veronica was one of the most charming creatures I had ever seen."

"You ought to be ashamed of yourself."

"*Tudieu, mon cher*, so ought you, if you come to that!" Montaut replied, taking his hand out of my arm.

"It's just what I am. We're a pair of scoundrels."

"Speak for yourself. I wouldn't have missed it for the world."

"You wouldn't have missed what?"

"His visit to me to-day — such an exhibition!"

"What did he exhibit?"

"The desire to be correct — but in a degree! You're a race apart, *vous autres.*"

"Don't lump him and me together," I said: "the immeasurable ocean divides us. Besides, it's you who

were stickling for correctness. It was your insistence
to me on what he ought to do — on what the family
would have a right to expect him to do — that was the
origin of the inquiry in which (yesterday, when I met
him at St. Peter's,) I so rashly embarked."

"My dear fellow, the beauty of it is that the family
have brought no pressure: that's an element I was
taking for granted. He has no claim to recognise, because none has been made. He tells me that the Honourable Blanche, after her daughter's escapade with him,
didn't open her mouth. *Ces Anglaises!*"

"Perhaps that's the way she made her claim," I suggested. "But why the deuce, then, couldn't *he* be
quiet?"

"It's exactly what he thinks — that she may have
been quiet out of delicacy. He's inimitable!"

"Fancy, in such a matter, his wanting advice!" I
groaned, much troubled. We had stopped outside, under
the palace windows; the sly porter, from the doorway,
was still looking at us.

"Call it information," said Montaut.

"But I gave him lots, last night. He came to me."

"He wanted more — he wanted to be sure! He wanted
an honest impression; he begged me, as a favour to him,
to be very frank. Had he definitely, yes or no, according to my idea, excited expectations? I told him, definitely, yes — according to my idea!"

"I shall go after him," I declared; "I shall overtake
him — I shall bring him back."

"You'll not play fair, then."

"Play be hanged! The fellow mustn't sacrifice his
life."

"Where's the sacrifice? — she's quite as good as he.
I don't detest poor Veronica — she has possibilities, and

also very pretty hair. What pretensions can *he* have? He's touching, but he's only a cotton-spinner and a block-head. Besides, it offends an *aimable Français* to see three unmated virgins withering in a row. You people don't mind that sort of thing, but it violates our sense of form — of proper arrangement. Girls marry, *que diable!*"

"I notice they don't marry you!" I cried.

"I don't go and hide in the bushes with them. Let him arrange it — I like to see people act out their character. Don't spoil this — it will be perfect. Such a story to tell!"

"*To tell?* We shall blush for it for ever. Besides, we can tell it even if he does nothing."

"Not I — I shall boast of it. I shall have done a good action, I shall have *assuré un sort* to a portionless girl." Montaut took hold of me again, for I threatened to run after Wilmerding, and he made me walk about with him for half an hour. He took some trouble to persuade me that further interference would be an unwarranted injury to Veronica Goldie. She had apparently got a husband — I had no right to dash him from her lips.

"Getting her a husband was none of my business."

"You did it by accident, and so you can leave it."

"I had no business to try him."

"You believed he would resist."

"I don't find it so amusing as you," I said, gloomily.

"What's amusing is that he has had no equivalent," Montaut broke out.

"No equivalent?"

"He's paying for what he didn't have, I gather, eh? *L'imbécile!* It's a reparation without an injury."

"It's an injury without a provocation!" I answered, breaking away from him.

I went straight to the stables at which I kept my horse — we all kept horses in Rome, in those days, for the Campagna was an incomparable riding-ground — and ordered the animal to be brought immediately to Porta San Giovanni. There was some delay, for I reached this point, even after the time it took me to change my dress, a good while before he came. When he did arrive I sprang into the saddle and dashed out of the gate. I soon got upon the grass and put the good beast to his speed, and I shall never forget that rich afternoon's ride. It seemed to me almost historic, at the time, and I thought of all the celebrated gallops, or those of poetry and fiction, that had been taken to bring good news or bad, to warn of dangers, to save cities, to stay executions. I felt as if staying an execution were now the object of mine. I took the direction of the Appian Way, where so many panting steeds, in the succession of ages, had struck fire from the stones; the ghostly aqueducts watched me as I passed, and these romantic associations gave me a sense of heroism. It was dark when I strained up the hill to Frascati, but there were lights in the windows of Wilmerding's villa, toward which I first pressed my course. I rode straight into the court, and called up to him — there was a window open; and he looked out and asked in unconcealed surprise what had brought me from Rome. "Let me in and I'll tell you," I said; and his servant came down and admitted me, summoning another member of the establishment to look after my horse.

It was very well to say to Wilmerding that I would tell him what had brought me: that was not so easy after I had been introduced into his room. Then I saw that something very important had happened: his whole aspect instantly told me so. He was half undressed —

he was preparing for dinner — he was to dine at Mrs. Goldie's. This he explained to me without any question of mine, and it led me to say to him, with, I suspect, a tremor in my voice: "Then you have not yet seen her?"

"On the contrary: I drove to their villa as soon as I got here. I've been there these two hours. I promised them to go back to dine — I only came round here to tidy myself a little." I looked at him hard, and he added: "I'm engaged to be married."

"To which of them?" I asked; and the question seemed to me absurd as soon as I had spoken it.

"Why, to Veronica."

"Any of them would do," I rejoined, though this was not much better. And I turned round and looked out of the window into the dark. The tears rose to my eyes — I had ridden heroically, but I had not saved the city.

"What did you desire to say to me?" Wilmerding went on.

"Only that I wish you all the happiness you deserve," I answered, facing him again.

"Did you gallop out here for *that?*" he inquired.

"I might have done it for less!" I laughed, awkwardly; but he was very mild — he didn't fly at me. They had evidently been very nice to him at the other house — well they might be! Veronica had shaken her hair in his eyes, and for the moment he had accepted his fate.

"You had better come back and dine with me," he said.

"On an occasion so private — so peculiar — when you want them all to yourself? Never in the world."

"What then will you do here — alone?"

"I'll wash and dress first, if you'll lend me some things."

"My man will give you everything you need."

His kindness, his courtesy, his extraordinary subjection to his unnecessary doom filled me with a kind of anguish, and I determined that I would save him even yet. I had a sudden inspiration — it was at least an image of help. "To tell the truth, I didn't ride from Rome at such a rate only to be the first to congratulate you. I've taken you on the way; but a considerable part of my business is to go and see Mrs. Rushbrook."

"Mrs. Rushbrook? Do you call this on your way? She lives at Albano."

"Precisely; and when I've brushed myself up a bit and had a little bread and wine I shall drive over there."

"It will take you a full hour, in the dark."

"I don't care for that — I want to see her. It came over me this afternoon."

Wilmerding looked at me a moment — without any visible irony — and demanded, with positive solemnity: "Do you wish to propose to her?"

"Oh, if she'd marry me it would suit me! But she won't. At least she won't yet. She makes me wait too long. All the same, I want to see her."

"She's very charming," said Wilmerding, simply. He finished dressing and went off to dine with Veronica, while I passed into another room to repair my own disorder. His servant gave me some things that would serve me for the night; for it was my purpose, at Albano, to sleep at the inn. I was so horrified at what I had done, or at what I had not succeeded in undoing, that I hungered for consolation, or at least for advice. Mrs. Rushbrook shone before me in the gloom as a generous dispenser of that sort of comfort.

III.

There was nothing extraordinary in my going to see her, but there was something very extraordinary in my taking such an hour for the purpose. I was supposed to be settled in Rome again, but it was ten o'clock at night when I turned up at the old inn at Albano. Mrs. Rushbrook had not gone to bed, and she greeted me with a certain alarm, though the theory of our intercourse was that she was always glad to see me. I ordered supper and a room for the night, but I couldn't touch the repast before I had been ushered into the vast and vaulted apartment which she used as a parlour, the florid bareness of which would have been vulgar in any country but Italy. She asked me immediately if I had brought bad news, and I replied: "Yes, but only about myself. That's not exactly it," I added; "it's about Henry Wilmerding."

"Henry Wilmerding?" She appeared for the moment not to recognise the name.

"He's going to marry Veronica Goldie."

Mrs. Rushbrook stared. "*Que me contez-vous là?* Have you come all this way to tell me that?"

"But he is — it's all settled — it's awful!" I went on.

"What do I care, and what do you mean?"

"I've got into a mess, and I want you to advise me and to get me out of it," I persisted.

"My poor friend, you must make it a little clearer then," she smiled. "Sit down, please — and have you had your dinner?"

She had been sitting at one end of her faded saloon, where, as the autumn night was fresh at Albano, a fire of faggots was crackling in the big marble-framed cavern of the chimney. Her books, her work, her materials for writing and sketching, were scattered near: the place was a comfortable lamplit corner in the general blankness. There was a piano near at hand, and beyond it were the doors of further chambers, in one of which my hostess's little daughter was asleep. There was always something vaguely annoying to me in these signs of occupation and independence: they seemed to limit the ground on which one could appeal to her for oneself.

"I'm tired and I'm hungry," I said, "but I can't think of my dinner till I've talked to you."

"Have you come all the way from Rome?"

"More than all the way, because I've been at Frascati."

"And how did you get here?"

"I hired a chaise and pair at Frascati — the man drove me over."

"At this hour? You weren't afraid of brigands?"

"Not when it was a question of seeing you. You must do something for me — you must stop it."

"What must I do, and what must I stop?" said Mrs. Rushbrook, sitting down.

"This odious union — it's too unnatural."

"I see, then. Veronica's to marry some one, and you want her for yourself."

"Don't be cruel, and don't torment me — I'm sore enough already. You know well enough whom I want to marry!" I broke out.

"How can I stop anything?" Mrs Rushbrook asked.

"When I see you this way, at home, between the fire and the lamp, with the empty place beside you — an image of charming domesticity — do you suppose I have any doubt as to what I want?"

She rested her eyes on the fire, as if she were turning my words over as an act of decent courtesy and of pretty form. But immediately afterwards she said: "If you've come out here to make love to me, please say so at once, so that we may have it over on the spot. You will gain nothing whatever by it."

"I'm not such a fool as to have given you such a chance to snub me. That would have been presumptuous, and what is at the bottom of my errand this evening is extreme humility. Don't therefore think you've gained the advantage of putting me in my place. You've done nothing of the sort, for I haven't come out of it — except, indeed, so far as to try a bad joke on Wilmerding. It has turned out even worse than was probable. You're clever, you're sympathetic, you're kind."

"What has Wilmerding to do with that?"

"Try and get him off. That's the sort of thing a woman can do."

"I don't in the least follow you, you know. Who is Wilmerding?"

"Surely you remember him — you've seen him at Frascati, the young American secretary — you saw him a year ago in Rome. The fellow who is always opening the door for you and finding the things you lose."

"The things I lose?"

"I mean the things women lose. He went with us the other day to Monte Cavo."

"And got himself lost with the girl? Oh yes, I recall him," said Mrs. Rushbrook.

"It was the darkest hour of his life — or rather of mine. I told him that after that the only thing he could do was to marry Veronica. And he has believed me."

"Does he believe everything you tell him?" Mrs. Rushbrook asked.

"Don't be impertinent, because I feel very wretched. He loathes Veronica."

"Then why does he marry her?"

"Because I worked upon him. It's comical — yet it's dreadful."

"Is he an idiot — can't he judge for himself?" said Mrs. Rushbrook.

"He's marrying her for good manners. I persuaded him they require it."

"And don't they, then?"

"Not the least in the world!"

"Was that *your* idea of good manners? Why did you do it?"

"I didn't — I backed out, as soon as I saw he believed me. But it was too late. Besides, a friend of mine had a hand in *it* — he went further than I. I may as well tell you that it's Guy de Montaut, the little Frenchman of the embassy, whom you'll remember — he was of our party at Monte Cavo. Between us, in pure sport and without meaning any harm, we have brought this thing on. And now I'm devoured with remorse — it wasn't a creditable performance."

"What was the beauty of the joke?" Mrs. Rushbrook inquired, with exasperating serenity.

"Don't ask me now — I don't see it! It seems to me hideous."

"And M. de Montaut — has he any compunction?"

"Not a bit — he looks at it from the point of view of the Goldies. Veronica is a *fille sans dot*, and not generally liked; therefore with poor prospects. He has put a husband in her way — a rich, good-natured young man, without encumbrances and of high character. It's a service, where a service was needed, of which he is positively proud."

Mrs. Rushbrook looked at me reflectively, as if she were trying to give me her best attention and to straighten out this odd story.

"Mr. Wilmerding is rich?" she asked in a moment.

"Dear me, yes — very well off."

"And of high character?"

"An excellent fellow — without a fault."

"I don't understand him, then."

"No more do I!"

"Then what can we do? How can we interfere?" my companion went on.

"That's what I want you to tell me. It's a woman's business — that's why I've tumbled in on you here. You must invent something, you must attempt something."

"My dear friend, what on earth do I care for Mr. Wilmerding?"

"You ought to care — he's a knight of romance. Do it for me, then."

"Oh, for you!" my hostess laughed.

"Don't you pity me — doesn't my situation appeal to you?"

"Not a bit! It's grotesque."

"That's because you don't know."

"What is it I don't know?"

"Why, in the first place, what a particularly shabby thing it was to play such a trick on Wilmerding — a gentleman and a man that never injured a fly; and, in the second place, how miserable he'll be and how little comfort he'll have with Veronica."

"What's the matter with Veronica — is she so bad?"

"You know them all — one doesn't want to marry them. Fancy putting oneself deliberately under Mrs. Goldie's heel! The great matter with Veronica is that, left to himself, he would never have dreamed of her. That's enough."

"You say he hasn't a fault," Mrs. Rushbrook replied. "But isn't it rather a fault that he's such a booby?"

"I don't know whether it's because I'm rather exalted, rather morbid, in my reaction against my momentary levity, that he strikes me as so far from being a booby that I really think what he has engaged to do is very fine. If without intending it, and in ignorance of the social perspective of a country not his own, he has appeared to go so far that they have had a right to expect he would go further, he's willing to pay the penalty. Poor fellow, he pays for all of us."

"Surely he's very meek," said Mrs. Rushbrook. "He's what you call a muff."

"*Que voulez-vous?* He's simple — he's generous."

"I see what you mean — I like that."

"You would like him if you knew him. He has acted like a gallant gentleman — from a sense of duty."

"It *is* rather fine," Mrs. Rushbrook murmured.

"He's too good for Veronica," I continued.

"And you want me to tell her so?"

"Well, something of that sort. I want you to arrange it."

"I'm much obliged — that's a fine large order!" my companion laughed.

"Go and see Mrs. Goldie, intercede with her, entreat her to let him go, tell her that they really oughtn't to take advantage of a momentary aberration, an extravagance of magnanimity."

"Don't you think it's *your* place to do all that?"

"Do you imagine it would do any good — that they would release him?" I demanded.

"How can I tell? You could try. Is Veronica very fond of him?" Mrs. Rushbrook pursued.

"I don't think any of them can really be very fond of any one who isn't 'smart.' They want certain things that don't belong to Wilmerding at all — to his nationality or his type. He isn't at all 'smart,' in their sense."

"Oh yes, *their* sense: I know it. It's not a nice sense!" Mrs. Rushbrook exclaimed, with a critical sigh.

"At the same time Veronica is dying to be married, and they are delighted with his money. It makes up for deficiencies," I explained.

"And is there so much of it?"

"Lots and lots. I know by the way he lives."

"An American, you say? One doesn't know Americans."

"How do you mean, one doesn't know them?"

"They're vague to me. One doesn't meet many."

"More's the pity, if they're all like Wilmerding. But they can't be. You must know him — I'm sure you'll like him."

"He comes back to me; I see his face now," said Mrs. Rushbrook. "Isn't he rather good-looking?"

"Well enough; but I'll say he's another Antinous if it will interest you for him."

"What I don't understand is *your* responsibility," my friend remarked after a moment. "If he insists and persists, how is it your fault?"

"Oh, it all comes back to that. I put it into his head — I perverted his mind. I started him on the fatal course — I administered the primary push."

"Why can't you confess your misdemeanour to him, then?"

"I *have* confessed — that is, almost. I attenuated, I retracted, when I saw how seriously he took it; I did what I could to pull him back. I rode after him to-day and almost killed my horse. But it was no use — he had moved so abominably fast."

"How fast do you mean?"

"I mean that he had proposed to Veronica a few hours after I first spoke to him. He couldn't bear it a moment longer — I mean the construction of his behaviour as shabby."

"He *is* rather a knight!" murmured Mrs. Rushbrook.

"*Il est impayable*, as Montaut says. Montaut practiced upon him without scruple. I really think it was Montaut who settled him."

"Have you told him, then, it was a trick?" my hostess demanded.

I hesitated. "No, not quite that."

"Are you afraid he'll cut your throat?"

"Not in the least. I would give him my throat if it would do any good. But he would cut it and then cut his own. I mean he'd still marry the girl."

"Perhaps he *does* love her," Mrs. Rushbrook suggested.

"I wish I could think it!"

She was silent a moment; then she asked: "Does he love some one else?"

"Not that I know of."

"Well then," said Mrs. Rushbrook, "the only thing for you to do, that I can see, is to take her off his hands."

"To take Veronica off?"

"That would be the only real reparation. Go to Mrs. Goldie to-morrow and tell her your little story. Say: 'I want to prevent the marriage, and I've thought of the most effective thing. If *I* will take her, she will let him go, won't she? Therefore consider that I *will* take her.'"

"I would almost do that; I have really thought of it," I answered. "But Veronica wouldn't take *me*."

"How do you know? It's your duty to try."

Q

"I've no money."

"No, but you're 'smart.' And then you're charming."

"Ah, you're cruel — you're not so sorry for me as I should like!" I returned.

"I thought that what you wanted was that I should be sorry for Mr. Wilmerding. You must bring him to see me," said Mrs. Rushbrook.

"And do you care so little about me that you could be witness of my marrying another woman? I enjoy the way you speak of it!" I cried.

"Wouldn't it all be for your honour? That's what I care about," she laughed.

"I'll bring Wilmerding to see you to-morrow: *he'll* make you serious," I declared.

"Do; I shall be delighted to see him. But go to Mrs. Goldie, too — it *is* your duty."

"Why mine only? Why shouldn't Montaut marry her?"

"You forget that he has no compunction."

"And is that the only thing you can recommend?"

"I'll think it over — I'll tell you to-morrow," Mrs. Rushbrook said. "Meanwhile, I do like your American — he sounds so unusual." I remember her exclaiming further, before we separated: "Your poor Wilmerding — he *is* a knight! But for a diplomatist — fancy!"

It was agreed between us the next day that she should drive over to Frascati with me; and the vehicle which had transported me to Albano and remained the night at the hotel conveyed us, before noon, in the opposite sense, along the side of the hills and the loveliest road in the world — through the groves and gardens, past the monuments and ruins and the brown old villages with feudal and papal gateways that overhang the historic plain. If I begged Mrs. Rushbrook to accompany me there was always reason enough for that in the extreme charm of her society. The day moreover was lovely, and a drive in those regions was always a drive. Besides, I still attached the idea of counsel and aid to Mrs. Rushbrook's presence, in spite of her not having as yet, in regard to my difficulty, any acceptable remedy to propose. She had told me she would try to think of something, and she now assured me she had tried, but the happy idea that would put everything right had not descended upon her. The most she could say was that probably the marriage wouldn't really take place. There was time for accidents; I should get off with my fright; the girl would see how little poor Wilmerding's heart was in it and wouldn't have the ferocity to drag him to the altar. I endeavoured to take that view, but through my magnifying spectacles I could only see Veronica as ferocious, and I remember saying to Mrs. Rushbrook, as we journeyed together: "I wonder if they would take money."

"Whose money — yours?"

"Mine — what money have I? I mean poor Wilmerding's."

"You can always ask them — it's a possibility," my companion answered; from which I saw that she quite took for granted I would intercede with the Honourable Blanche. This was a formidable prospect, a meeting on such delicate ground, but I steeled myself to it in proportion as I seemed to perceive that Mrs. Rushbrook held it to be the least effort I could reputably make. I desired so to remain in her good graces that I was ready to do anything that would strike her as gallant — I didn't want to be so much less of a "knight" than the wretched Wilmerding. What I most hoped for — secretly, however, clinging to the conception of a clever woman's tact as infinite — was that she would speak for me either to

Mrs. Goldie or to Veronica herself. She had powers of manipulation and she would manipulate. It was true that she protested against any such expectation, declaring that intercession on her part would be in the worst possible taste and would moreover be attributed to the most absurd motives: how could I fail to embrace a truth so flagrant? If she was still supposed to be trying to think of something, it was something that *I* could do. Fortunately she didn't say again to me that the solution was that I should "take over" Veronica; for I could scarcely have endured that. You may ask why, if she had nothing to suggest and wished to be out of it, if above all she didn't wish, in general, to encourage me, she should have gone with me on this occasion to Frascati. I can only reply that that was her own affair, and I was so far from quarrelling with such a favour that as we rolled together along the avenues of ilex, in the exquisite Roman weather, I was almost happy.

I went straight to Mrs. Goldie's residence, as I should have gone to a duel, and it was agreed that Mrs. Rushbrook should drive on to the Villa Mondragone, where I would rejoin her after the imperfect vindication of my honour. The Villa Mondragone — you probably remember its pompous, painted, faded extent and its magnificent terrace — was open to the public, and any lover of old Rome was grateful for a pretext for strolling in its picturesque, neglected, enchanted grounds. It had been a resource for all of us at Frascati, but Mrs. Rushbrook had not seen so much of it as the rest of us, or as she desired.

I may as well say at once that I shall not attempt to make my encounter with the terrible dowager a vivid scene to you, for to this day I see it only through a blur of embarrassment and confusion, a muddle of difficulties suspended like a sort of enlarging veil before a monstrous Gorgon face. What I had to say to Mrs. Goldie was in truth neither easy nor pleasant, and my story was so abnormal a one that she may well have been excused for staring at me, with a stony refusal to comprehend, while I stammered it forth. I was even rather sorry for her, inasmuch as it was not the kind of appeal that she had reason to expect, and as her imagination had surely never before been led such a dance. I think it glimmered upon her at first, from my strange manner, that I had come to ask for one of the other girls; but that illusion cannot have lasted long. I have no idea of the order or succession of the remarks that we exchanged; I only recall that at a given moment Mrs. Goldie rose, in righteous wrath, to cast me out of her presence. Everything was a part of the general agitation; for the house had been startled by the sudden determination of its mistress to return to Rome. Of this she informed me as soon as I presented myself, and she apprised me in the same breath, you may be sure, of the important cause. Veronica's engagement had altered all their plans; she was to be married immediately, absence and delay being incompatible with dear Henry's official work (I winced at "dear Henry"), and they had no time to lose for conference with dressmakers and shopkeepers. Veronica had gone out for a walk with dear Henry; and the other girls, with one of the maids, had driven to Rome, at an early hour, to see about putting to rights the apartment in Via Babuino. It struck me as characteristic of the Honourable Blanche that *she* had remained on the spot, as if to keep hold of dear Henry.

These announcements gave me, of course, my opening. "Can't you see he is only going through with it as a duty? Do you mean to say you were not very much surprised when he proposed?" I fearlessly demanded.

I maintained that it was *not* a duty — that Wilmerding had a morbid sense of obligation and that at that rate any one of us might be hauled up for the simple sociability, the innocent conviviality of youth. I made a clean breast of it and tried to explain the little history of my unhappy friend's mistake. I am not very proud of any part of my connection with this episode; but though it was a delicate matter to tell a lady that it had been a blunder to offer marriage to her daughter, what I am on the whole least ashamed of is the manner in which I fronted the Honourable Blanche. I was supported by the sense that she was dishonest in pretending that she had not been surprised — that she had regarded our young man as committed to such a step. This was rubbish — her surprise had been at least equal to her satisfaction. I was irritated by her quick assumption, at first, that if I wanted the engagement broken it was because I myself was secretly enamoured of the girl.

Before I went away she put me to the real test, so that I was not able to say afterwards to Mrs. Rushbrook that the opportunity to be fully heroic had not been offered me. She gave me the queerest look I had ever seen a worldly old woman give, and proffered an observation of which the general copious sense was this:

"Come, I do see what you mean, and though you have made a pretty mess with your French monkey-tricks, it may be that if dear Henry's heart isn't in it it simply isn't, and that my sweet, sensitive girl will in the long run have to pay too much for what looks now like a tolerably good match. It isn't so brilliant after all, for what do we really know about him or about his obscure relations in the impossible country to which he may wish to transplant my beloved? He has money, or rather expectations, but he has nothing else, and who knows about American fortunes? Nothing appears to be settled or entailed. Take her yourself and you may have her — I'll engage to make it straight with Mr. Wilmerding. You're impecunious and you're disagreeable, but you're clever and well-connected; you'll rise in your profession — you'll become an ambassador."

All this (it was a good deal), Mrs. Goldie communicated to me in the strange, prolonged, confidential leer with which she suddenly honoured me. It was a good deal, but it was not all, for I understood her still to subjoin: "That will show whether you are sincere or not in wishing to get your friend out of this scrape. It's the only condition on which you can do it. Accept this condition and I will kindly overlook the outrage of your present intrusion and your inexpressible affront to my child."

No, I couldn't tell Mrs. Rushbrook that I had not had my chance to do something fine, for I definitely apprehended this proposition, I looked it well in the face and I sadly shook my head. I wanted to get Wilmerding off, but I didn't want to get him off so much as that.

"Pray, is he aware of your present extraordinary proceeding?" Mrs. Goldie demanded, as she stood there to give me my *congé*.

"He hasn't the faintest suspicion of it."

"And may I take the liberty of inquiring whether it is your design to acquaint him with the scandalous manner in which you have betrayed his confidence?" She was wonderfully majestic and *digne*.

"How can I?" I asked, piteously. "How can I, without uttering words not respectful to the young lady he now stands pledged to marry? Don't you see how that has altered my position?" I wailed.

"Yes, it has given you a delicacy that is wondrous indeed!" cried my hostess, with a laugh of derision which rang in my ears as I withdrew — which rings in my ears at this hour.

I went to the Villa Mondragone, and there, at the end of a quarter of an hour's quest, I saw three persons — two ladies and a gentleman — coming toward me in the distance. I recognised them in a moment as Mrs. Rushbrook, Veronica Goldie, and Wilmerding. The combination amused and even gratified me, as it fell upon my sight, for it immediately suggested that, by the favour of accident, Mrs. Rushbrook would already have had the advantage of judging for herself how little one of her companions was pleased with his bargain, and be proportionately stimulated to come to his rescue. Wilmerding had turned out to spend a perfunctory hour with his betrothed; Mrs. Rushbrook, strolling there and waiting for me, had met them, and she had remained with them on perceiving how glad they were to be relieved of the grimness of their union. I pitied the mismated couple, pitied Veronica almost as much as my more particular victim, and reflected as they came up to me that unfortunately our charming friend would not always be there to render them this delicate service. She seemed pleased, however, with the good turn she had already done them and even disposed to continue the benevolent work. I looked at her hard, with a perceptible headshake, trying to communicate in this way the fact that nothing had come of my attack on Mrs. Goldie; and she smiled back as if to say: "Oh, no matter; I daresay I shall think of something now."

Wilmerding struck me as rather less miserable than I had expected; though of course I knew that he was the man to make an heroic effort not to appear miserable.

He immediately proposed that we should all go home with him to luncheon; upon which Veronica said, hesitating with responsibility: "Do you suppose, for me, mamma will mind?" Her intended made no reply to this; his silence was almost a suggestion that if she were in doubt she had perhaps better go home. But Mrs. Rushbrook settled the question by declaring that it was, on the contrary, exactly what mamma would like. Besides, was not she, Mrs. Rushbrook, the most satisfactory of duennas? We walked slowly together to Wilmerding's villa, and I was not surprised at his allowing me complete possession of Veronica. He fell behind us with Mrs. Rushbrook and succeeded, at any rate, in shaking off his gloom sufficiently to manifest the proper elation at her having consented to partake of his hospitality. As I moved beside Veronica I wondered whether she had an incipient sense that it was to me she owed her sudden prospect of a husband. I think she must have wondered to what she owed it. I said nothing to awaken that conjecture: I didn't even allude to her engagement — much less did I utter hollow words of congratulation. She had a right to expect something of that sort, and my silence disconcerted her and made her stiff. She felt important now, and she was the kind of girl who likes to show the importance that she feels. I was sorry for her — it was not *her* fault, poor child — but I couldn't flatly lie to her, couldn't tell her I was "delighted." I was conscious that she was waiting for me to speak, and I was even afraid that she would end by asking me if I didn't know what had happened to her. Her pride, however, kept her from this, and I continued to be dumb and to pity her — to pity her the more as I was sure her mystification would not be cleared up by any revelation in regard to my visit to her mother. Mrs. Goldie would never tell her of that.

Our extemporised repast at Wilmerding's was almost merry; our sociability healed my soreness and I forgot for the moment that I had grounds of discomposure. Wilmerding had always the prettiest courtesy in his own house, with pressing, preoccupied, literal ways of playing the master, and Mrs. Rushbrook enjoyed anything that was unexpected and casual. Our carriage was in waiting, to convey us back to Albano, and we offered our companions a lift, as it was time for Wilmerding to take Veronica home. We put them down at the gate of Mrs. Goldie's villa, after I had noticed the double-dyed sweetness with which Mrs. Rushbrook said to Veronica, as the carriage stopped: "You must bring him over to Albano to return my visit." This was spoken in my interest, but even then the finished feminine hypocrisy of it made me wince a little. I should have winced still more had I foreseen what was to follow.

Mrs. Rushbrook was silent during much of the rest of our drive. She had begun by saying: "Now that I see them together I understand what you mean"; and she had also requested me to tell her all I could about poor Wilmerding — his situation in life, his character, his family, his history, his prospects — since, if she were really to go into the matter, she must have the facts in her hand. When I had told her everything I knew, she sat turning my instructions over in her mind, as she looked vaguely at the purple Campagna: she was lovely with that expression. I intimated to her that there was very little time to lose: every day that we left him in his predicament he would sink deeper and be more difficult to extricate.

"Don't you like him—don't you think he's worthy to marry some woman he's really fond of?" I remember asking.

Her answer was rather short: "Oh yes, he's a good creature." But before we reached Albano she said to me: "And is he really rich?"

"I don't know what you call ' really ' — I only wish I had his pocket-money."

"And is he generous — free-handed?"

"Try him and you'll see."

"How can I try him?"

"Well then, ask Mrs. Goldie."

"Perhaps he'd pay to get off," mused Mrs. Rushbrook.

"Oh, they'd ask a fortune!"

"Well, he's perfect to her." And Mrs. Rushbrook repeated that he was a good creature.

That afternoon I rode back to Rome, having reminded my friend at Albano that I gave her *carte-blanche* and that delay would not improve matters. We had a little discussion about this, she maintaining, as a possible view, that if one left the affair alone a rupture would come of itself.

"Why should it come when, as you say, he's perfect?"

"Yes, he's very provoking," said Mrs. Rushbrook: which made me laugh as I got into the saddle.

IV.

IN Rome I kept quiet three or four days, hoping to hear from Mrs. Rushbrook; I even removed myself as much as possible from the path of Guy de Montaut. I observed preparations going forward in the house occupied during the winter by Mrs. Goldie, and, in passing, I went so far as to question a servant who was tinkering a flower-stand in the doorway and from whom I learned that the *padrona* was expected at any hour. Wilmerding, however, returned to Rome without her; I perceived

it from meeting him in the Corso — he didn't come to see
me.   This might have been accidental, but I was willing
to consider that he avoided me, for it saved me the
trouble of avoiding him.   I couldn't bear to see him —
it made me too uncomfortable; I was always thinking
that I ought to say something to him that I couldn't say,
or that he would say something to me that he didn't.
As I had remarked to Mrs. Goldie, it was impossible
for me now to allude in invidious terms to Veronica, and
the same licence on his side would have been still less
becoming.   And yet it hardly seemed as if we could go
on like that.   He couldn't quarrel with me avowedly
about his prospective wife, but he might have quarrelled
with me ostensibly about something else.   Such subtleties however (I began to divine), had no place in his
mind, which was presumably occupied with the con-
scientious effort to like Veronica — as a matter of duty
— since he was doomed to spend his life with her.   Wilmerding was capable, for a time, of giving himself up to
this effort: I don't know how long it would have lasted.
Our relations were sensibly changed, inasmuch as after
my singular interview with Mrs. Goldie, the day following her daughter's betrothal, I had scruples about
presenting myself at her house as if on the old footing.

   She came back to town with the girls, immediately
showing herself in her old cardinalesque chariot of the
former winters, which was now standing half the time
before the smart shops in the Corso and Via Condotti.
Wilmerding perceived of course that I had suddenly
begun to stay away from his future mother-in-law's; but
he made no observation about it — a reserve of which I
afterwards understood the reason.   This was not, I may
say at once, any revelation from Mrs. Goldie of my un-

mannerly appeal to her. Montaut amused himself with again taking up his habits under her roof; the entertainment might surely have seemed mild to a man of his temper, but he let me know that it was richer than it had ever been before — poor Wilmerding showed such a face there. When I answered that it was just his face that I didn't want to see, he declared that I was the best sport of all, with my tergiversations and superstitions. He pronounced Veronica *très-embellie* and said that he was only waiting for her to be married to make love to her himself. I wrote to Mrs. Rushbrook that I couldn't say she had served me very well, and that now the Goldies had quitted her neighbourhood I was in despair of her doing anything. She took no notice of my letter, and I availed myself of the very first Sunday to drive out to Albano and breakfast with her. Riding across the Campagna now suddenly appeared to me too hot and too vain.

Mrs. Rushbrook told me she had not replied to me because she was about to return to Rome: she expected to see me almost as soon as, with the Holy Father's postal arrangements, a letter would be delivered to me. Meanwhile she couldn't pretend that she had done anything for me; and she confessed that the more she thought of what I wanted the more difficult it seemed. She added however that she now had a project, which she declined to disclose to me. She contradicted herself a little, for she said at one moment that she hadn't the heart to spoil poor Veronica's happiness and at the next that it was precisely to carry out her device (such a secret as it was, even from the girl!) that she had decided to quit Albano earlier than she had intended.

"How can you spoil Veronica's happiness when she won't have any happiness? How can she have any

happiness with a man who will have married her in such
absurd conditions?"

"Oh, he's charming, Mr. Wilmerding — everything
you told me of him is true: it's a case of pure chivalry.
He'll be very kind to her — he'll be sorry for her. Besides, when once he takes her away from her mother
Veronica will be all right. Seeing more of them that
way, before they left Frascati, I became ever so much
interested in them. There's something in Veronica;
when once she's free it will come out."

"How will she ever be free? Her mother will be on
top of them — she'll stick to them — she'll live with
them."

"Why so, when she has her other daughters to work
for?"

"Veronica will be rich — I'm sure Mrs. Goldie will
want to enjoy that."

"They'll give her money — Mr. Wilmerding won't
haggle!"

"How do you know — have you asked him?"

"Oh, I know," smiled Mrs. Rushbrook. "You know
I saw them again. Besides," she added, "he'll escape
with his wife — he'll take her to America."

"Veronica won't go — she'll hate that part of it."

"Why will she hate it?"

"Oh, it isn't 'smart.'"

"So much the better. I should like to go there."

"Very good," said I. "I daresay I shall be sent there
by the Foreign Office some day. I'll take you over."

"Oh, I don't want to go with *you*," said Mrs. Rushbrook, plainly. And then she added that she should try
to get back to Rome by the Thursday.

"How was it you saw so much of them before they
went away?" I suddenly inquired.

"Why, they returned my visit — the queer young couple. Mr. Wilmerding brought her over to see me the day after we breakfasted with him. They stayed three or four hours — they were charming."

"Oh, I see; he didn't tell me."

Mrs. Rushbrook coloured a little. "You say that in a tone! *I* didn't ask him not to."

"I didn't say you did. However, he has had very little chance: we've scarcely spoken since that day."

"You're very wrong — he's such a good fellow."

"I like the way you give me information about him, because you've seen him three times."

"I've seen him four — I've seen him five," Mrs. Rushbrook protested. "After they had been here I went over to Mrs. Goldie's."

"Oh, to speak to her?" I cried, eagerly.

"I spoke to her, of course — it was to bid her good-bye. Mr. Wilmerding was there — that made another time. Then he came here once again. In fact, the next day —— " Mrs. Rushbrook continued.

"He came alone?"

She hesitated a moment. "Yes, he walked over. He said he was so nervous."

"Ah, to talk it over, you mean?" I exclaimed.

"To talk it over?"

"Your interference, your rescue."

Mrs. Rushbrook stared; then she burst into merriment. "You don't suppose we've spoken of that! Imagine his knowing it!"

I stood corrected — I perceived that wouldn't have done. "But what then did he come for?" I asked.

"He came to see me — as you do."

"Oh, as I do!" I laughed.

"He came because he feels so awkward with the girl."

"Did he tell you that?"

"You told me yourself! We never spoke of Veronica."

"Then what *did* you speak of?"

"Of other things. How you catechise!"

"If I catechise it's because I thought it was all for me."

"For you — and for him. I went to Frascati again," said Mrs. Rushbrook.

"Lord, and what was that for?"

"It was for you," she smiled. "It was a kindness, if they're so uncomfortable together. I relieve them, I know I do!"

"Gracious, you might live with them! Perhaps that's the way out of it."

"We took another walk to Villa Mondragone," my hostess continued. "Augusta Goldie went with us. It went off beautifully."

"Oh, then it's all right," I said, picking up my hat.

Before I took leave of her Mrs. Rushbrook told me that she certainly would move to Rome on the Thursday — or on the Friday. She would give me a sign as soon as she was settled. And she added: "I daresay I shall be able to put my idea into execution. But I shall tell you only if it succeeds."

I don't know why I felt, at this, a slight movement of contrariety; at any rate I replied: "Oh, you had better leave them alone."

On the Wednesday night of that week I found, on coming in to go to bed, Wilmerding's card on my table, with "Good-bye — I'm off to-morrow for a couple of months" scrawled on it. I thought it an odd time for him to be "off" — I wondered whether anything had happened. My servant had not seen him; the card had been transmitted by the porter, and I was obliged to sleep upon my mystification. As soon as possible the next morning I went to his house, where I found a post-chaise, in charge of one of the old *vetturini* and prepared for a journey, drawn up at the door. While I was in the act of asking for him Wilmerding came down, but to my regret, for it was an obstacle to explanations, he was accompanied by his venerable chief. The American Minister had lately come back, and he leaned affectionately on his young secretary's shoulder. He took, or almost took, the explanations off our hands; he was oratorically cheerful, said that his young friend wanted to escape from the Roman past — to breathe a less tainted air, that he had fixed it all right and was going to see him off, to ride with him a part of the way. The General (have I not mentioned that he was a general?) climbed into the vehicle and waited, like a sitting Cicero, while Wilmerding gave directions for the stowage of two or three more parcels. I looked at him hard as he did this and thought him flushed and excited. Then he put out his hand to me and I held it, with my eyes still on his face. We were a little behind the carriage, out of sight of the General.

"Frankly — what's the matter?" I asked.

"It's all over — they don't want me."

"Don't want you?"

"Veronica can't — she told me yesterday. I mean she can't marry me," Wilmerding explained, with touching lucidity. "She doesn't care for me enough."

"Ah, thank God!" I murmured, with great relief, pressing his hand.

The General put his head out of the chaise. "If there was a railroad in this queer country I guess we should miss the train."

"All the same, I'm glad," said Wilmerding.

R

"I should think you would be."

"I mean I'm glad I did it."

"You're a *preux chevalier*."

"No, I ain't." And, blushing, he got into the carriage, which rolled away.

Mrs. Rushbrook failed to give me the "sign" she promised, and two days after this I went, to get news of her, to the small hotel at which she intended to alight and to which she had told me, on my last seeing her at Albano, that she had sent her maid to make arrangements. When I asked if her advent had been postponed the people of the inn exclaimed that she was already there — she had been there since the beginning of the week. Moreover she was at home, and on my sending up my name she responded that she should be happy to see me. There was something in her face, when I came in, that I didn't like, though I was struck with her looking unusually pretty. I can't tell you now why I should have objected to that. The first words I said to her savoured, no doubt, of irritation: "Will you kindly tell me why you have been nearly a week in Rome without letting me know?"

"Oh, I've been occupied — I've had other things to do."

"You don't keep your promises."

"Don't I? You shouldn't say that," she answered, with an amused air.

"Why haven't I met you out — in this place where people meet every day?"

"I've been busy at home — I haven't been running about."

I looked round me, asked about her little girl, congratulated her on the brightness she imparted to the most *banal* room as soon as she began to live in it, took up her books, fidgeted, waited for her to say something about

Henry Wilmerding. For this, however, I waited in vain; so that at last I broke out: "I suppose you know he's gone?"

"Whom are you talking about?"

"Veronica's *promesso sposo*. He quitted Rome yesterday."

She was silent a moment; then she replied — "I didn't know it."

I thought this odd, but I believed what she said, and even now I have no doubt it was true. "It's all off," I went on: "I suppose you know that."

"How do *you* know it?" she smiled.

"From his own lips; he told me, at his door, when I bade him good-bye. Didn't you really know he had gone?" I continued.

"My dear friend, do you accuse me of lying?"

"*Jamais de la vie* — only of joking. I thought you and he had become so intimate."

"Intimate — in three or four days? We've had very little communication."

"How then did you know his marriage was off?"

"How you cross-examine one! I knew it from Veronica."

"And is it *your* work?"

"Ah, mine — call it rather yours: you set me on."

"Is that what you've been so busy with that you couldn't send me a message?" I asked.

"What shall I say? It didn't take long."

"And how did you do it?"

"How shall I tell you — how shall I tell?"

"You said you would tell me. Did you go to Mrs. Goldie?"

"No, I went to the girl herself."

"And what did you say?"

"Don't ask me — it's my secret.   Or rather it's hers."

"Ah, but you promised to let me know if you succeeded."

"Who can tell?   It's too soon to speak of success."

"Why so — if he's gone away?"

"He may come back."

"What will that matter if she won't take him?"

"Very true — she won't."

"Ah, what did you do to her?" I demanded, very curious.

Mrs. Rushbrook looked at me with strange, smiling eyes.   "I played a bold game."

"Did you offer her money?"

"I offered her yours."

"Mine?   I have none.   The bargain won't hold."

"I offered her mine, then."

"You might be serious — you promised to tell me," I repeated.

"Surely not.   All I said was that if my attempt didn't succeed I wouldn't tell you."

"That's an equivocation.   If there was no promise and it was so disagreeable, why did you make the attempt?"

"It was disagreeable to me, but it was agreeable to you. And now, though you goaded me on, you don't seem delighted."

"Ah, I'm too curious — I wonder too much!"

"Well, be patient," said Mrs. Rushbrook, "and with time everything will probably be clear to you."

I endeavoured to conform to this injunction, and my patience was so far rewarded that a month later I began to have a suspicion of the note that Mrs. Rushbrook had sounded.   I quite gave up Mrs. Goldie's house, but Montaut was in and out of it enough to give me occa-

sional news of *ces dames*. He had been infinitely puzzled
by Veronica's retractation and Wilmerding's departure:
he took it almost as a personal injury, the postponement
of the event that would render it proper for him to make
love to the girl. Poor Montaut was destined never to
see that attitude legitimated, for Veronica Goldie never
married. Mrs. Rushbrook, somewhat to my surprise,
accepted on various occasions the hospitality of the
Honourable Blanche — she became a frequent visitor at
Casa Goldie. I was therefore in a situation not to be
ignorant of matters relating to it, the more especially as
for many weeks after the conversation I have last related
my charming friend was remarkably humane in her
treatment of me — kind, communicative, sociable, encouraging me to come and see her and consenting often to
some delightful rummaging Roman stroll. But she
would never tolerate, on my lips, the slightest argu-
ment in favour of a union more systematic; she once
said, laughing: "How can we possibly marry when
we're so impoverished? Didn't we spend every penny
we possess to buy off Veronica?" This was highly fantastic, of course, but there was just a sufficient symbolism
in it to minister to my unsatisfied desire to know what
had really taken place.

I seemed to make that out a little better when, before
the winter had fairly begun, I learned from both of my
friends that Mrs. Goldie had decided upon a change of
base, a new campaign altogether. She had got some
friends to take her house off her hands; she was quitting
Rome, embarking on a scheme of foreign travel, going
to Naples, proposing to visit the East, to get back to
England for the summer, to *promener* her daughters, in
short, in regions hitherto inaccessible and unattempted.
This news pointed to a considerable augmentation of

fortune on the part of the Honourable Blanche, whose
conspicuous thrift we all knew to be funded on slender
possessions. If she was undertaking expensive journeys
it was because she had "come into" money — a reflection
that didn't make Mrs. Rushbrook's refusal to enlighten
my ignorance a whit less tormenting. When I said to
this whimsical woman, as I did several times, that she
really oughtn't to leave me so in the dark, her reply was
always the same, that the matter was all too delicate —
she didn't know how she had done, there were some
transactions so tacit, so made up of subtle *sousentendus*,
that you couldn't describe them. So I groped for the
missing link without finding it — the secret of how it
had been possible for Mrs. Rushbrook to put the key of
Wilmerding's coffers into Mrs. Goldie's hand.

I was present at the large party the latter lady gave
as her leave-taking of her Roman friends, and as soon as
I stood face to face with her I recognised that she had had
much less "feeling" than I about our meeting again.   I
might have come at any time. She was good-natured,
in her way, she forgot things and was not rancorous: it
had now quite escaped her that she had turned me out of
the house. The air of prosperity was in the place, the
shabby past was sponged out. The tea was potent, the
girls had all new frocks, and Mrs. Goldie looked at me
with an eye that seemed to say that I might still have
Veronica if I wanted. Veronica was now a fortune, but
I didn't take it up.

Wilmerding came back to Rome in February, after
Casa Goldie, as we had known it, was closed. In his
absence I had been at the American Legation on various occasions — no *chancellerie* in Europe was steeped
in dustier leisure — and the good General confided to me
that he missed his young friend *as* a friend, but so far as

missing him as a worker went (there *was* no work),
"Uncle Sam" might save his salary. He repeated that
he had fixed it all right: Wilmerding had taken three
months to cross the Atlantic and see his people. He had
doubtless important arrangements to make and copious
drafts to explain. They must have been extraordinarily
obliging, his people, for Mrs. Goldie (to finish with her),
was for the rest of her days able to abjure cheap capitals
and follow the chase where it was doubtless keenest —
among the lordly herds of her native land. If Veronica
never married the other girls did, and Miss Goldie, dis-
encumbered and bedizened, reigned as a beauty, a good
deal contested, for a great many years. I think that
after her sisters went off she got her mother much under
control, and she grew more and more to resemble her.
She is dead, poor girl, her mother is dead — I told you
every one is dead. Wilmerding is dead — his wife is
dead.

The subsequent life of this ingenious woman was
short: I doubt whether she liked America as well as she
had had an idea she should, or whether it agreed with
her. She had put me off my guard that winter, and she
put Wilmerding a little off his, too, I think, by going
down to Naples just before he came back to Rome. She
reappeared there, however, late in the spring — though
I don't know how long she stayed. At the end of May,
that year, my own residence in Rome terminated. I
was assigned to a post in the north of Europe, with
orders to proceed to it with speed. I saw them together
before I quitted Italy, my two good friends, and then
the truth suddenly came over me. As she said herself
— for I had it out with her fearfully before I left — I
had only myself to thank for it. I had made her think of
him, I had made her look at him, I had made her do

extraordinary things. You won't be surprised to hear
they were married less than two years after the service
I had induced her to render me.

Ah, don't ask me what really passed between them —
that was their own affair. There are " i's " in the matter
that have never been dotted, and in later years, when my
soreness had subsided sufficiently to allow me a certain
liberty of mind, I often wondered and theorised. I was
sore for a long time and I never even thought of marrying another woman: that " i " at least I can dot. It
made no difference that she probably never would have
had me. She fell in love with him, of course — with the
idea of him, secretly, in her heart of hearts — the hour
I told her, in my distress, of the *beau trait* of which he
had been capable. She didn't know him, hadn't seen
him, positively speaking; but she took a fancy to the
man who had that sort of sense of conduct. Some
women would have despised it, but I was careful to pick
out the one to whom it happened most to appeal. I
dragged them together, I kept them together. When
they met he liked her for the interest he was conscious
she already took in him, and it all went as softly as
when you tread on velvet. Of course I had myself to
thank for it, for I not only shut her up with Wilmerding — I shut her up with Veronica.

What she said to Veronica in this situation was no
doubt that it was all a mistake (she appealed to the girl's
conscience to justify her there), but that he would pay
largely for his mistake. Her warrant for that was
simply one of the subtle *sousentendus* of which she spoke
to me when I attacked her and which are the medium of
communication of people in love. She took upon herself
to speak for him — she despoiled him, at a stroke, in
advance, so that when she married him she married a

man of relatively small fortune. This was disinterested at least. There was no bargain between them, as I read it — it all passed in the air. He divined what she had promised for him and he immediately performed. Fancy how she must have liked him then! Veronica believed, her mother believed, because he had already given them a specimen of his disposition to do the handsome thing. I had arranged it all in perfection. My only consolation was that I had done what I wanted; but do you suppose that was sufficient?

SIR EDMUND ORME.[1]

THE statement appears to have been written, though
the fragment is undated, long after the death of his wife,
whom I take to have been one of the persons referred to.
There is, however, nothing in the strange story to
establish this point, which is, perhaps, not of importance. When I took possession of his effects I found
these pages, in a locked drawer, among papers relating
to the unfortunate lady's too brief career (she died in
childbirth a year after her marriage), letters, memo-
randa, accounts, faded photographs, cards of invitation.
That is the only connection I can point to, and you may
easily and will probably say that the tale is too extravagant to have had a demonstrable origin. I cannot, I
admit, vouch for his having intended it as a report of
real occurrence — I can only vouch for his general veracity. In any case it was written for himself, not for
others. I offer it to others — having full option — precisely because it is so singular. Let them, in respect to
the form of the thing, bear in mind that it was written
quite for himself. I have altered nothing but the names.

IF there's a story in the matter I recognise the exact
moment at which it began. This was on a soft, still

[1] Copyright, 1891, by Macmillan & Co.

Sunday noon in November, just after church, on the sunny Parade. Brighton was full of people; it was the height of the season, and the day was even more respectable than lovely — which helped to account for the multitude of walkers. The blue sea itself was decorous; it seemed to doze, with a gentle snore (if that *be* decorum), as if nature were preaching a sermon. After writing letters all the morning I had come out to take a look at it before luncheon. I was leaning over the rail which separates the King's Road from the beach, and I think I was smoking a cigarette, when I became conscious of an intended joke in the shape of a light walking-stick laid across my shoulders. The idea, I found, had been thrown off by Teddy Bostwick, of the Rifles and was intended as a contribution to talk. Our talk came off as we strolled together — he always took your arm to show you he forgave your obtuseness about his humour — and looked at the people, and bowed to some of them, and wondered who others were, and differed in opinion as to the prettiness of the girls. About Charlotte Marden we agreed, however, as we saw her coming toward us with her mother; and there surely could have been no one who wouldn't have agreed with us. The Brighton air, of old, used to make plain girls pretty and pretty girls prettier still — I don't know whether it works the spell now. The place, at any rate, was rare for complexions, and Miss Marden's was one that made people turn round. It made *us* stop, heaven knows — at least, it was one of the things, for we already knew the ladies.

We turned with them, we joined them, we went where they were going. They were only going to the end and back — they had just come out of church. It was another manifestation of Teddy's humour that he got immediate possession of Charlotte, leaving me to walk with her mother. However, I was not unhappy; the girl was before me and I had her to talk about. We prolonged our walk, Mrs. Marden kept me, and presently she said she was tired and must sit down. We found a place on a sheltered bench — we gossiped as the people passed. It had already struck me, in this pair, that the resemblance between the mother and the daughter was wonderful even among such resemblances — the more so that it took so little account of a difference of nature. One often hears mature mothers spoken of as warnings — signposts, more or less discouraging, of the way daughters may go. But there was nothing deterrent in the idea that Charlotte, at fifty-five, should be as beautiful, even though it were conditioned on her being as pale and preoccupied, as Mrs. Marden. At twenty-two she had a kind of rosy blankness and she was admirably handsome. Her head had the charming shape of her mother's, and her features the same fine order. Then there were looks and movements and tones (moments when you could scarcely say whether it were aspect or sound), which, between the two personalities, were a reflection, a recall.

These ladies had a small fortune and a cheerful little house at Brighton, full of portraits and tokens and trophies (stuffed animals on the top of bookcases, and sallow, varnished fish under glass), to which Mrs. Marden professed herself attached by pious memories. Her husband had been "ordered" there in ill-health, to spend the last years of his life, and she had already mentioned to me that it was a place in which she felt herself still under the protection of his goodness. His goodness appeared to have been great, and she sometimes had the air of defending it against mysterious imputations. Some sense of protection, of an influence invoked and cherished, was evidently necessary to her; she had a dim wistfulness, a longing for security. She wanted friends and she had a good many. She was kind to me on our first meeting, and I never suspected her of the vulgar purpose of "making up" to me — a suspicion, of course, unduly frequent in conceited young men. It never struck me that she wanted me for her daughter, nor yet, like some unnatural mammas, for herself. It was as if they had had a common deep, shy need and had been ready to say: "Oh, be friendly to us and be trustful! Don't be afraid, you won't be expected to marry us." "Of course there's something about mamma; that's really what makes her such a dear!" Charlotte said to me, confidentially, at an early stage of our acquaintance. She worshipped her mother's appearance. It was the only thing she was vain of; she accepted the raised eyebrows as a charming ultimate fact. "She looks as if she were waiting for the doctor, dear mamma," she said on another occasion. "Perhaps *you're* the doctor; do you think you are?" It appeared in the event that I had some healing power. At any rate when I learned, for she once dropped the remark, that Mrs. Marden also thought there was something "awfully strange" about Charlotte, the relation between the two ladies became extremely interesting. It was happy enough, at bottom; each had the other so much on her mind.

On the Parade the stream of strollers held its course, and Charlotte presently went by with Teddy Bostwick. She smiled and nodded and continued, but when she came back she stopped and spoke to us. Captain Bostwick positively declined to go in, he said the occasion was too jolly: might they therefore take another turn? Her mother dropped a "Do as you like," and the girl gave me an impertinent smile over her shoulder as they quitted us. Teddy looked at me with his glass in one eye; but I didn't mind that; it was only of Miss Marden I was thinking as I observed to my companion, laughing:

"She's a bit of a coquette, you know."

"Don't say that — don't say that!" Mrs. Marden murmured.

"The nicest girls always are — just a little," I was magnanimous enough to plead.

"Then why are they always punished?"

The intensity of the question startled me — it had come out in such a vivid flash. Therefore I had to think a moment before I inquired: "What do you know about it?"

"I was a bad girl myself."

"And were you punished?"

"I carry it through life," said Mrs. Marden, looking away from me. "Ah!" she suddenly panted, in the next breath, rising to her feet and staring at her daughter, who had reappeared again with Captain Bostwick. She stood a few seconds, with the queerest expression in her face; then she sank upon the seat again and I saw that she had blushed crimson. Charlotte, who had observed her movement, came straight up to her and, taking her hand with quick tenderness, seated herself on the other side of her. The girl had turned pale — she gave her mother a fixed, frightened look. Mrs. Marden, who had had some shock which escaped our detection, recovered herself; that is she sat quiet and inexpressive, gazing at the indifferent crowd, the sunny air, the slumbering sea. My eye happened to fall, however, on the interlocked hands of the two ladies, and I quickly guessed that the grasp of the elder one was violent. Bostwick stood before them, wondering what was the matter and asking me from his little vacant disk if *I* knew; which led Charlotte to say to him after a moment, with a certain irritation:

"Don't stand there that way, Captain Bostwick; go away — *please* go away."

I got up at this, hoping that Mrs. Marden wasn't ill; but she immediately begged that we would *not* go away, that we would particularly stay and that we would presently come home to lunch. She drew me down beside her and for a moment I felt her hand pressing my arm in a way that might have been an involuntary betrayal of distress and might have been a private signal. What she might have wished to point out to me I couldn't divine: perhaps she had seen somebody or something abnormal in the crowd. She explained to us in a few minutes that she was all right; that she was only liable to palpitations — they came as quickly as they went. It was time to move, and we moved. The incident was felt to be closed. Bostwick and I lunched with our sociable friends, and when I walked away with him he declared that he had never seen such dear kind creatures.

Mrs. Marden had made us promise to come back the next day to tea, and had exhorted us in general to come as often as we could. Yet the next day, when at five o'clock I knocked at the door of the pretty house, it was to learn that the ladies had gone up to town. They had left a message for us with the butler: he was to say that they had suddenly been called — were very sorry. They would be absent a few days. This was all I could extract from the dumb domestic. I went again three days later, but they were still away; and it was not till the end of a week that I got a note from Mrs. Marden, saying "We are back; do come and forgive us." It was on this occasion, I remember (the occasion of my going

just after getting the note), that she told me she had
intuitions. I don't know how many people there were
in England at that time in that predicament, but there
were very few who would have mentioned it; so that
the announcement struck me as original, especially as
her point was that some of these uncanny promptings
were connected with me. There were other people present — idle Brighton folk, old women with frightened
eyes and irrelevant interjections — and I had but a few
minutes' talk with Charlotte; but the day after this I
met them both at dinner and had the satisfaction of
sitting next to Miss Marden. I recall that hour as the
hour on which it first completely came over me that she
was a beautiful, liberal creature. I had seen her per-
sonality in patches and gleams, like a song sung in
snatches, but now it was before me in a large rosy glow,
as if it had been a full volume of sound — I heard the
whole of the air. It was sweet, fresh music — I was
often to hum it over.

After dinner I had a few words with Mrs. Marden; it
was at the moment, late in the evening, when tea was
handed about. A servant passed near us with a tray, I
asked her if she would have a cup, and, on her assenting,
took one and handed it to her. She put out her hand for
it and I gave it to her, safely as I supposed; but as she
was in the act of receiving it she started and faltered, so
that the cup and saucer dropped with a crash of porcelain
and without, on the part of my interlocutress, the usual
woman's movement to save her dress. I stooped to pick
up the fragments and when I raised myself Mrs. Marden
was looking across the room at her daughter, who looked
back at her smiling, but with an anxious light in her
eyes. "Dear mamma, what on earth *is* the matter with
you?" the silent question seemed to say. Mrs. Marden

coloured, just as she had done after her strange movement on the Parade the other week, and I was therefore
surprised when she said to me with unexpected assurance: "You should really have a steadier hand!" I had
begun to stammer a defence of my hand when I became
aware that she had fixed her eyes upon me with an intense appeal. It was ambiguous at first and only added
to my confusion; then suddenly I understood, as plainly
as if she had murmured "Make believe it was you —
make believe it was you." The servant came back to
take the morsels of the cup and wipe up the spilt tea,
and while I was in the midst of making believe Mrs.
Marden abruptly brushed away from me and from her
daughter's attention and went into another room. I
noticed that she gave no heed to the state of her dress.

I saw nothing more of either of them that evening,
but the next morning, in the King's Road, I met
Miss Marden with a roll of music in her muff. She told
me she had been a little way alone, to practice duets
with a friend, and I asked her if she would go a little
way further in company. She gave me leave to attend
her to her door, and as we stood before it I inquired if
I might go in. "No, not to-day — I don't want you,"
she said, candidly, though not roughly; while the words
caused me to direct a wistful, disconcerted gaze at one
of the windows of the house. It fell upon the white
face of Mrs. Marden, who was looking out at us from the
drawing-room. She stood there long enough for me to
see that it *was* she and not an apparition, as I had
thought for a second, and then she vanished before her
daughter had observed her. The girl, during our walk,
had said nothing about her. As I had been told they
didn't want me I left them alone a little, after which circumstances supervened that kept us still longer apart. I

S

finally went up to London, and while there I received a pressing invitation to come immediately down to Tranton, a pretty old place in Sussex belonging to a couple whose acquaintance I had lately made.

I went to Tranton from town, and on arriving found the Mardens, with a dozen other people, in the house. The first thing Mrs. Marden said was: "Will you forgive me?" and when I asked what I had to forgive she answered: "My throwing my tea over you." I replied that it had gone over herself; whereupon she said: "At any rate I was very rude; but some day I think you'll understand, and then you'll make allowances for me." The first day I was there she dropped two or three of these references (she had already indulged in more than one), to the mystic initiation that was in store for me; so that I began, as the phrase is, to chaff her about it, to say I would rather it were less wonderful and take it out at once. She answered that when it should come to me I would have to take it out — there would be little enough option. That it *would* come was privately clear to her, a deep presentiment, which was the only reason she had ever mentioned the matter. Didn't I remember she had told me she had intuitions? From the first time of her seeing me she had been sure there were things I should not escape knowing. Meanwhile there was nothing to do but wait and keep cool, not to be precipitate. She particularly wished not to be any more nervous than she was. And I was above all not to be nervous myself — one got used to everything. I declared that though I couldn't make out what she was talking about I was terribly frightened; the absence of a clue gave such a range to one's imagination. I exaggerated on purpose; for if Mrs. Marden was mystifying I can scarcely say she was alarming. I couldn't imagine what she meant, but I wondered more than I shuddered. I might have said to myself that she was a little wrong in the upper story; but that never occurred to me. She struck me as hopelessly right.

There were other girls in the house, but Charlotte Marden was the most charming; which was so generally felt to be the case that she really interfered with the slaughter of ground game. There were two or three men, and I was of the number, who actually preferred her to the society of the beaters. In short she was recognised as a form of sport superior and exquisite. She was kind to all of us — she made us go out late and come in early. I don't know whether she flirted, but several other members of the party thought *they* did. Indeed, as regards himself, Teddy Bostwick, who had come over from Brighton, was visibly sure.

The third day I was at Tranton was a Sunday, and there was a very pretty walk to morning service over the fields. It was grey, windless weather, and the bell of the little old church that nestled in the hollow of the Sussex down sounded near and domestic. We were a straggling procession, in the mild damp air (which, as always at that season, gave one the feeling that after the trees were bare there was more of it — a larger sky), and I managed to fall a good way behind with Miss Marden. I remember entertaining, as we moved together over the turf, a strong impulse to say something intensely personal, something violent and important — important for *me*, such as that I had never seen her so lovely, or that that particular moment was the sweetest of my life. But always, in youth, such words have been on the lips many times before they are spoken; and I had the sense, not that I didn't know her well enough (I cared little for that), but that she didn't know *me* well enough. In the church, where there were old Tranton tombs and brasses, the big Tranton pew was full. Several of us were scattered, and I found a seat for Miss Marden, and another for myself beside it, at a distance from her mother and from most of our friends. There were two or three decent rustics on the bench, who moved in further to make room for us, and I took my place first, to cut off my companion from our neighbours. After she was seated there was still a space left, which remained empty till service was about half over.

This at least was the moment at which I became aware that another person had entered and had taken the seat. When I noticed him he had apparently been for some minutes in the pew, for he had settled himself and put down his hat beside him, and, with his hands crossed on the nob of his cane, was gazing before him at the altar. He was a pale young man in black, with the air of a gentleman. I was slightly startled on perceiving him, for Miss Marden had not attracted my attention to his entrance by moving to make room for him. After a few minutes, observing that he had no prayer-book, I reached across my neighbour and placed mine before him, on the ledge of the pew; a manœuvre the motive of which was not unconnected with the possibility that, in my own destitution, Miss Marden would give me one side of *her* velvet volume to hold. The pretext, however, was destined to fail, for at the moment I offered him the book the intruder — whose intrusion I had so condoned — rose from his place without thanking me, stepped noiselessly out of the pew (it had no door), and, so discreetly as to attract no attention, passed down the centre of the church. A few minutes had sufficed for his devotions. His behaviour was unbecoming, his early departure even more than his late arrival; but he managed so quietly

that we were not incommoded, and I perceived, on turning a little to glance after him, that nobody was disturbed
by his withdrawal. I only noticed, and with surprise,
that Mrs. Marden had been so affected by it as to rise,
involuntarily, an instant, in her place. She stared at
him as he passed, but he passed very quickly, and she
as quickly dropped down again, though not too soon to
catch my eye across the church. Five minutes later I
asked Miss Marden, in a low voice, if she would kindly
pass me back my prayer-book — I had waited to see if
she would spontaneously perform the act. She restored
this aid to devotion, but had been so far from troubling
herself about it that she could say to me as she did so:
"Why on earth did you put it there?" I was on the
point of answering her when she dropped on her knees,
and I held my tongue. I had only been going to say:
"To be decently civil."

After the benediction, as we were leaving our places,
I was slightly surprised, again, to see that Mrs. Marden,
instead of going out with her companions, had come up
the aisle to join us, having apparently something to say
to her daughter. She said it, but in an instant I observed that it was only a pretext — her real business was
with me. She pushed Charlotte forward and suddenly
murmured to me: "Did you see him?"

"The gentleman who sat down here? How could I
help seeing him?"

"Hush!" she said, with the intensest excitement;
"don't *speak* to her — don't tell her!" She slipped her
hand into my arm, to keep me near her, to keep me, it
seemed, away from her daughter. The precaution was
unnecessary, for Teddy Bostwick had already taken
possession of Miss Marden, and as they passed out of
church in front of me I saw one of the other men close

up on her other hand. It appeared to be considered that I had had my turn. Mrs. Marden withdrew her hand from my arm as soon as we got out, but not before I felt that she had really needed the support. "Don't speak to any one — don't tell any one!" she went on.

"I don't understand. Tell them what?"

"Why, that you saw him."

"Surely they saw him for themselves."

"Not one of them, not one of them." She spoke in a tone of such passionate decision that I glanced at her — she was staring straight before her. But she felt the challenge of my eyes and she stopped short, in the old brown timber porch of the church, with the others well in advance of us, and said, looking at me now and in a quite extraordinary manner: "You're the only person, the only person in the world."

"But *you*, dear madam?"

"Oh me — of course. That's my curse!" And with this she moved rapidly away from me to join the body of the party. I hovered on its outskirts on the way home, for I had food for rumination. Whom had I seen and why was the apparition — it rose before my mind's eye very vividly again — invisible to the others? If an exception had been made for Mrs. Marden, why did it constitute a curse, and why was I to share so questionable an advantage? This inquiry, carried on in my own locked breast, kept me doubtless silent enough during luncheon. After luncheon I went out on the old terrace to smoke a cigarette, but I had only taken a couple of turns when I perceived Mrs. Marden's moulded mask at the window of one of the rooms which opened on the crooked flags. It reminded me of the same flitting presence at the window at Brighton the day I met Charlotte and walked home with her. But this time my ambiguous friend didn't vanish; she tapped on the pane and motioned me to come in. She was in a queer little apartment, one of the many reception-rooms of which the ground-floor at Tranton consisted; it was known as the Indian room and had a decoration vaguely Oriental — bamboo lounges, lacquered screens, lanterns with long fringes and strange idols in cabinets, objects not held to conduce to sociability. The place was little used, and when I went round to her we had it to ourselves. As soon as I entered she said to me: "Please tell me this; are you in love with my daughter?"

I hesitated a moment. "Before I answer your question will you kindly tell me what gives you the idea? I don't consider that I have been very forward."

Mrs. Marden, contradicting me with her beautiful anxious eyes, gave me no satisfaction on the point I mentioned; she only went on strenuously:

"Did you say nothing to her on the way to church?"

"What makes you think I said anything?"

"The fact that you saw him."

"Saw whom, dear Mrs. Marden?"

"Oh, you know," she answered, gravely, even a little reproachfully, as if I were trying to humiliate her by making her phrase the unphraseable.

"Do you mean the gentleman who formed the subject of your strange statement in church — the one who came into the pew?"

"You saw him, you saw him!" Mrs. Marden panted, with a strange mixture of dismay and relief.

"Of course I saw him; and so did you."

"It didn't follow. Did you feel it to be inevitable?"

I was puzzled again. "Inevitable?"

"That you *should* see him?"

"Certainly, since I'm not blind."

"You might have been; every one else is." I was wonderfully at sea, and I frankly confessed it to my interlocutress; but the case was not made clearer by her presently exclaiming: "I knew you would, from the moment you should be really in love with her! I knew it would be the test — what do I mean? — the proof."

"Are there such strange bewilderments attached to that high state?" I asked, smiling.

"You perceive there are. You see him, you see him!" Mrs. Marden announced, with tremendous exaltation. "You'll see him again."

"I've no objection; but I shall take more interest in him if you'll kindly tell me who he is."

She hesitated, looking down a moment; then she said, raising her eyes: "I'll tell you if you'll tell me first what you said to her on the way to church."

"Has she told you I said anything?"

"Do I need that?" smiled Mrs. Marden.

"Oh yes, I remember — your intuitions! But I'm sorry to see they're at fault this time; because I really said nothing to your daughter that was the least out of the way."

"Are you very sure?"

"On my honour, Mrs. Marden."

"Then you consider that you're not in love with her?"

"That's another affair!" I laughed.

"You are — you *are!* You wouldn't have seen him if you hadn't been."

"Who the deuce *is* he, then, madam?" I inquired with some irritation.

She would still only answer me with another question. "Didn't you at least *want* to say something to her — didn't you come very near it?"

The question was much to the point; it justified the famous intuitions. "Very near it — it was the turn of a hair. I don't know what kept me quiet."

"That was quite enough," said Mrs. Marden. "It isn't what you say that determines it; it's what you feel. *That's* what he goes by."

I was annoyed, at last, by her reiterated reference to an identity yet to be established, and I clasped my hands with an air of supplication which covered much real impatience, a sharper curiosity and even the first short throbs of a certain sacred dread. "I entreat you to tell me whom you're talking about."

She threw up her arms, looking away from me, as if to shake off both reserve and responsibility. "Sir Edmund Orme."

"And who is Sir Edmund Orme?"

At the moment I spoke she gave a start. "Hush, here they come." Then as, following the direction of her eyes, I saw Charlotte Marden on the terrace, at the window, she added, with an intensity of warning: "Don't notice him — *never!*"

Charlotte, who had had her hands beside her eyes, peering into the room and smiling, made a sign that she was to be admitted, on which I went and opened the long window. Her mother turned away, and the girl came in with a laughing challenge: "What plot, in the world are you two hatching here?" Some plan — I forget what — was in prospect for the afternoon, as to which Mrs. Marden's participation or consent was solicited — *my* adhesion was taken for granted — and she had been half over the place in her quest. I was flurried, because I saw that Mrs. Marden was flurried (when she turned round to meet her daughter she covered it by a kind of extravagance, throwing herself on the girl's neck and embracing her), and to pass it off I said, fancifully, to Charlotte:

"I've been asking your mother for your hand."

"Oh, indeed, and has she given it?" Miss Marden answered, gayly.

"She was just going to when you appeared there."

"Well, it's only for a moment — I'll leave you free."

"Do you like him, Charlotte?" Mrs. Marden asked, with a candour I scarcely expected.

"It's difficult to say it *before* him isn't it?" the girl replied, entering into the humour of the thing, but looking at me as if she didn't like me.

She would have had to say it before another person as well, for at that moment there stepped into the room from the terrace (the window had been left open), a gentleman who had come into sight, at least into mine, only within the instant. Mrs. Marden had said "Here *they* come," but he appeared to have followed her daughter at a certain distance. I immediately recognised him as the personage who had sat beside us in church. This time I saw him better, saw that his face and his whole air were strange. I speak of him as a personage, because one felt, indescribably, as if a reigning prince had come into the room. He held himself with a kind of habitual majesty, as if he were different from us. Yet he looked fixedly and gravely at me, till I wondered what he expected of me. Did he consider that I should bend my knee or kiss his hand? He turned his eyes in the same way on Mrs. Marden, but she knew what to do. After the first agitation produced by his approach she took no notice of him whatever; it made me remember her passionate adjuration to me. I had to achieve a great effort to imitate her, for though I knew nothing about him but that he was Sir Edmund Orme I felt his presence as a strong appeal, almost as an oppression. He stood there without speaking — young, pale, handsome, clean-shaven, decorous, with extraordinary light blue eyes and something old-fashioned, like a portrait of years ago, in his head, his manner of wearing his hair. He was in complete mourning (one immediately felt that he was very well dressed), and he carried his hat in his hand. He looked again strangely hard at me, harder than any one in the world had ever looked before; and I remember feeling rather cold and wishing he would say something. No silence had ever seemed to me so soundless. All this was of course an impression intensely rapid; but that it had consumed some instants was proved to me suddenly by the aspect of Charlotte Marden, who stared from her mother to me and back again (he never looked at her, and she had no appearance of looking at him), and then broke out with: "What on earth is the matter with you? You've such odd faces!" I felt the colour come back to mine, and when she went on in the same tone: "One would think you had seen a ghost!" I was conscious that I had turned very red. Sir Edmund Orme never blushed, and I could see that he had no capacity for embarrassment. One had met people of that sort, but never any one with such a grand indifference.

"Don't be impertinent; and go and tell them all that I'll join them," said Mrs. Marden with much dignity, but with a quaver in her voice.

"And will you come — *you?*" the girl asked, turning away. I made no answer, taking the question, somehow, as meant for her companion. But he was more silent than I, and when she reached the door (she was going out that way), she stopped, with her hand on the knob, and looked at me, repeating it. I assented, springing for-

ward to open the door for her, and as she passed out she
exclaimed to me mockingly: "You haven't got your wits
about you — you sha'n't have my hand!"

I closed the door and turned round to find that Sir
Edmund Orme had during the moment my back was
presented to him retired by the window. Mrs. Marden
stood there and we looked at each other long. It had
only then — as the girl flitted away — come home to me
that her daughter was unconscious of what had happened.
It was *that*, oddly enough, that gave me a sudden, sharp
shake, and not my own perception of our visitor, which
appeared perfectly natural. It made the fact vivid to
me that she had been equally unaware of him in church,
and the two facts together — now that they were over —
set my heart more sensibly beating. I wiped my fore-
head, and Mrs. Marden broke out with a low distressful
wail: "Now you know my life — now you know my life!"

"In God's name who is he — *what* is he?"

"He's a man I wronged."

"How did you wrong him?"

"Oh, awfully — years ago."

"Years ago? Why, he's very young."

"Young — young?" cried Mrs. Marden. "He was
born before *I* was!"

"Then why does he look so?"

She came nearer to me, she laid her hand on my arm,
and there was something in her face that made me shrink
a little. "Don't you understand — don't you *feel?*" she
murmured, reproachfully.

"I feel very queer!" I laughed; and I was conscious
that my laugh betrayed it.

"He's dead!" said Mrs. Marden, from her white face.

"Dead?" I panted. "Then that gentleman was — ?"
I couldn't even say the word.

"Call him what you like — there are twenty vulgar names. He's a perfect presence."

"He's a splendid presence!" I cried. "The place is haunted — *haunted!*" I exulted in the word as if it represented the fulfilment of my dearest dream.

"It isn't the place — more's the pity! That has nothing to do with it!"

"Then it's you, dear lady?" I said, as if this were still better.

"No, nor me either — I wish it were!"

"Perhaps it's me," I suggested with a sickly smile.

"It's nobody but my child — my innocent, innocent child!" And with this Mrs. Marden broke down — she dropped into a chair and burst into tears. I stammered some question — I pressed on her some bewildered appeal, but she waved me off, unexpectedly and passionately. I persisted — couldn't I help her, couldn't I intervene? "You *have* intervened," she sobbed; "you're *in* it, you're *in* it."

"I'm very glad to be in anything so curious," I boldly declared.

"Glad or not, you can't get out of it."

"I don't want to get out of it — it's too interesting."

"I'm glad you like it. Go away."

"But I want to know more about it."

"You'll see all you want — go away!"

"But I want to understand what I see."

"How can you — when I don't understand myself?"

"We'll do so together — we'll make it out."

At this she got up, doing what she could to obliterate her tears. "Yes, it will be better together — that's why I've liked you."

"Oh, we'll see it through!" I declared.

"Then you must control yourself better."

"I will, I will — with practice."

"You'll get used to it," said Mrs. Marden, in a tone I never forgot. "But go and join them — I'll come in a moment."

I passed out to the terrace and I felt that I had a part to play. So far from dreading another encounter with the "perfect presence," as Mrs. Marden called it, I was filled with an excitement that was positively joyous. I desired a renewal of the sensation — I opened myself wide to the impression, I went round the house as quickly as if I expected to overtake Sir Edmund Orme. I didn't overtake him just then, but the day was not to close without my recognising that, as Mrs. Marden had said, I should see all I wanted of him.

We took, or most of us took, the collective sociable walk which, in the English country-house, is the consecrated pastime on Sunday afternoons. We were restricted to such a regulated ramble as the ladies were good for; the afternoons, moreover, were short, and by five o'clock we were restored to the fireside in the hall, with a sense, on my part at least, that we might have done a little more for our tea. Mrs. Marden had said she would join us, but she had not appeared; her daughter, who had seen her again before we went out, only explained that she was tired. She remained invisible all the afternoon, but this was a detail to which I gave as little heed as I had given to the circumstance of my not having Miss Marden to myself during all our walk. I was too much taken up with another emotion to care; I felt beneath my feet the threshold of the strange door, in my life, which had suddenly been thrown open and out of which unspeakable vibrations played up through me like a fountain. I had heard all my days of apparitions, but it was a different thing to have seen one and to know that I should in all probability see it familiarly, as it were, again. I was on the look-out for it, as a pilot for the flash of a revolving light, and I was ready to generalise on the sinister subject, to declare that ghosts were much less alarming and much more amusing than was commonly supposed. There is no doubt that I was extremely nervous. I couldn't get over the distinction conferred upon me — the exception (in the way of mystic enlargement of vision), made in my favour. At the same time I think I did justice to Mrs. Marden's absence; it was a commentary on what she had said to me — "Now you know my life." She had probably been seeing Sir Edmund Orme for years, and, not having my firm fibre, she had broken down under him. Her nerve was gone, though she had also been able to attest that, in a degree, one got used to him. She had got used to breaking down.

Afternoon tea, when the dusk fell early, was a friendly hour at Tranton; the firelight played into the wide, white last-century hall; sympathies almost confessed themselves, lingering together, before dressing, on deep sofas, in muddy boots, for last words, after walks; and even solitary absorption in the third volume of a novel that was wanted by some one else seemed a form of geniality. I watched my moment and went over to Charlotte Marden when I saw she was about to withdraw. The ladies had left the place one by one, and after I had addressed myself particularly to Miss Marden the three men who were near her gradually dispersed. We had a little vague talk — she appeared preoccupied, and heaven knows *I* was — after which she said she must go: she should be late for dinner. I proved to her by book that she had plenty of time, and she objected that she must at any rate go up to see her mother: she was afraid she was unwell.

"On the contrary, she's better than she has been for a long time — I'll guarantee that," I said. "She has found out that she can have confidence in me, and that has done her good." Miss Marden had dropped into her chair again. I was standing before her, and she looked up at me without a smile — with a dim distress in her beautiful eyes; not exactly as if I were hurting her, but as if she were no longer disposed to treat as a joke what had passed (whatever it was, it was at the same time difficult to be serious about it), between her mother and myself. But I could answer her inquiry in all kindness and candour, for I was really conscious that the poor lady had put off a part of her burden on me and was proportionately relieved and eased. "I'm sure she has slept all the afternoon as she hasn't slept for years," I went on. "You have only to ask her."

Charlotte got up again. "You make yourself out very useful."

"You've a good quarter of an hour," I said. "Haven't I a right to talk to you a little this way, alone, when your mother has given me your hand?"

"And is it *your* mother who has given me yours? I'm much obliged to her, but I don't want it. I think our hands are not our mothers' — they happen to be our own!" laughed the girl.

"Sit down, sit down and let me tell you!" I pleaded.

I still stood before her, urgently, to see if she wouldn't oblige me. She hesitated a moment, looking vaguely this way and that, as if under a compulsion that was slightly painful. The empty hall was quiet — we heard the loud ticking of the great clock. Then she slowly sank down and I drew a chair close to her. This made me face round to the fire again, and with the movement I perceived, disconcertedly, that we were not alone.

The next instant, more strangely than I can say, my discomposure, instead of increasing, dropped, for the person before the fire was Sir Edmund Orme. He stood there as I had seen him in the Indian room, looking at me with the expressionless attention which borrowed its sternness from his sombre distinction. I knew so much more about him now that I had to check a movement of recognition, an acknowledgment of his presence. When once I was aware of it, and that it lasted, the sense that we had company, Charlotte and I, quitted me; it was impressed on me on the contrary that I was more intensely alone with Miss Marden. She evidently saw nothing to look at, and I made a tremendous and very nearly successful effort to conceal from her that my own situation was different. I say "very nearly," because she watched me an instant — while my words were arrested — in a way that made me fear she was going to say again, as she had said in the Indian room: "What on earth is the matter with you?"

What the matter with me was I quickly told her, for the full knowledge of it rolled over me with the touching spectacle of her unconsciousness. It was touching that she became, in the presence of this extraordinary portent. What was portended, danger or sorrow, bliss or bane, was a minor question; all I saw, as she sat there, was that, innocent and charming, she was close to a horror, as she might have thought it, that happened to be veiled from her but that might at any moment be disclosed. I didn't mind it now, as I found, but nothing was more possible than she should, and if it wasn't curious and interesting it might easily be very dreadful. If I didn't mind it for myself, as I afterwards saw, this was largely because I was so taken up with the idea of protecting *her*. My heart beat high with this idea, on the spot; I determined to do everything I could to keep her sense sealed. What I could do might have been very obscure to me if I had not, in all this, become more aware than of anything else that I loved her. The way to save her was to love her, and the way to love her was to tell her, now and here, that I did so. Sir Edmund Orme didn't prevent me, especially as after a moment he turned his back to us and stood looking discreetly at the fire. At the end of another moment he leaned his head on his arm, against the chimneypiece, with an air of gradual dejection, like a spirit still more weary than discreet. Charlotte Marden was startled by what I said to her, and she jumped up to escape it; but she took no offence — my tenderness was too real. She only moved about the room with a deprecating murmur, and I was so busy following up any little advantage that I might have obtained that I didn't notice in what manner Sir Edmund Orme disappeared. I only observed presently that he had gone. This made no difference — he had been so small a hindrance; I only remember being struck, suddenly, with something inexorable in the slow, sweet, sad headshake that Miss Marden gave me.

"I don't ask for an answer now," I said; "I only want you to be sure — to know how much depends on it."

"Oh, I don't want to give it to you, now or ever!" she replied. "I hate the subject, please — I wish one could be let alone." And then, as if I might have found something harsh in this irrepressible, artless cry of beauty beset, she added quickly, vaguely, kindly, as she left the room: "Thank you, thank you — thank you so much!"

At dinner I could be generous enough to be glad, for her, that I was placed on the same side of the table with her, where she couldn't see me. Her mother was nearly opposite to me, and just after we had sat down Mrs. Marden gave me one long, deep look, in which all our strange communion was expressed. It meant of course "She has told me," but it meant other things beside. At any rate I know what my answering look to her conveyed: "I've seen him again — I've seen him again!" This didn't prevent Mrs. Marden from treating her neighbours with her usual scrupulous blandness. After dinner, when, in the drawing-room, the men joined the ladies and I went straight up to her to tell her how I wished we could have some private conversation, she said immediately, in a low tone, looking down at her fan while she opened and shut it:

"He's here — he's here."

"Here?" I looked round the room, but I was disappointed.

"Look where *she* is," said Mrs. Marden, with just the faintest asperity. Charlotte was in fact not in the main saloon, but in an apartment into which it opened and which was known as the morning-room. I took a few steps and saw her, through a doorway, upright in the middle of the room, talking with three gentlemen whose backs were practically turned to me. For a moment my quest seemed vain; then I recognised that one of the gentlemen — the middle one — was Sir Edmund Orme. This time it *was* surprising that the others didn't see him. Charlotte seemed to be looking straight at him, addressing her conversation to him. She saw me after an instant, however, and immediately turned her eyes away. I went back to her mother with an annoyed sense that the girl would think I was watching *her*, which would be unjust. Mrs. Marden had found a small sofa — a little apart — and I sat down beside her. There were some questions I had so wanted to go into that I wished we were once more in the Indian room. I presently gathered, however, that our privacy was all-sufficient. We communicated so closely and completely now, and with such silent reciprocities, that it would in every circumstance be adequate.

"Oh, yes, he's there," I said; "and at about a quarter-past seven he was in the hall."

"I knew it at the time, and I was so glad!"

"So glad?"

"That it was your affair, this time, and not mine. It's a rest for me."

"Did you sleep all the afternoon?" I asked.

"As I haven't done for months. But how did you know that?"

"As *you* knew, I take it, that Sir Edmund was in the hall. We shall evidently each of us know things now — where the other is concerned."

"Where *he* is concerned," Mrs. Marden amended. "It's a blessing, the way you take it," she added, with a long, mild sigh.

"I take it as a man who's in love with your daughter."

"Of course — of course." Intense as I now felt my desire for the girl to be, I couldn't help laughing a little at the tone of these words; and it led my companion immediately to say: "Otherwise you wouldn't have seen him."

"But every one doesn't see him who's in love with her, or there would be dozens."

"They're not in love with her as you are."

"I can, of course, only speak for myself; and I found a moment, before dinner, to do so."

"She told me immediately."

"And have I any hope — any chance?"

"That's what *I* long for, what I pray for."

"Ah, how can I thank you enough?" I murmured.

"I believe it will all pass — if she loves you," Mrs. Marden continued.

"It will all pass?"

"We shall never see him again."

"Oh, if she loves me I don't care how often I see him!"

"Ah, you take it better than I could," said my companion. "You have the happiness not to know — not to understand."

"I don't indeed. What on earth does he want?"

"He wants to make me suffer." She turned her wan face upon me with this, and I saw now for the first time, fully, how perfectly, if this had been Sir Edmund Orme's purpose, he had succeeded. "For what I did to him," Mrs. Marden explained.

"And what did you do to him?"

She looked at me a moment. "I killed him." As I had seen him fifty yards away only five minutes before the words gave me a start. "Yes, I make you jump; be careful. He's there still, but he killed himself. I broke his heart — he thought me awfully bad. We were to have been married, but I broke it off — just at the last. I saw some one I liked better; I had no reason but that. It wasn't for interest, or money, or position, or anything of that sort. All *those* things were his. It was simply that I fell in love with Captain Marden. When I saw him I felt that I couldn't marry any one else. I wasn't in love with Edmund Orme — my mother, my elder sister had brought it about. But he did love me. I told him I didn't care — that I couldn't, that I *wouldn't*. I threw him over, and he took something, some abominable drug or draught that proved fatal. It was dreadful, it was horrible, he was found that way — he died in agony. I married Captain Marden, but not for five years. I was happy, perfectly happy; time obliterates. But when my husband died I began to see him."

I had listened intently, but I wondered. "To see your husband?"

"Never, never *that* way, thank God! To see *him*, with Chartie — always with Chartie. The first time it nearly killed me — about seven years ago, when she first came out. Never when I'm by myself — only with her. Sometimes not for months, then every day for a week. I've tried everything to break the spell — doctors and *régimes* and climates; I've prayed to God on my knees. That day at Brighton, on the Parade with you, when you thought I was ill, that was the first for an age. And then, in the evening, when I knocked my tea over you, and the day you were at the door with Charlotte and I saw you from the window — each time he was there."

"I see, I see." I was more thrilled than I could say.

"It's an apparition like another."

"Like another? Have you ever seen another?"

"No, I mean the sort of thing one has heard of. It's tremendously interesting to encounter a case."

"Do you call me a 'case'?" Mrs. Marden asked, with exquisite resentment.

"I mean myself."

"Oh, you're the right one!" she exclaimed. "I was right when I trusted you."

"I'm devoutly grateful you did; but what made you do it?"

"I had thought the whole thing out — I had had time to in those dreadful years, while he was punishing me in my daughter."

"Hardly that," I objected, "if she never knew."

"That has been my terror, that she *will*, from one occasion to another. I've an unspeakable dread of the effect on her."

"She sha'n't, she sha'n't!" I declared, so loud that several people looked round. Mrs. Marden made me get up, and I had no more talk with her that evening. The next day I told her I must take my departure from Tranton — it was neither comfortable nor considerate to remain as a rejected suitor. She was disconcerted, but she accepted my reasons, only saying to me out of her mournful eyes: "You'll leave me alone then with my burden?" It was of course understood between us that for many weeks to come there would be no discretion in "worrying poor Charlotte": such were the terms in which, with odd feminine and maternal inconsistency, she alluded to an attitude on my part that she favoured. I was prepared to be heroically considerate, but it seemed to me that even this delicacy permitted me to say a word to Miss Marden before I went. I begged her, after breakfast, to take a turn with me on the terrace, and as she hesitated, looking at me distantly, I informed her that it was only to ask her a question and to say good-bye — I was leaving Tranton for *her*.

She came out with me, and we passed slowly round the house three or four times. Nothing is finer than this great airy platform, from which every look is a sweep of the country, with the sea on the furthest edge. It might have been that as we passed the windows we were conspicuous to our friends in the house, who would divine, sarcastically, why I was so significantly bolting. But I didn't care; I only wondered whether they wouldn't really this time make out Sir Edmund Orme, who joined us on one of our turns and strolled slowly on the other side of my companion. Of what transcendent essence

he was composed I knew not; I have no theory about
him (leaving that to others), any more than I have one
about such or such another of my fellow-mortals whom
I have elbowed in life. He was as positive, as individ-
ual, as ultimate a fact as any of these. Above all he
was as respectable, as sensitive a fact; so that I should
no more have thought of taking a liberty, of practicing
an experiment with him, of touching him, for instance,
or speaking to him, since he set the example of silence,
than I should have thought of committing any other
social grossness. He had always, as I saw more fully
later, the perfect propriety of his position — had always
the appearance of being dressed and, in attitude and
aspect, of comporting himself, as the occasion demanded.
He looked strange, incontestably, but somehow he always
looked *right*. I very soon came to attach an idea of
beauty to his unmentionable presence, the beauty of an
old story of love and pain. What I ended by feeling
was that he was on my side, that he was watching over
my interest, that he was looking to it that my heart
shouldn't be broken. Oh, he had taken it seriously, his
own catastrophe — he had certainly proved that in his day.
If poor Mrs. Marden, as she told me, had thought it out,
I also subjected the case to the finest analysis of which
my intellect was capable. It was a case of retributive
justice. The mother was to pay, in suffering, for the
suffering she had inflicted, and as the disposition to jilt
a lover might have been transmitted to the daughter,
the daughter was to be watched, so that *she* might be
made to suffer should she do an equal wrong. She might
reproduce her mother in character as vividly as she did
in face. On the day she should transgress, in other
words, her eyes would be opened suddenly and unpit-
iedly to the "perfect presence," which she would have

to work as she could into her conception of a young lady's universe. I had no great fear for her, because I didn't believe she was, in any cruel degree, a coquette. We should have a good deal of ground to get over before I, at least, should be in a position to be sacrificed by her. She couldn't throw me over before she had made a little more of me.

The question I asked her on the terrace that morning was whether I might continue, during the winter, to come to Mrs. Marden's house. I promised not to come too often and not to speak to her for three months of the question I had raised the day before. She replied that I might do as I liked, and on this we parted.

I carried out the vow I had made her; I held my tongue for my three months. Unexpectedly to myself there were moments of this time when she struck me as capable of playing with a man. I wanted so to make her like me that I became subtle and ingenious, wonderfully alert, patiently diplomatic. Sometimes I thought I had earned my reward, brought her to the point of saying: "Well, well, you're the best of them all — you may speak to me now." Then there was a greater blankness than ever in her beauty, and on certain days a mocking light in her eyes, of which the meaning seemed to be: "If you don't take care, I *will* accept you, to have done with you the more effectually." Mrs. Marden was a great help to me simply by believing in me, and I valued her faith all the more that it continued even though there was a sudden intermission of the miracle that had been wrought for me. After our visit to Tranton Sir Edmund Orme gave us a holiday, and I confess it was at first a disappointment to me. I felt less designated, less connected with Charlotte. "Oh, don't cry till you're out of the wood," her mother said; "he has let me off sometimes for six months.   He'll break out again when you least expect it — he knows what he's about."   For her these weeks were happy, and she was wise enough not to talk about me to the girl.   She was so good as to assure me that I was taking the right way, that I looked as if I felt secure and that in the long run women give way to that.   She had known them do it even when the man was a fool for looking so — or was a fool on any terms.   For herself she felt it to be a good time, a sort of St. Martin's summer of the soul.   She was better than she had been for years, and she had me to thank for it. The sense of visitation was light upon her — she wasn't in anguish every time she looked round.   Charlotte contradicted me very often, but she contradicted herself still more.   That winter was a wonder of mildness, and we often sat out in the sun.   I walked up and down with Charlotte, and Mrs. Marden, sometimes on a bench, sometimes in a bath-chair, waited for us and smiled at us as we passed.   I always looked out for a sign in her face — "He's with you, he's with you" (she would see him before I should), but nothing came; the season had brought us also a sort of spiritual softness.   Toward the end of April the air was so like June that, meeting my two friends one night at some Brighton sociability — an evening party with amateur music — I drew Miss Marden unresistingly out upon a balcony to which a window in one of the rooms stood open.   The night was close and thick, the stars were dim, and below us, under the cliff, we heard the regular rumble of the sea.   We listened to it a little and we heard mixed with it, from within the house, the sound of a violin accompanied by a piano — a performance which had been our pretext for passing out.

"Do you like me a little better?" I asked, abruptly, after a minute.   "Could you listen to me again?"

I had no sooner spoken than she laid her hand quickly, with a certain force, on my arm. "Hush! — isn't there some one there?" She was looking into the gloom of the far end of the balcony. This balcony ran the whole width of the house, a width very great in the best of the old houses at Brighton. We were lighted a little by the open window behind us, but the other windows, curtained within, left the darkness undiminished, so that I made out but dimly the figure of a gentleman standing there and looking at us. He was in evening dress, like a guest — I saw the vague shine of his white shirt and the pale oval of his face — and he might perfectly have been a guest who had stepped out in advance of us to take the air. Miss Marden took him for one at first — then evidently, even in a few seconds, she saw that the intensity of his gaze was unconventional. What else she saw I couldn't determine; I was too taken up with my own impression to do more than feel the quick contact of her uneasiness. My own impression was in fact the strongest of sensations, a sensation of horror; for what could the thing mean but that the girl at last *saw?* I heard her give a sudden, gasping "Ah!" and move quickly into the house. It was only afterwards that I knew that I myself had had a totally new emotion — my horror passing into anger, and my anger into a stride along the balcony with a gesture of reprobation. The case was simplified to the vision of a frightened girl whom I loved. I advanced to vindicate her security, but I found nothing there to meet me. It was either all a mistake or Sir Edmund Orme had vanished.

I followed Miss Marden immediately, but there were symptoms of confusion in the drawing-room when I passed in. A lady had fainted, the music had stopped; there was a shuffling of chairs and a pressing forward.

The lady was not Charlotte, as I feared, but Mrs. Marden, who had suddenly been taken ill. I remember the relief with which I learned this, for to see Charlotte stricken would have been anguish, and her mother's condition gave a channel to her agitation. It was of course all a matter for the people of the house and for the ladies, and I could have no share in attending to my friends or in conducting them to their carriage. Mrs. Marden revived and insisted on going home, after which I uneasily withdrew.

I called the next morning to ask about her and was informed that she was better, but when I asked if Miss Marden would see me the message sent down was that it was impossible. There was nothing for me to do all day but to roam about with a beating heart. But toward evening I received a line in pencil, brought by hand — "Please come; mother wishes you." Five minutes afterward I was at the door again and ushered into the drawing-room. Mrs. Marden lay upon the sofa, and as soon as I looked at her I saw the shadow of death in her face. But the first thing she said was that she was better, ever so much better; her poor old heart had been behaving queerly again, but now it was quiet. She gave me her hand and I bent over her with my eyes in hers, and in this way I was able to read what she didn't speak — "I'm really very ill, but appear to take what I say exactly as I say it." Charlotte stood there beside her, looking not frightened now, but intensely grave, and not meeting my eyes. "She has told me — she has told me!" her mother went on.

"She has told you?" I stared from one of them to the other, wondering if Mrs. Marden meant that the girl had spoken to her of the circumstances on the balcony.

"That you spoke to her again — that you're admirably faithful."

I felt a thrill of joy at this; it showed me that that memory had been uppermost, and also that Charlotte had wished to say the thing that would soothe her mother most, not the thing that would alarm her. Yet I now knew, myself, as well as if Mrs. Marden had told me, that she knew and had known at the moment what her daughter had seen. "I spoke — I spoke, but she gave me no answer," I said.

"She will now, won't you, Chartie? I want it so, I want it!" the poor lady murmured, with ineffable wistfulness.

"You're very good to me," Charlotte said to me, seriously and sweetly, looking fixedly on the carpet. There was something different in her, different from all the past. She had recognised something, she felt a coercion. I could see that she was trembling.

"Ah, if you would let me show you *how* good I can be!" I exclaimed, holding out my hands to her. As I uttered the words I was touched with the knowledge that something had happened. A form had constituted itself on the other side of the bed, and the form leaned over Mrs. Marden. My whole being went forth into a mute prayer that Charlotte shouldn't see it and that I should be able to betray nothing. The impulse to glance toward Mrs. Marden was even stronger than the involuntary movement of taking in Sir Edmund Orme; but I could resist even that, and Mrs. Marden was perfectly still. Charlotte got up to give me her hand, and with the definite act she saw. She gave, with a shriek, one stare of dismay, and another sound, like a wail of one of the lost, fell at the same instant on my ear. But I had already sprung toward the girl to cover her, to veil her face. She had already thrown herself into my arms. I held her there a moment — bending over her, given up to her, feeling

each of her throbs with my own and not knowing which
was which; then, all of a sudden, coldly, I gathered
that we were alone. She released herself. The figure
beside the sofa had vanished; but Mrs. Marden lay in
her place with closed eyes, with something in her stillness that gave us both another terror. Charlotte expressed it in the cry of "Mother, mother!" with which
she flung herself down. I fell on my knees beside her.
Mrs. Marden had passed away.

Was the sound I heard when Chartie shrieked — the
other and still more tragic sound I mean — the despairing cry of the poor lady's death-shock or the articulate
sob (it was like a waft from a great tempest), of the
exorcised and pacified spirit? Possibly the latter, for
that was, mercifully, the last of Sir Edmund Orme.

MACMILLAN'S DOLLAR SERIES

OF

WORKS BY POPULAR AUTHORS.

Crown 8vo. Cloth extra. $1.00 each.

By F. MARION CRAWFORD.

With the solitary exception of Mrs. Oliphant, we have no living novelist more distinguished for variety of theme and range of imaginative outlook than Mr. Marion Crawford. — *Spectator*.

THE CHILDREN OF THE KING. (*Ready in January.*)
MR. ISAACS: A Tale of Modern India.
DR. CLAUDIUS: A True Story.
ZOROASTER.
A TALE OF A LONELY PARISH.
SARACINESCA. A New Novel.
MARZIO'S CRUCIFIX.

WITH THE IMMORTALS.
GREIFENSTEIN.
SANT' ILARIO.
A CIGARETTE-MAKER'S ROMANCE.
KHALED: A Tale of Arabia.
THE WITCH OF PRAGUE. With numerous Illustrations by W. J. HENNESSY.
THE THREE FATES.

By CHARLES DICKENS.

It would be difficult to imagine a better edition of Dickens at the price than that which is now appearing in Macmillan's Series of Dollar Novels. — *Boston Beacon*.

THE PICKWICK PAPERS. 50 Illustrations. (*Ready.*)
OLIVER TWIST. 27 Illustrations. (*Ready.*)
NICHOLAS NICKLEBY. 44 Illustrations. (*Ready.*)
MARTIN CHUZZLEWIT. 41 Illustrations. (*Ready.*)
THE OLD CURIOSITY SHOP. 97 Illustrations. (*Ready.*)

BARNABY RUDGE. 76 Illustrations. (*Ready.*)
SKETCHES BY BOZ. 44 Illustrations. (*Ready.*)
DOMBEY AND SON. 40 Illustrations. (*Ready.*)
CHRISTMAS BOOKS. 65 Illustrations. (*December.*)
DAVID COPPERFIELD. 41 Illustrations. (*January.*)

AMERICAN NOTES, AND PICTURES FROM ITALY. 4 Illustrations. (*Feb.*)

By CHARLES KINGSLEY.

ALTON LOCKE.	HYPATIA.
HEREWARD.	TWO YEARS AGO.
HEROES.	WATER BABIES. Illustrated.
WESTWARD HO!	YEAST.

By HENRY JAMES.

He has the power of seeing with the artistic perception of the few, and of writing about what he has seen, so that the many can understand and feel with him. — *Saturday Review.*

THE LESSON OF THE MASTER AND OTHER STORIES.	THE ASPEN PAPERS AND OTHER STORIES.
THE REVERBERATOR.	A LONDON LIFE.

By ANNIE KEARY.

In our opinion there have not been many novels published better worth reading. The literary workmanship is excellent, and all the windings of the stories are worked with patient fulness and a skill not often found. — *Spectator*.

JANET'S HOME.	A DOUBTING HEART.
CLEMENCY FRANKLYN.	THE HEROES OF ASGARD.
A YORK AND LANCASTER ROSE.	

By D. CHRISTIE MURRAY.

Few modern novelists can tell a story of English country life better than Mr. D. Christie Murray. — *Spectator*.

AUNT RACHEL.	THE WEAKER VESSEL.
SCHWARZ.	

By MRS. OLIPHANT.

Has the charm of style, the literary quality and flavour that never fails to please. — *Saturday Review.*

At her best she is, with one or two exceptions, the best of living English novelists. — *Academy.*

A SON OF THE SOIL. New Edition.	THE WIZARD'S SON. New Edition.
THE CURATE IN CHARGE. New Edition.	A COUNTRY GENTLEMAN AND HIS FAMILY. New Edition.
YOUNG MUSGRAVE. New Edition.	NEIGHBOURS ON THE GREEN. New Edition.
HE THAT WILL NOT WHEN HE MAY. New and Cheaper Edition.	AGNES HOPETOUN'S SCHOOLS AND HOLIDAYS. With Illustrations.
SIR TOM. New Edition.	
HESTER. A Story of Contemporary Life.	

By J. H. SHORTHOUSE.

Powerful, striking, and fascinating romances. — *Anti-Jacobin.*

BLANCHE, LADY FALAISE.
JOHN INGLESANT.
SIR PERCIVAL.

THE COUNTESS EVE.
A TEACHER OF THE VIOLIN.
THE LITTLE SCHOOLMASTER MARK.

By MRS. CRAIK.

(The Author of "John Halifax, Gentleman.")

LITTLE SUNSHINE'S HOLIDAY.
ADVENTURES OF A BROWNIE.

ALICE LEARMONT.
OUR YEAR.

By MRS. HUMPHRY WARD.

Mrs. Ward, with her "Robert Elsmere" and "David Grieve," has established with extraordinary rapidity an enduring reputation as one who has expressed what is deepest and most real in the thought of the time. . . . They are dramas of the time vitalized by the hopes, fears, doubts, and despairing struggles after higher ideals which are swaying the minds of men and women of this generation. — *New York Tribune.*

ROBERT ELSMERE. | THE HISTORY OF DAVID GRIEVE.
MILLY AND OLLY.

By RUDYARD KIPLING.

Every one knows that it is not easy to write good short stories. Mr. Kipling has changed all that. Here are forty of them, averaging less than eight pages apiece; there is not a dull one in the lot. Some are tragedy, some broad comedy, some tolerably sharp satire. The time has passed to ignore or undervalue Mr. Kipling. He has won his spurs and taken his prominent place in the arena. This, as the legitimate edition, should be preferred to the pirated ones by all such as care for honesty in letters. — *Churchman,* New York.

PLAIN TALES FROM THE HILLS. | LIFE'S HANDICAP.

By AMY LEVY.

REUBEN SACHS.

By M. McLENNAN.

MUCKLE JOCK, AND OTHER STORIES.

3

By THOMAS HUGHES.

TOM BROWN'S SCHOOLDAYS. RUGBY, TENNESSE.
Illustrated.

By ROLF BOLDREWOOD.

Mr. Boldrewood can tell what he knows with great point and vigour, and there is no better reading than the adventurous parts of his books. — *Saturday Review.*

ROBBERY UNDER ARMS.   NEVERMORE.
SYDNEY-SIDE SAXON.

By SIR HENRY CUNNINGHAM, K.C.I.E.

Interesting as specimens of romance, the style of writing is so excellent — scholarly and at the same time easy and natural — that the volumes are worth reading on that account alone. But there is also masterly description of persons, places, and things; skilful analysis of character; a constant play of wit and humour; and a happy gift of instantaneous portraiture. — *St. James's Gazette.*

THE CŒRULEANS: A VACATION IDYLL.

By GEORGE GISSING.

We earnestly commend the book for its high literary merit, its deep bright interest, and for the important and healthful lessons that it teaches. — *Boston Home Journal.*

DENZIL QUARRIER.

By W. CLARK RUSSELL.

The descriptions are wonderfully realistic . . . and the breath of the ocean is over and through every page. The plot is very novel indeed, and is developed with skill and tact. Altogether one of the cleverest and most entertaining of Mr. Russell's many works. — *Boston Times.*

A STRANGE ELOPEMENT.

By the Hon. EMILY LAWLESS.

It is a charming story, full of natural life, fresh in style and thought, pure in tone, and refined in feeling. — *Nineteenth Century.*
A strong and original story. It is marked by originality, freshness, insight, a rare graphic power, and as rare a psychological perception. It is in fact a better story than "Hurrish," and that is saying a good deal. — *New York Tribune.*

GRANIA : THE STORY OF AN ISLAND.

4

By A NEW AUTHOR.

We should not be surprised if this should prove to be the most popular book of the present season; it cannot fail to be one of the most remarkable. — *Literary World*.

TIM : A STORY OF SCHOOL LIFE.

By LANOE FALCONER.

(Author of " Mademoiselle Ixe.")

It is written with cleverness and brightness, and there is so much human nature in it that the attention of the reader is held to the end. . . . The book shows far greater powers than were evident in " Mademoiselle Ixe," and if the writer who is hidden behind the *nom de guerre* Lanoe Falconer goes on, she is likely to make for herself no inconsiderable name in fiction. — *Boston Courier*.

CECILIA DE NOËL.

By THE REV. PROF. ALFRED J. CHURCH.

Rev. Alfred J. Church, M.A., has long been doing valiant service in literature in presenting his stories of the early centuries, so clear is his style and so remarkable his gift of enfolding historical events and personages with the fabric of a romance, entertaining and oftentimes fascinating. . . . One has the feeling that he is reading an accurate description of real scenes, that the characters are living — so masterly is Professor Church's ability to reclothe history and make it as interesting as a romance. — *Boston Times*.

Just ready.

STORIES FROM THE

GREEK COMEDIANS.

ARISTOPHANES.   PHILEMON.

DIPHILUS.   MENANDER.   APOLLODORUS.

With Sixteen Illustrations after the Antique.

THE STORY OF THE ILIAD. | THE STORY OF THE ODYSSEY.
With Coloured Illustrations. | With Coloured Illustrations.
THE BURNING OF ROME.

5

BY

MISS CHARLOTTE M. YONGE.

AN OLD WOMAN'S OUTLOOK.

(Just ready.)

NOVELS AND TALES.

THE HEIR OF REDCLYFFE. Illustrated.

HEARTSEASE; OR, THE BROTHER'S WIFE. Illustrated.

HOPES AND FEARS. Illustrated.

DYNEVOR TERRACE. Illustrated.

THE DAISY CHAIN. Illustrated.

THE TRIAL: MORE LINKS OF THE DAISY CHAIN. Illustrated.

PILLARS OF THE HOUSE; OR, UNDER WODE UNDER RODE. 2 Vols. Illustrated.

THE YOUNG STEPMOTHER. Illustrated.

THE CLEVER WOMAN OF THE FAMILY. Illustrated.

THE THREE BRIDES. Illustrated.

MY YOUNG ALCIDES. Illustrated.

THE CAGED LION. Illustrated.

THE DOVE IN THE EAGLE'S NEST. Illustrated.

THE CHAPLET OF PEARLS. Illustrated.

LADY HESTER, AND THE DANVERS PAPERS. Illustrated.

MAGNUM BONUM. Illustrated.

LOVE AND LIFE. Illustrated.

UNKNOWN TO HISTORY. A Story of the Captivity of Mary of Scotland.

STRAY PEARLS. Memoirs of Margaret de Ribaumont, Viscountess of Belaise.

THE ARMOURER'S 'PRENTICES.

THE TWO SIDES OF THE SHIELD.

NUTTIE'S FATHER.

SCENES AND CHARACTERS: OR, EIGHTEEN MONTHS AT BEECHCROFT.

CHANTRY HOUSE.

A MODERN TELEMACHUS.

BEECHCROFT AT ROCKSTONE.

WOMANKIND. A Book for Mothers and Daughters.

A REPUTED CHANGELING; OR, THREE SEVENTH YEARS, TWO CENTURIES AGO.

THE TWO PENNILESS PRINCESSES. A Story of the Time of James I. of Scotland.

THAT STICK.

MACMILLAN & CO.,

112 FOURTH AVENUE, NEW YORK.

6

GOLDEN TREASURY SERIES.

Uniformly Printed in 18mo, with Vignette Titles
Engraved on Steel.

New and Cheaper Edition. $1.00 each volume.

THE GOLDEN TREASURY OF THE BEST SONGS AND LYR–ICAL POEMS. By F. T. Palgrave.

THE CHILDREN'S GARLAND. Selected by Coventry Patmore.

THE BOOK OF PRAISE. Selected by the Earl of Selborne.

THE FAIRY BOOK. By the Author of "John Halifax, Gentleman."

THE BALLAD BOOK. Edited by William Allingham.

THE JEST BOOK. Selected by Mark Lemon.

BACON'S ESSAYS. By W. Aldis Wright, M.A.

THE PILGRIM'S PROGRESS. By John Bunyan.

THE SUNDAY BOOK OF POETRY. Selected by C. F. Alexander.

A BOOK OF GOLDEN DEEDS. By the Author of "The Heir of Redclyffe."

THE ADVENTURES OF ROBIN–SON CRUSOE. Edited by J. W. Clark, M.A.

THE REPUBLIC OF PLATO. Translated by J. Ll. Davies, M.A., and D. J. Vaughan.

THE SONG BOOK. Words and Tunes selected by John Hullah.

LA LYRE FRANÇAISE. Selected, with Notes, by G. Masson.

TOM BROWN'S SCHOOL DAYS. By An Old Boy.

A BOOK OF WORTHIES. Written anew by the Author of "The Heir of Redclyffe."

GUESSES AT TRUTH. By Two Brothers.

THE CAVALIER AND HIS LADY.

SCOTTISH SONG. Compiled by Mary Carlyle Aitken.

DEUTSCHE LYRIK. Selected by Dr. Buchheim.

CHRYSOMELA. A Selection from the Lyrical Poems of Robert Herrick. Arranged by F. T. Palgrave.

SELECTED POEMS OF MATTHEW ARNOLD.

THE STORY OF THE CHRISTIANS AND MOORS IN SPAIN. By Charlotte M. Yonge.

LAMB'S TALES FROM SHAKESPEARE. Edited by the Rev. A. Ainger.

GOLDEN TREASURY SERIES.

UNIFORMLY PRINTED IN 18MO, WITH VIGNETTE TITLES
ENGRAVED ON STEEL.

New and Cheaper Edition. $1.00 each volume.

SHAKESPEARE'S SONGS AND SONNETS. Edited, with Notes, by F. T. PALGRAVE.

POEMS OF WORDSWORTH. Chosen and Edited by MATTHEW ARNOLD.

POEMS OF SHELLEY. Edited by STOPFORD A. BROOKE.

THE ESSAYS OF JOSEPH ADDISON. Chosen and Edited by JOHN RICHARD GREEN.

POETRY OF BYRON. Chosen and Arranged by MATTHEW ARNOLD.

SIR THOMAS BROWNE'S RELIGIO MEDICI, ETC. Edited by W. A. GREENHILL.

THE SPEECHES AND TABLE-TALK OF THE PROPHET MOHAMMED. Chosen and Translated by STANLEY LANE POOLE.

SELECTIONS FROM THE WRITINGS OF WALTER SAVAGE LANDOR. Edited by SIDNEY COLVIN.

SELECTIONS FROM COWPER'S POEMS. With an Introduction by Mrs. OLIPHANT.

LETTERS OF WILLIAM COWPER. Edited by Rev. W. BENHAM.

THE POETICAL WORKS OF JOHN KEATS. Edited by F. T. PALGRAVE.

THE TRIAL AND DEATH OF SOCRATES. Translated into English by E. J. CHURCH, M.A.

CHILDREN'S TREASURY OF ENGLISH SONG. Edited by F. T. PALGRAVE.

IN MEMORIAM.

TENNYSON'S LYRICAL POEMS. Edited by F. T. PALGRAVE.

PLATO, PHÆDRUS, LYSIS, AND PROTAGORAS. Translated by Rev. J. WRIGHT.

THEOCRITUS, BION, AND MOSCHUS. In English Prose. By ANDREW LANG, M.A.

BALLADEN UND ROMANZEN. Edited by C. A. BUCHHEIM, Ph.D.

LYRIC LOVE. Edited by WILLIAM WATSON.

HYMNS AND OTHER POEMS. By F. T. PALGRAVE.

THE ART OF WORLDLY WISDOM. BALTHASAS GRACIAN.

MACMILLAN & CO.,

112 FOURTH AVENUE, NEW YORK.

8